Without a Prayer

Religious Expression in Public Schools

Robert S. Alley

PB Prometheus Books

59 John Glenn Drive
Amherst, New York 14228-2197

Published 1996 by Prometheus Books

00 99 98 97 96   5 4 3 2 1

Library of Congress Cataloging-in-Publication Data

Alley, Robert S., 1932–
     Without a prayer : religious expression in public schools / by Robert S. Alley.
          p.   cm.
     Includes bibliographical references and index.
     ISBN 1–57392–097–5 (alk. paper)
     1. Prayer in the public schools—Law and legislation—United States.
I. Title.
KF4162.A944   1996
344.73'0796—dc20
[347.304796]   96–27812
                                                                              CIP

Printed in the United States of America on acid-free paper

"In all cases where a majority are united by a common interest or passion, the rights of the minority are in danger. What motives are to restrain them? . . . Religion itself may become a motive to persecution and oppression."

James Madison, 1787

"In all of his (Madison's) experience, moreover, nothing had disturbed him quite so much as the demand for an assessment to support religion."

Lance Banning, 1995

Dedicated, with grateful appreciation

To those families and particularly those young children and teenagers who, under threat of criticism, slander, ostracism, and violence, have steadfastly sought to maintain and preserve their First Amendment rights in the public schools

Contents

9

Acknowledgments

In preparing this manuscript for publication I am indebted first to the participants in these human dramas who have shared with me their memories of exceedingly painful moments in their lives: Lisa and Kevin Herdahl; Rachel Bauchman; Joann Bell; Beverly and Phyllis Harris; Deborah, David, and Rebecca Weisman; William Jager; Lucille McCord; Jim McCollum; and Ellery Schempp. Without their willingness to make themselves available when I needed them, this volume would not have been possible. They generously listened to my questions and replied with care and precision. In addition, a word of special appreciation to two young tots, Elizabeth and Christine Herdahl, whose warm welcome made my visit to their home in Mississippi very special indeed.

The assistance of attorneys Steven Green, Elliot Mincberg, Eddie Tabash, Brent Walker, Steve Pershing, Judith Schaeffer, Buzz Thomas, Steven Pevar, David Ingebretsen, Joe Cook, and Andrew Hruska provided the legal perspective necessary to put these accounts in context. My good friend Lisa Thurau, director of Public Education and Religious Liberty (PEARL), has been a vigorous supporter of this project from its inception and has provided access to a wealth of people and information. The Virginia Chapter of the American Civil Liberties Union has been a constant source of help and encouragement in the persons of Director Kent Willis and staff member Julie McConnell. I owe a special debt to Americans United for Separation of Church and State and its remarkable staff, including director Barry Lynn, Rob Boston, Joe Conn, Bunnie Riedel, and Julie Segal. Gregg Ivers, a professor at American University, has inspired me by his dedication to scholarship, teaching, and sound reasoning. A particular word of thanks for numerous kindnesses and insights goes to James Dunn, director of the Baptist Joint Committee on Public Affairs; Sam Rabinov of the American Jewish Committee; Edd Doerr, director of Americans for Religious Liberty; and Paul Kurtz, editor of *Free Inquiry,* an indefatigable advocate of freethought.

Nadine Strossen, national president of the ACLU, the staunchest of advocates of religious freedom, has encouraged this book from its inception. Loren Siegel, national ACLU director of public education opened all doors to which I needed access. Courtenay Morris, assistant in media relations, supplied me with a mountain of material from the ACLU files as well as providing daily information on the people with whom I should speak.

A special word of appreciation is extended to editor in chief Steven Mitchell and to assistant editor Kathy McGuinness for her careful perusal of the final manuscript.

In retirement I have had the privilege of continuing each semester to teach a course on church and state at the University of Richmond. I am indebted to librarian Lit Maxwell, who knew what I needed in the way of research tools and found the way to provide them. I am grateful to the students, the administration, and my colleagues and friends in the Department of Religion for continuing encouragement of my work in this area. Dean David Leary and Provost Zeddie Bowen provided both support and encouragement.

First and last, my family (Norma, Bob, Pam, John, and Vickie) has been the mainstay of my life and career, and especially on this book, as the six of us, all teachers, talked through the situations I encountered. The exchanges and insights gave precision to my words and excitement to the project. Norma, my wife, loving companion, and friend for over thirty-five years, constantly provided positive criticism, direction, and a sounding board for ideas. One idea in particular we have shared our whole lives together: We believe that all parents and children should have the opportunity to develop their minds and consciences without intimidation from self-righteous persons seeking to impose their own peculiar, exclusivistic definitions on individuals, families, and communities. We are convinced most of all that democratic and social values are at risk when our minds and spirits are threatened with indoctrination into "the truth" by some brand of dogmatic religion.

Introduction

In the fall of 1966 one of our two sons was enrolled in a public school first grade in the County of Henrico in metropolitan Richmond, Virginia. Early in the school year our son informed us that his teacher was reading the Bible to his class. His description made it clear that she was interpreting, in a literal fashion, biblical stories from the Book of Genesis. As he recounted events, we learned that the teacher had informed him that the story of Noah's ark was not only a historical event, but a warning that God kills people who are "bad." He asked if that were true. When his mother and I tried to explain, in terms he could understand, that the Noah tale was a myth developed three thousand years ago by ancient people to explain natural events in a nonscientific world, we discovered we were creating an emotional conflict that was disturbing to our six-year-old. No person in a first grader's life has more credibility than the teacher, and we were not prepared, based on the information we had gathered, to undermine that trust. If, as we suspected, the teacher had indeed betrayed that trust, then we had to confront the situation with the school officials.

As we contemplated what action we should take, we were well aware that we could, even by a visit to the principal, generate a confrontation that might easily adversely affect our child's relationships both in the school and in the community. After careful analysis, together we agreed that I would visit the principal in an effort to resolve the problem.

I had only a casual acquaintance with the gentleman who was in charge of my son's school, but I was hardly prepared for the conversation that ensued. When he learned why I was in his office, his first question was, "What are you, a Jew?" I found that inquiry astounding. I responded by saying, "No, but why do you ask?" He replied, "Well, you know how they are." This slurring attack on a minority community agitated me and I became angry. I called his attention to the fact that the teacher's actions were a clear violation of constitutional interpretations set forth in 1962 and 1963 by the Supreme Court in the *Engel* v. *Vitale* and *Abington* v. *Schempp* cases. He said he knew that to be the case, but he allowed the violations to continue anyway. I asked what other lessons in civics he encouraged for the students. Recognizing that I was not mollified, he told me that if my wife and I insisted, the actions of the one teacher would be curtailed. However, he added, our son would suffer if we persisted. Children in the classroom, he said, would know that our son was responsible for the loss of the Bible stories. He assured me that our son's classmates would make it uncomfortable for the troublemaker. I asked him how the children would know whose parents had complained. Brashly, he announced that he would tell them.

I left the school and returned home to discuss the conversation with my wife, Norma. We both knew the potential price that might result from any legal action. We had followed the cases of similar nature that had been decided by the Supreme Court. We knew about the resulting abuse from school officials, teachers, and citizens in the community. This was a particularly difficult problem because of our son's age. How would we explain the complex issues of First Amendment jurisprudence to him?

In the situation facing us, not unlike many of the cases recorded in this volume, our conflict with the teacher pitted two markedly different Christian traditions against each other, in this instance, two distinct Baptist traditions. Indeed, we are reminded that most of the religious persecution so common in the American colonies in the seventeenth and eighteenth centuries was perpetrated by Protestants in power against Protestants not in power. That was the case in 1801 in Connecticut when the established Congregational Church dominated government and only begrudgingly tolerated Baptists. Counting President Jefferson an ally, members of the Danbury Baptist Association wrote to him concerning religious persecution in their state, a correspondence that receives a more thorough examination later in this book. They observed,

> Our antient [*sic*] charter together with the Laws made coincident therewith, were adopted as the Basis of our government, at the time of our revolution; and such had been our Laws & usages, and such still are; that Religion is considered as the first object of Legislation; and therefore what religious privileges we enjoy (as a minor part of the State) we enjoy as favors granted, and not as inalienable rights: and these favors we receive at the expense of such degrading acknowledgements, as are inconsistent with the rights of freemen.[1]

The last thing we wanted to do was to embroil our children in a lawsuit. Yet, with a commitment to religious freedom that had been nurtured by Baptist and Methodist parents, we knew what we had to do.

During this time we were planning to build a new home on the University of Richmond campus. Our choice of a building site in Henrico County, a location that would have left us in the same school district, was changed at the last moment because we could not obtain a building permit for the chosen lot. In our effort to find an alternative site and still keep the builder on schedule, we had to select a location in the city of Richmond. This placed us in a new public school jurisdiction. Thus, we no longer had standing in the county where any suit would have been brought.

In the summer of 1967, we relocated and we encountered no problems about classroom prayer and religious proselytizing at the new school.

There has not been a year since the events recounted here when we have failed to speculate on what would have occurred had we remained in our former residence. Would we have been risking our boys' childhoods for a principle they could only vaguely grasp? We knew how harshly parents and children had been treated in communities across the country when, dedicated to religious liberty, they challenged prayer and Bible reading in public schools.[2] Only little more than four years after the 1962 *Engel* decision, the evidence was growing that advocates of public school prayers and Bible reading were readily prepared to persecute citizens who dared to challenge the old ways of a presumed Protestant establishment.

Sadly, as we survey the national landscape in the year 1996, thirty years after our experience, we find that those citizens who have sought to implement the Bill of Rights in public schools against the prevailing cultural mores continue to suffer discrimination. It is noteworthy that the most egregious abuses against fellow citizens have occurred in those communities where the overwhelming number of residents belonged to a single religious tradition.

As we work our way through the experiences of young girls and boys, along with their parents, seeking constitutional protection from sustained efforts to establish religion in the schools, a sense of the history of the constitutional guarantees we possess will occasionally take us back to founders such as James Madison. For instance, the tendency of local and state jurisdictions to impose legislatively a majoritarian dogma in matters of public policy would have come as no surprise to James Madison. It was in the first Congress, meeting in New York in 1789, that he made a valiant and unsuccessful effort to persuade his colleagues to apply the proposed religion clauses of the First Amendment to the states.[3] He reasoned that it was in the smaller, more homogeneous political jurisdictions that the greatest threat to religious freedom existed. It was reasonably clear that the forces and counterforces at the federal level, born from political factions, would likely prevent a religious establishment. In contrast, the often near-monolithic religious environments of local communities easily translated into the tyranny of a majority that often threatened democracy itself. It was in those jurisdictions that a majority of citizens, driven by religious zeal, unrestrained by democratic principles, often did and still do impose upon others their own definitions of faith.

Only with the passage of the Fourteenth Amendment in 1868 was the Supreme Court provided the means to apply the Bill of Rights at the state and local level, thereby guarding individual freedom. The Supreme Court did not invoke the amendment's jurisdiction concerning the religion clauses until 1940, more than seventy years later, however.[4] This led, in turn, to the prayer and Bible reading cases of the 1960s. Nevertheless, facing the full force of the Court's opinion, many local jurisdictions that had created traditions of religion in the public schools, frequently encouraged by state governing authorities, have all too often remained recalcitrant, daring anyone to tamper with local custom.

Most often, when the First Amendment religion clauses are addressed in the public arena, debates turn on historical precedents and constitutional principles. That is proper and appropriate if we, as a nation, are to remain a country of laws, not sins. Sins are defined by religious dogma, thus while one may be convicted of breaking a law, our legal system does not concern itself with committing a sin. Yet there is a fundamental moral issue that is frequently ignored when public school prayer advocates claim the right to promote religion by distorting the meaning of "free exercise." Most commonly this leads to a degrading of the concept of separation of religious institutions from government by relegating the First Amendment prohibition of religious establishment to a secondary status. While the historical and constitutional arguments thrust against such thinking are formidable and altogether persuasive, it is equally essential that we consider the willful violations of human rights that inevitably result when school policy, ignoring the establishment clause, is justified by asking, "What's wrong with a little prayer in school?"

For three decades now knowledge of the personal suffering of dissenters and of the human rights violations associated with the "school prayer" issue have been largely confined to court records. A major purpose of relating the real-life situations that follow is to expose the personal suffering inflicted upon some American citizens by others in the name of prayer. A common theme running through all the accounts is the use of prayer as a weapon against the minority.

Frequently today when the matter of establishment of religion is raised in public discourse, those favorable to some form of organized religion in the public schools argue that their majority right to have prayer is violated by applying the establishment principle. This argument fails completely to distinguish between inconvenience (their inability to pray in a government-run public school, though they may pray elsewhere) and indoctrination (forcing others to participate against their will). Without a strict prohibition of established religion in public schools, the entire concept of religious freedom erodes into nothingness. In its place comes government largesse and toleration, creating a two-tiered society.

Again, Madison knew this to be the case. In one of his earliest letters, addressed to his friend William Bradford of Philadelphia, Madison asked Bradford, "when you have obtained sufficient insight into the Constitution of your Country . . . send me a draft of the Origin and fundamental principles of legislation, particularly the extent of your religious Toleration." He inquired, "Is an Ecclesiastical Establishment absolutely necessary to support civil society in a supream [*sic*] Government & how far is it harmful to a dependent State?" He wanted his friend to reply after reading and "consulting experienced Lawyers & Politicians. . . ."[5]

Without waiting for a reply, Madison made clear in his next letter, in January 1774, why he had written his earlier request. In the interim he had thought through a response to his own question. With crystal clear logic, Madison set forth his own perceptions regarding religious toleration and why that concept was totally flawed. His was a new and revolutionary pattern of thought based upon his observations of the evils of religious establishment in Virginia. The laws he would encourage, the constitutional protections he would champion respecting religious exercise were born and bred in moral outrage. Laws infused with the principle of religious freedom would become a means to alleviate human misery and despair. It is imperative that today we continue to listen to Madison's plaintive cry over the suffering of his fellow human beings and heed his warnings about religion as an engine of political power.

Madison accused the established Anglican Church of insinuating "slavery and Subjection" in Virginia. "Ecclesiastical Establishments" he wrote, "tend to great ignorance and Corruption all of which facilitate the Execution of mischievous Projects." Then Madison announced that in his native colony he had "nothing to brag of as to the State and Liberty of my Country. Poverty and Luxury prevail among all sorts: Pride ignorance and Knavery among the Priesthood and Vice and Wickedness among the Laity." He would conclude that no assurance of religious freedom was possible without a complete separation of religious institutions from the governing body. In his letter to Bradford he wrote, "That diabolical Hell conceived principle of persecution rages among some and to their eternal Infamy the Clergy can furnish their quota of Imps for such business. This vexes me the most of any thing whatever."[6]

Lest Bradford be left in doubt about that vexation, Madison continued by stating that, there are at this [time] in the adjacent County not less than 5 or 6 well meaning men in close Goal [jail] for publishing their religious Sentiments which in the main are very orthodox. I have neither patience to hear talk or think any thing relative to this matter, for I have squabbled and scolded abused and ridiculed so long about it, [to so lit]tle purpose that I am without common patience. So I [leave you] to pity me and pray for Liberty of Conscience [to revive among us.][7]

But history has neither convinced nor persuaded citizens in hundreds of communities across the nation to abandon a lingering notion that somehow their own religion should have preeminence. The imposition of some type of religious practice, no matter how innocuous, in public schools has never ceased to be a problem in spite of *Engel* and its progeny. Respect for the rule of law is frequently left in tatters by communities, regularly led by clergy, insisting upon obeisance to the religious practices dominant in the area. Congressman Roger Wicker of Ecru, Mississippi, in speaking about the struggle of the Herdahl family to have religious instruction removed from public schools in Pontotoc County, Mississippi, remarked, "I want to know where in the Constitution does it guarantee anybody the right not to be offended?"[8] And being offended was only the beginning for the Herdahls.

The consequences of self-righteous imposition of religious ritual by the government is damaging enough. But what of those who resist? Unlike the eighteenth century, citizens are no longer imprisoned or hounded by the law. Our modern forms of persecution are no less damaging and are far more insidious. Over and over again throughout this book we witness the majority of citizens in a given community, in the name of prayer, abusing and tyrannizing those who have challenged local- or state-endorsed religious practices. And these represent only a few examples; the problem itself is far too widespread for every instance to be included here. Establishment in the name of the majority has bred hooligans ready to threaten fellow citizens, harassing both adults and children alike in the name of prayer. The disease of de facto religious establishment is evident today in the vicious treatment by community majorities of those courageous citizens who seek protection under the First Amendment.

The moral rot engendered by those who piously claim the need for "just a little prayer" is a daily specter in communities across the nation. When the law prevails in a community and prayers are removed from schools, twentieth-century "imps" take the law into their own hands, encouraging severe community persecution of those who have sought legal redress for tyrannical behavior by the majority.

As a nation we have revisited that bitter lesson all too often since the school prayer decision of 1962. In the name of prayer and "family values," large numbers of citizens have reacted to their neighbors with hate and anger when public school religious practices have been challenged as violating the Bill of Rights. It is astounding and depressing to witness people who claim that school prayer is necessary to return the nation to spiritual and religious values, attacking with vicious and intemperate behavior fellow citizens who disagree with their solution. In the name of their deity, these self-styled keepers of public morality exhibit the most outrageous forms of discrimination, hate, and intimidation against those who challenge organized prayer in public schools. And the venom has not been diluted over the thirty-four years since *Engel*. Further, on those occasions where the challenge to school prayer originated with Jewish citizens, the ugly head of anti-Semitism lurks all too close to the surface.

As an example of that bias on the part of Christians, one might read the editorial in the August 1962 issue of the journal *America*. On the heels of *Engel* the editor warned "our Jewish friends" that there have been "disturbing hints of heightened anti-Semitism" as a result of Jewish support of the Court decision. The editorial writer asked, "What will have been accomplished if our Jewish friends win all the legal immunities they seek," and bring upon themselves "social and cultural alienation?" Bring upon themselves? At the time, the American Jewish Congress saw this as "thinly veiled threat(s) of anti-Semitism."[9]

From *Engel* in 1962 to Ecru, Mississippi, in 1996 is a tortured trail. Today in Ecru, resident Lisa Herdahl and her family face the same challenges that confronted their predecessors who fought to keep the wall of separation between church and state. And the Herdahls' story will only be a prologue to greater abuses unless, as a nation, we can find the means and the will to practice the principles laid out so effectively by the nation's founders.

The events herein described are documented, and generally not denied by the perpetrators. Some names have been withheld because the victims are still experiencing harassment and abuse. These unembellished accounts certify the use of religion in the service of hate and anger. They also clearly describe valor and dedication to the values of freedom and democracy.

In 1966, dealing with that first grade class experience, our family did not have to face the consequences of a difficult choice. The accounts in this book are dedicated to those vigilant and caring parents, and their children, who challenged unlawful and unconstitutional behavior in public classrooms across the nation. It is hoped that the reader will come to appreciate the words of Lisa Herdahl: "They are not going to drive me out of this community." And of Rachel Bauchman: "I was told not to make waves by my teachers, peers, members of the Jewish community, etc. Basically, it was a feeble attempt to silence me—a hope that I would go away. The problem is that I will *not* go away. I am in for the long haul. Whether I'm forty-five or one hundred and five, I'll still be here." The valor and love of freedom expressed by such citizens are legacies upon which to build.

As we engage these heroic citizens from public schools across the nation in dialogue, students and parents alike, we will hear a constant refrain from prevailing majorities about the need to accommodate their wishes concerning religion in the public schools. Majority rights becomes a mantra for justified offenses perpetrated upon children. When Rep. Wicker told his audience there was no guarantee against being offended, he was fundamentally wrong as well as grossly insensitive.[10] The establishment clause, as it relates to public education, is a guarantee against the government giving offense to the tender consciences of children who are required by law to be in school. And those who press for some form of publicly endorsed religion in the public schools make matters worse by employing that public institution whose primary purpose historically has been to provide an educated electorate complete with its remarkable diversity. Using those schools to offend children and then branding them as malcontents when they exercise their civic responsibility and seek redress of grievances in a federal court is a fundamental constitutional issue.

Unfortunately, all too often "moralists," flaunting some plan to restore "old-time values," are willing to abandon the natural right of religious free exercise for some simple notion of majority rule. Thus is a natural right reduced to a privilege conferred by the current prevailing majority of the community at its pleasure. And of course what the state can confer, it can also deny. Thomas Jefferson, in his classic Act for the Establishment of Religious Freedom, reminded all legislatures and citizens of this fact when he concluded the bill with these words: "We are free to declare, and do declare, that the rights hereby asserted are of the natural rights of mankind, and that if any act shall be hereafter passed to repeal the present, or to narrow its operation, such act will be an infringement of natural right."[11]

The First Amendment to the Constitution of the United States informs us that there shall be no laws "respecting the establishment of religion or prohibiting the free exercise thereof." The Supreme Court, for the past fifty years, has been consistent in informing citizens that, in accord with those principles, government-administered public schools *don't* have a right to endorse or organize prayer by public school children. The Court also makes crystal clear that, within the reasonable need for order and decorum, a child *does* have the right to pray during the school day as his or her conscience dictates. This remarkable confluence of rights is the bedrock of an educational system that must always protect the tender consciences of children against indoctrination, abuse, and offense. Our constitutional guarantees should breed respect for each citizen's reason and conscientious belief.

To reiterate, this volume examines the roots of precious constitutional rights and tells the real-life stories of parents and children who, in exercising those rights, have been harassed, taunted, insulted, and harmed by zealous citizens seeking to impose a particular definition of religion in public institutions both in rituals and in instruction. Here are accounts of Baptist, Lutheran, agnostic, Nazarene, Catholic, Christian Science, Jewish, and Church of Christ Americans facing menacing local majorities bent on imposing rigid dogma by employing government agencies to impose rules and practices in public schools. The portrait of heroism exhibited by this select group of children and adults discussed in these pages, in the face of unbridled, hateful words and deeds by many of their neighbors, paints the truest picture at our disposal of what constitutes a patriotic citizen. I have attempted both to relate their experiences and honor their commitment. However, I leave unanswered the question directed to the majority of citizens in Pontotoc County, Mississippi, by *USA Today* correspondent Barbara Reynolds: "How can Christians have such evil ways?"[12]

Notes

1. This passage was transcribed by the author from the original letter in the Manuscript Archives of the Library of Congress, Madison Building, Washington, D.C. See Robert S. Alley, "Public Education and the Public Good," *William & Mary Bill of Rights Journal*, 4, iss. 1 (1995): 310.

2. My wife and I were aware that, following the filing of the *Abington* v. *Schempp* case in 1958, Ellery Schempp was abused by his high school principal, W. Eugene Stuhl. Schempp was seventeen years old and made his own decision, in consultation with his parents, to challenge the Pennsylvania law that required Bible reading in public schools. He was preparing to graduate from high school when the unprincipled principal attacked him. Schempp had applied for admission to Tufts University, and Stuhl contacted the university urging them to reject Schempp as a "troublemaker." Of course, Tufts ignored the offensive warning and accepted Schempp. A different set of circumstances prevails when younger children are involved, as is indicated in the case of Lisa Herdahl in Mississippi, noted below and in chapter 10.

3. Robert S. Alley, *James Madison on Religious Liberty* (Amherst, N.Y.: Prometheus Books, 1985), p. 76.

4. *Cantwell* v. *Connecticut*, 310 US 296 (1940).

5. *The Papers of James Madison*, vol. 1 (Chicago: University of Chicago Press, 1962), p. 100; hereafter cited as *JMPapers*. (The University of Chicago published *JMPapers*, vols. 1–10, 1962–1977, and the University Press of Virginia published vols. 11– , 1977– .)

6. *JMPapers*, vol. 1, p. 106.

7. Ibid., p. 107. The use of brackets indicates some difficulty on the part of the editors as to the exact reading.

8. Bartholomew Sullivan, "Prayer Furor Crescendos in Pontotoc," *Memphis Commercial Appeal,* 29 January 1995. See chapter 10 of this book for details of the account of Lisa Herdahl's encounters with her neighbors in Ecru, Mississippi.

9. John Wicklein, "Warning to Jews by Jesuits," *New York Times*, 27 August 1962, p. 26.

10. Stephanie Saul, "A Lonely Battle in Bible Belt," *Newsday*, 13 March 1995, p. 8.

11. Thomas Jefferson, *An Act for the Establishment of Religious Freedom*, signed into law in January 1786 in the Virginia legislature. See *JMPapers,* vol. 8, p. 399.

12. Barbara Reynolds, "Closed Minds, Cold Hearts, Make School Prayer a Mockery," *USA Today*, 10 February 1995, p. 11A.

1

The Context of the Current Crisis

The personal accounts offered in this volume are not *isolated, unrelated* incidents of courage displayed by dedicated parents and children against local recalcitrance on the part of a determined majority. In each individual set of experiences there are common threads that bind together those persons who have challenged the tyrannical majorities in localities across the nation. What has happened and is happening in dozens of communities respecting religion in public schools must be viewed as a national story with emerging patterns that have major significance for our constitutional democracy. Each account is, to be sure, unique, but the overarching conflict has roots in our nation's recent and distant past.

Because this is a national phenomenon to which we address ourselves, before examining the personal experiences it is necessary to explore two historical periods: first the era that gave us the Bill of Rights, and second, the past half century in which the Supreme Court undertook to interpret the First Amendment as it applies to state and local legislation. In considering these two eras we will reverse the historical order as a means of identifying those eighteenth-century events that have a critical bearing upon our subject. We open the inquiry then with a discussion of the past fifty-five years of Supreme Court precedents related to the religion clauses of the First Amendment and their application to the public schools. Only after the recent decisions have been explained will we direct attention to the Founders and their constitution building.

The Supreme Court Addresses Religion: 1940-1996

When the Supreme Court first rendered its decisions in *Engel* v. *Vitale* (1962) and *Abington* v. *Schempp* (1963), declaring unconstitutional public school-sponsored prayer and Bible reading, it sent shock waves through large portions of the citizenry. Particularly in the South, these opinions were quickly linked to what was perceived to be a "liberal" Court that had already "offended" that region with its *Brown* v. *Board of Education* desegregation decision of 1954. And all too frequently the *Brown* decision was equated by its critics with atheistic communism.* Protests against the unanimous *Brown* opinion, evident in large portions of the South, did not play as well in other sections of the country, particularly when those protests were flavored with bald bigotry, violence, and hatred. To many residents in the South, it appeared that the editorial policies of newspapers supporting local demagogic political leaders created an environment that threatened democracy itself. Particularly noxious was the intentional demeaning of the federal judiciary.

Drawing on my own experience as an example, in the summer of 1955 the combined political power of the School Board and the Board of Supervisors of Henrico County, Virginia, arranged for a public hearing to address the question of whether or not the public schools should be closed to avoid integration. As a citizen of the county I attended. It was the closest I have ever been to sensing what a lynch mob might be like. These were angry, outraged citizens, ignorant of constitutional law and, it seemed, of the democratic heritage, who had been driven to a fever pitch by politicians and newspapers intent upon sucking every drop of prejudice from the populace. The result that night was an unruly mob.[1]

---

*Many people believed that segregation was the will of God, and therefore desegregation was seen as an act of atheism. Also, at this stage of the cold war, when "atheistic communism" was blamed for everything, desegregation was perceived by segregationist zealots as the first step on a path leading to the downfall of democracy and the United States.

As I gained the floor to give verbal support to the *Brown* decision as both morally and politically sound, I was greeted with yells that I go back to Russia. Of the some 250 persons crowded into that courtroom, only two of us vocally supported the Court ruling. There was a single black citizen in attendance and to this day I have no idea how he mustered the fortitude to listen to the irrational ravings of that mob for some two hours. The history of the South is forever inextricably entwined with those ten years following *Brown* when reason and justice were not in the land. Once again "states' rights" became a political battle cry and every federal action seemed suspect. Defiance of federal authority was widespread as a reply to the morality-based nonviolent resistance movement.

Today we are witness to that "states' rights" mentality being promoted by persons who are delighted to urge the federal officials and courts to micro-manage our lives. This movement, so vigorously championed by the Christian Coalition,* demeans the central government in Washington while championing fifty smaller editions coast to coast. The result is a growing sense of dual citizenship where loyalty seems all to often to be defined by regional mores and prejudices. This

---

*The Christian Coalition, one of the largest and most active organizations of the Religious Right, was founded in 1989, a creation and creature of Pat Robertson, who is president of the organization. Ralph Reed, while the executive director, makes clear that Robertson is the boss. Critics of Robertson suggest that this new vehicle is a form of occlusion, seeking to distance his political agenda from the hundreds of extreme statements associated with him over the past twenty years. Reed is young, smiling, pleasant, seemingly reasonable, but ultimately consistent with Robertson's agenda. Early in his tenure he told his followers that the Coalition would be involved in "stealth" activities to take over school boards. In the election of 1994 the Coalition played a major role in supporting the Republican Contract with America. In 1995 it claimed a membership of 1.7 million. Americans United for Separation of Church and State, one of the Coalition's many critics, was skeptical. The Coalition sends its publication, *Christian American,* to anyone who contributes as little as $15 a year. The U.S. Postal Service must publish sales information for all second-class postage. Americans United asked for that data for *Christian American* and according to the postal service 310,293 copies of the magazine were mailed in September 1995 by the Coalition. if the 1.7 million figure were correct, then 1.3 million would not have paid their dues and did not receive the publication. Replying to that charge, the Coalition claimed that the other 1.3 million were "supporters." They were people who signed nothing and contributed nothing but were "known" to be sympathetic.

current contempt for federal jurisdiction builds on pockets of regional resentment focussed at Congress, the Court, and the president.

The momentum for this new states' rights agenda is fueled by a fear of the very thing that once was so proudly hailed—diversity. Religiously and culturally we are tearing ourselves asunder. And the one cement still standing is a public school system that has imbibed deeply of the themes of diversity. The protection of that diversity is now the issue before the nation, for there appears to be a growing resistance to federal enforcement of the Bill of Rights.

As we look back approximately thirty years, two themes dominated political discourse in the late 1950s and early 1960s—race and communism. One drove wedges in national unity, the other enhanced a nationalism, albeit frequently irrational, in the face of atheistic communism. The latter threat seems dead, and currently there is no national cause or center of loyalty. However, the racial divisions have expanded to include numerous demands for majority power over both cultural and religious minorities. This, in turn, gravitates inevitably to a states' rights argument.

To be sure, the issue of race and the angry response to *Brown* v. *Board of Education* by an entire generation of southern leadership sowed the seeds of post-World War II hatred against the Warren Court.* A tight southern political alliance against the Court bears much of the blame for lost opportunities and lost children. The decade of the 1950s may rank as the time of the greatest irresponsibility in our history. In spite of all the good will manifest in the character of Martin Luther King, Jr., so movingly expressed in his letter from the Birmingham jail, in which he wrote, "Oppressed people cannot remain oppressed forever. The yearning for freedom eventually manifests itself, and that is what has happened to the American Negro," a deaf ear was turned by white politicians who, a decade later, would be in a lather over public school prayer. Nothing in our recent past so clearly identifies the shallowness of the public religious sentiments of that era than does the fundamentally unjust treatment of black citizens and the attempted dismantling of public education following the *Brown* decision.

---

*Earl Warren served as chief justice of the Supreme Court from 1953 to 1969. Along with the *Brown* decision, he is noted for his opinions in *Reynolds* v. *Sims* requiring state legislative reapportionment and *Miranda* v. *Arizona* regarding the rights of police suspects.

The sentiments unleashed in those years, so filled with hatred against the Supreme Court, cannot be recalled. The influence is permanent. So it was a great deal easier for other citizens to draw on that condemnation to equate the *Engel* decision with an atheist, secular Court. That association still persists in the rhetoric of millions of Americans and many of their chosen political leaders.

It would be the height of folly to argue that the call for public school prayer is always linked to racism. That is simply not true. Many of my acquaintances believe that the public schools should be about moral education. Furthermore, they believe that such a task is impossible without a formal religious foundation. However, they do not think the public schools are the place to build that foundation. These are the citizens who will listen to alternative arguments and do not dismiss out of hand Supreme Court decisions that run counter to their own convictions. Indeed, it is only with the support of such persons that the public schools have a chance for survival. But the millions of citizens in this category are not natural allies to those, claiming divine insight, who seek the imposition of their own "true" faith on the whole society. The Religious Right is in the business of creating a political disconnection in the United States that will permanently create second-class citizenship for those who disagree with them. The linking of an exclusivistic claim to religious truth, no matter how mildly affirmed, with the public school curriculum drives many advocates of school prayer to high pitched denunciations of their opponents as persons without faith, perhaps agents of the "antichrist."

For many who arrogantly claim to have cornered the market on "truth," the prayer and Bible reading issues were a godsend. States' rights coupled with religious indignation was perceived as making possible an amendment to the Constitution which would repudiate and chastise the Court. From 1962 through 1971 there was an all-out attack on the Court church/state opinions combined with hundreds of suggested "prayer" amendments. Court bashing became nationally respectable to the extent that by the fall of 1962 the House of Representatives voted unanimously to replace some stars on the wall above the Speaker of the House's chair with the motto "In God We Trust." If one missed the significance of that action, a Democratic Representative from Missouri was on hand to clarify the matter. He asserted that one of the "byproducts of our act today is that we have given perhaps not too directly, but in not too subtle a way, our answer to the recent decision of the U.S. Supreme Court banning the Regents' Prayer from the New York public schools."[2] In other words, although the Supreme Court refused, in their interpretation of the decision, to allow prescribed prayer to God in public school classrooms, the House of Representatives would proudly announce His presence in their chambers.

Of course, the paranoia concerning the Soviet Union had grown exponentially to its climax with the building of the Berlin Wall and the Cuban Missile crisis. People like evangelist Billy Graham, Reformed minister; Norman Vincent Peale, author of *The Power of Positive Thinking*; and Catholic Bishop Fulton J. Sheen drew a cross in the sand. "Christian America versus atheistic communism" was their war cry. It takes no pundit to understand how that sentiment was used to attack the Court's prayer decisions. It also generated an inordinate fear of secular education among millions. The term "secular" became fixed in the popular mind with "antireligion," an association totally at odds with the facts.

Volumes of testimony before House and Senate committees from 1962 to the present make clear the level of anger directed toward the Court resulting from its decisions to address the issue of organized prayer in the public schools. Of all the cases over the past several decades, four will claim significant attention here. They are *Engel* v. *Vitale* (1962), *Abington Township School District* v. *Schempp* (1963), *Wallace* v. *Jaffree* (1985), and *Lee* v. *Weisman* (1992).[3] It is important to observe that there was a monumental effort by some of the most prominent political leaders of the day, encouraged by Evangelist Billy Graham and Episcopal Bishop James Pike, to alter the First Amendment. All such efforts have failed. Equally important is the fact that mainline Protestant ministers and leaders largely applauded the Court actions. Southern Baptists were conspicuous in their voiced approval of the *Engel* and *Schempp* decisions.

There was a lull in the prayer debate after the emotionally charged days of the 1960s, and school prayer never really became a serious platform issue for either party in the 1970s. The public furor over the Court's opinions seemed to have diminished. Few new "prayer" amendments were introduced in Congress and the political climate, heavily affected by the Vietnam conflict in Southeast Asia and by Watergate, was not as receptive to shrill attacks on the Court. Further, following the *Lemon* v. *Kurtzman* and *Committee for Public Education* and *Religious Liberty* v. *Nyquist* decisions of 1971 and 1973, respectively (both of which are discussed below), establishment questions were generally absent from the Court agenda for more than a decade.

Furthermore, these two cases together seriously blunted moves by proponents of public aid to parochial schools. *Lemon* laid out a three-part test for the constitutionality of a statute: "First, the statute must have a secular legislative purpose; second, its principal or primary effect must be one that neither advances nor inhibits religion; finally, the statute must not foster 'an excessive government entanglement with religion.' " On the basis of these three tests, *Lemon* found unconstitutional parochial school aid programs in Pennsylvania and Rhode Island. Two years later, in *Nyquist*, Justice Lewis Powell, relying on *Lemon*, wrote in his majority opinion that three New York parochial school aid programs were unconstitutional because they advanced religion. It is worth noting that the *Nyquist* decision appears to have been a watershed for what was to become a deeply divided Court. Justices Byron White, Warren Burger, and William Rehnquist were to become a minority bloc, joined in the 1980s by Justice Antonin Scalia.

At the time of *Nyquist* there were few private schools under the control of Religious Right churches, and the primary loser in these cases was the Roman Catholic Church. It was one more round in a struggle that began with *Everson* in 1947 (a case in which the Court upheld the use of tax dollars to provide public transportation for parochial schools), and the Catholic leadership did not seek to polarize the nation politically when it lost in Court. Protestant fundamentalism had its eye on another 1973 decision, *Roe* v. *Wade*.*

Why, one might ask, in the face of overwhelming Protestant denominational support for church/state separation in the 1960s and 1970s, is there a seemingly massive movement across the nation today among religious people to impose religion in the public schools? Perhaps it is due to the fact that while many Christian leaders are fully aware that individuals voluntarily associate with religious institutions with no government establishment, in a free, democratic, secular state, and that this has produced perhaps the most religious nation on the

---

*The *Roe* v. *Wade* decision in January 1973 made abortion legal throughout the United States.

globe; their constituents in the pews have not been so easily persuaded. That may explain the prognosis by John Bennett, distinguished Protestant scholar of the 1960s, who warned of the dangers of the Court's reading of the religious establishment clause. While suggesting that the Supreme Court decisions "may not in themselves be objectionable," Bennett called for "less absolutistic terms" in defining church/state issues. He feared the nation turning its back on public education.[4] And if that was a dilemma in 1962, it is a crisis in 1996.[5]

Upon reflection we can see that, free of government established religion, the Protestant denominations in the 1960s and 1970s had a national leadership fully cognizant of the advantages of such an arrangement. We owe the blocking of all the efforts to amend the First Amendment in the 1960s to them and their persuasive power. Today current leadership is only a dim reminder of the dynamic voices of twenty years ago. The power center has shifted. While Congress once listened to the elected leadership of American Protestantism on the subject of church and state, its conservative members now relish the opinion of the political-religious organization called the Christian Coalition. And while the presidents of the American Baptist Convention and the National Council of Churches appealed to reason with no promises of future political support by their constituents, the Christian Coalition's executive director, Ralph Reed, makes political threats while he promises support only to those congressmen who vote positively on the wide-ranging Christian Coalition agenda. The Pat Robertson/Ralph Reed movement *is* an incipient established religion, collecting political favors in exchange for votes.

Whence the Wall?

One of the central aspects of this debate, establishment, revolves around the commonly used phrase "separation of church and state" employed first by President Jefferson in an 1802 letter to a group of Connecticut Baptists. In Justice William Rehnquist's dissenting opinion in the case of *Wallace* v. *Jaffree* (1985) he dismissed the Jeffersonian "separation" phrase as irrelevant to the First Amendment, a metaphor based on bad history that should be abandoned. In examining the context of that letter we find that the current chief justice and one of his most vigorous advocates, Pat Robertson, choose to ignore the indisputable facts surrounding that correspondence.

Some fourteen years ago Robertson, in a 1982 appearance before the Senate Judiciary Committee, testified on behalf of Ronald Reagan's school prayer amendment. On that occasion he asserted that separation of church and state was more compatible with the Soviet Union than the United States.[6] In order to enhance his argument, he sought to discredit the 1802 Jefferson letter to the Danbury Baptist Association. Robertson, lacking a single shred of evidence, said the letter resulted from the Danbury Baptists having "aroused his [Jefferson's] ire by criticism of one of his policies."[7] In his oral testimony Robertson spoke of Jefferson having "some pique, because of criticism."[8] The conclusion to be drawn was that the separation metaphor resulted from anger and was to be dismissed. (While there is no evidence to link Justice Rehnquist with this uninformed view of history, Rehnquist has also abused the record by writing in *Jaffree* that the "separation" letter "was a short note of courtesy." His advocacy for the abandonment of that term has galvanized those who yearn for a theory of church and state consistent with their notion of a Christian nation.)

Implicit in Robertson's claim was the notion that Jefferson was merely telling the Baptists to leave him alone since the First Amendment separated him from the need to listen to their criticism. Robertson's whole premise demonstrates a misreading of history, the Constitution, and the intentions of the founders.

Anyone who has read the letter from the Danbury Baptist Association can categorically state that there is not a single shred of criticism of Jefferson in the entire letter. It began by expressing "our great satisfaction in your appointment to the chief Magistracy in the United States." Quickly the writers moved to assert "Our Sentiments are uniformly on the side of Religious Liberty—That Religion is at all times and places a matter between God and individuals . . .—That the legitimate Power of civil government extends no further than to punish the man who *works ill to his neighbor* [emphasis in original]." Turning from that ideal, as stated before, the letter calls attention to Connecticut laws made at the time of the Revolution and asserts, "that religion is considered as the first object of legislation; and therefore what religious privileges we enjoy (as a minor part of the State) we enjoy as favors granted and not as inalienable rights."[9]

Turning to the state legislators, the Baptists noted, "It is not to be wondered at therefore; if those who seek after power and gain under the pretense of *government and Religion* should reproach" us and President Jefferson, as being enemies of religion, law, and good order because Jefferson would not dare to "assume the prerogatives of Jehovah and make Laws to govern the Kingdom of Christ." The Baptists, recognizing Jefferson's opposition to all forms of religious establishment, thus confirmed, "our hopes are strong that the sentiments of our beloved President, which have had such genial Effect already, like the radiant beams of the Sun, will shine and prevail through all these states and all the world till Hierarchy and tyranny be destroyed from the Earth [emphasis in original]." The Baptists expounded on their hopes by asserting, "May God strengthen you for the arduous task which providence and the voice of the people have called you to sustain and support you in your Administration against all the predetermined opposition of those who wish to rise to wealth & importance on the poverty and subjection of the people."[10]

This message to the new president reflected the sentiments of most Baptists in Connecticut where the "Standing Order," the established Congregational ministers, dominated the political scene. Most established clergy of Connecticut were firmly opposed to Jefferson's election in 1800 because he wished to separate religion and government. The Connecticut establishment survived until 1818,[11] when these words were included in the state constitution: "That the exercise and enjoyment of religious profession and worship without discrimination, shall forever be free to all persons in this State. . . ."[12]

It is no wonder that President Jefferson, who received the letter on December 30, 1801, replied on January 1, 1802, "The affectionate sentiments of esteem and approbation you are so good as to express towards me, on behalf of the Danbury Baptist Association, give me the highest satisfaction." Then Jefferson turned to the association's concerns about majoritarian religion's tyranny in Connecticut and stated:

> Believing with you that religion is a matter which lies solely between man and his God, that he owes account to none other for his faith or his worship, that the legislative powers of government reach actions only, and not opinions, I contemplate with sovereign reverence that act of the whole American people which declared that their legislature should "make no law respecting an establishment of religion, or prohibiting the free exercise thereof," thus building a wall of separation between church and state.[13]

Contrary to several claims, the Jefferson letter was not dashed off in haste. The president received the Danbury letter on December 30, 1801. On January 1, 1802, he sent the association's letter, a draft of his response, and a request to Attorney General Levi Lincoln. He wrote:

> The Baptist address, now enclosed, admits of a condemnation of the alliance between Church and State, under the authority of the Constitution. It furnishes an occasion, too, which I have long wished to find, of saying why I do not proclaim fastings and thanksgivings, as my predecessor did. The address, to be sure, does not point at this, and its introduction is awkward.[14] But I foresee no opportunity of doing it more pertinently. I know it will give great offense to the New England clergy; but the advocate of religious freedom is to expect neither peace nor forgiveness from them. Will you be so good as to examine the answer and suggest any alterations which might prevent an ill effect, or promote a good one, among the people?[15]

Lincoln replied on the same day with the suggestion that Jefferson alter his comments on proclamations because, with the exception of Rhode Island, the other New England states were accustomed to "proclamations from their respective executives." Lincoln went on, "This custom is venerable, being handed down from our ancestors" and "they regreted very much the late conduct of the legislature of Rhode Island on this subject." Based on Lincoln's advice, Jefferson deleted, "Congress thus inhibited from acts respecting religion and the Executive authorized only to execute their acts, I have refrained from prescribing even those occasional performances of devotion." Explaining his decision, Jefferson wrote in the margin of the original draft, "This paragraph was omitted on the suggestion that it might give uneasiness to some of our republican friends in the eastern states where the proclamation of thanksgivings etc. by their Executive is an antient [*sic*] habit and is respected."[16] Having concluded that he would remain with the issues raised by his Danbury correspondents, he composed the final draft with the strong separation language, waiting until another day to address the proclamation issue.

What a remarkable story this is. In 1801, Baptists in Connecticut were still persecuted under a "mild" establishment. Jefferson, as presi-

dent, could do nothing about the state laws except to anticipate seeing "the progress of those sentiments which tend to restore to man all
his natural rights, convinced he has no natural right in opposition to
his social duties."[17] In their hearts the Baptists knew that and so stated
when they wrote "we are sensible that the President of the United
States is not the national legislator, and also sensible that the national
government cannot destroy the laws of each State" but "our hopes are
strong that the sentiments of our beloved President, . . . will shine and
prevail through all these States and all the world till Hierarchy and
tyranny be destroyed from the Earth."[18]

These letters and events together reflect how seriously Jefferson
approached the plight of fellow citizens and, understood in that context, makes the separation metaphor profoundly significant. It was
born out of human suffering, not rational abstraction. How Pat
Robertson, with such disdain for facts, could callously violate the dedication and commitment of those Connecticut Baptist citizens is difficult to fathom. Sadly, in his current rhetoric, Robertson encourages
citizens in towns and counties across this nation to violate the character and molest the reputations of modern parents and children who
stand in the great tradition of the Danbury Baptists' dedication and
devotion to freedom.

A Wall by Any Other Name

Because Justice Rehnquist must be taken seriously as the nation's chief
justice, with a distinguished career on the federal bench, his effort to
dissociate Madison's thought from that of Jefferson needs close
scrutiny.

Although it is true that Jefferson did not participate in the first
Congress in which the Constitution was in force, he carried on constant discussion with Madison, via voluminous correspondence, during the entire period from 1784 through 1789.[19] Citizens of good will
may differ with Jefferson's insights, but to assert that his separationist
language has provided modern judges with a "mischievous diversion"
is bad history and poor legal reasoning.

Rehnquist seeks to expurgate the idea of a "wall" because it is an
impediment to a goal he espouses. In his quest he ignores the numerous times when James Madison employed variations on the separation

theme. In 1833 Madison wrote about "the line of separation between the rights of religion and the Civil authority . . ."[20] and most particularly, in a letter to Robert Walsh in 1819 Madison stated, "the number, the industry, and the morality of the Priesthood, & the devotion of the people have been manifestly increased by the total separation of the Church from the State."[21]

Unfortunately, the decision of Jefferson to use nonconstitutional language to define the religion clauses has become a means to divert the argument by those persons attached to what has been termed "nonpreferentialism."[22] In essence, nonpreferentialism is a call for plural religious establishments. Jefferson's central role in the struggle provides his credibility. However, his absence from the debates in Virginia, Pennsylvania, and New York causes critics to use that against him. The Court, however, from 1879 to the present, has found a reasonable correlation between the wall idea and the First Amendment. Chief Justice Morrison Waite* wrote for the Court in *Reynolds* v. *United States* (1879) that the Danbury letter, "Coming as it does from an acknowledged leader of the advocates of the measure, it may be accepted almost as an authoritative declaration of the scope and effect of the amendment thus secured."[23]

Note that Chief Justice Waite used the word "almost." This is important because none of the cases from that time forward have been based upon the Jefferson metaphor *alone*. The Court decisions also stem from clear and precise language of James Madison and other participants spanning a period from 1774 to 1834.

Madison frequently addressed the notion of plural establishments. He did so first while opposing the 1784 Virginia Assessment Bill which would have provided state funds to finance teaching religion by the Protestant churches. He did it for the last time around 1834 in a letter to Jasper Adams, a Charleston, South Carolina, minister. Adams wanted Madison to endorse the idea of a national religion, Christianity. Adams asserted that "the people of the United States have retained the Christian religion as the foundation of their civil, legal, and political institutions." Madison took up Adams's challenge, writing,

---

*Morrison R. Waite served as Chief Justice of the Supreme Court from 1874 to 1888, writing over one thousand opinions during that time.

[T]he simple question to be decided is whether a support of the best
& purest religion, the Xn [Christian] religion itself ought not so far at
least as pecuniary means are involved, to be provided for by the Govt.
rather than be left to the voluntary provisions of those who profess it.
And on this question experience will be an admitted Umpire, the
more adequate as the connection between Govts. & Religion have
existed in such various degrees & forms, and now can be compared
with examples where connection has been entirely dissolved.[24]

Madison here rejected a plural establishment of the "Xn religion."
He went on to reject all establishments. He noted, "the prevailing
opinion in Europe, England not excepted, has been that Religion could
not be preserved without the support of Govt." But he continued:

It remained for North America to bring the great & interesting subject to a fair, and finally to a decisive test. In the Colonial State of
the Country, there were four examples, R[hode] I[sland], N[ew]
J[ersey], Penn[sylvani]a and Delaware, & a greater part of N[ew]
Y[ork] where there were no religious Establishments, the support of
Religion being left to the voluntary associations & contributions of
individuals; and certainly the religious conditions of those Colonies
will well bear a comparison with that where establishment existed.
As it may be suggested that experiments made in Colonies more or
less under the Controul [*sic*] of a foreign Government had not the
full scope necessary to display their tendency, it is fortunate that the
appeal can now be made to their effects under a compleat [*sic*]
exemption from any such controul [*sic*].

Employing the separation idea, Madison concluded, "The tendency to a usurpation on one side or the other, or to a corrupting coalition or alliance between them, will be best guarded agst. by an entire
abstinence of the Govt. from interference in any way whatsoever,
beyond the necessity of preserving public order, & protecting each sect
agst. trespasses on its legal rights by others."[25]

Clearly, Madison was advocating a complete separation of church
and state. The point here, however, is not to insist that Madison must
be the only voice considered for interpreting the First Amendment.
Rather, it is to suggest that historical integrity and fairness demand that
the celebrated author of our constitutional right to free exercise and its

prohibition of establishment be taken quite seriously. We should rest on Madison's arguments, not his stature as a founder. It is not original intent at issue here, but experience with principles of freedom.

But, concluding that the "wall" metaphor is a good and useful one does not resolve the current debate. Proponents of alternate readings of the First Amendment have become focused not on history alone, but on new terminology as well.

Notes

1. Allan Jones, "Henrico's Dr. Smart Asks Study to Keep Segregation," *Richmond Times Dispatch*, 29 July 1955, p. 1.

2. Robert S. Alley, *School Prayer: The Court, the Congress, and the First Amendment* (Amherst, N.Y.: Prometheus Books, 1994), pp. 119–20.

3. We will have occasion to return to these cases in chapter 3.

4. Religious News Service in *The Religious Herald*, 23 August 1962, p. 20.

5. Robert S. Alley, *The Supreme Court on Church and State* (New York: Oxford University Press, 1988), p. 118.

6. Senate Committee on the Judiciary, *Hearings on S.J. 199,* 97th Congress, 2nd sess. August 18, 1982, pp. 264–79 (Pat Robertson testimony).

7. Ibid., p. 274.

8. Ibid. p. 265.

9. Robert S. Alley, "Public Education and the Public Good," *William & Mary Bill of Rights Journal* 4, iss. 1 (1995): 310.

10. Ibid.

11. Anson Phelps Stokes and Leo Pfeffer, *Church and State in the United States* (New York: Harper & Row, 1964), pp. 73–76.

12. Ibid., p. 75.

13. Thomas Jefferson to "a Committee of the Danbury Baptist Association," January 1, 1802. Published in *The Writings of Thomas Jefferson*, Merrill D. Peterson, ed. (New York: The Library of America, 1984), p. 510.

14. Jefferson undoubtedly felt "awkward" about the flowery language of the opening paragraph praising the president.

15. Letter from Jefferson to Levi Lincoln, January 1, 1802. Jefferson Papers, Library of Congress. In the course of the research preparatory to writing this section, the original handwritten documents noted in this discussion were examined at the Library of Congress, along with the microfilm copies on Reel #25.

16. Ibid. The note, in Jefferson's hand, does not alter Jefferson's consis-

tent refusal to make such proclamations. It merely reflects his awareness that the "antient" traditions of the New England states, except for Rhode Island, would require time before they were altered. At the national level religious exercises were subject "only to the voluntary regulations and discipline of each respective sect." These words were in the paragraph Jefferson omitted.

17. Jefferson, Danbury letter.

18. Ibid. We are reminded that James Madison anticipated just the problem the Danbury Baptists experienced, knowing, as he did, that it was at the state level that violations of rights were most likely to occur. Thus did he attempt, unsuccessfully, to pass a bill applying the religion clauses to state laws.

19. James Morton Smith, ed., *The Republic of Letters: The Correspondence between Thomas Jefferson and James Madison 1776–1826,* vol. 1 (New York: W. W. Norton, 1995).

20. Gaillard Hunt, ed., *The Writings of James Madison*, vol. 9 (New York: G. P. Putnam, 1910), p. 487 (letter to Rev. Adams). Internal evidence would place the date of this letter in 1834 or later.

21. See Letter to Robert Walsh from James Madison, March 2, 1819, in Gaillard Hunt, ed., *The Writings of James Madison*, vol. 8 (New York: G. P. Putnam, 1908). p. 432.

22. This will be discussed further in chapter 2.

23. Alley, *The Supreme Court on Church and State*, p. 353.

24. Hunt, *The Writings of James Madison* (letter to Rev. Adams), p. 487.

25. Ibid.

2

Interpreting the Religion Clauses

Toleration versus Freedom: New Terms, Old Debate

There should be, I think, an "old saying" that warns, "Beware of scholars redefining terms lest they rewrite history in the bargain."

Respecting the Supreme Court, a new era emerged with the election of President Ronald Reagan in 1980. In that year the Reverend Jerry Falwell was anointed by several conservative political operatives, including Richard Vigurie, Howard Phillips, and Paul Weyrich, to head the so-called Moral Majority. Claiming to represent what the press dubbed the "Religious Right," Falwell emerged as a new political force in the nation. Although difficult to count or define, the Religious Right at least refers to those Christian adherents of biblical literalism who favor public school-sponsored prayer, who demand banning the teaching of evolution in the public schools, and who oppose, often violently, abortion. As I suggest in chapter 3, this was the time when the significant influence of Billy Graham was declining even as the new voices of Jerry Falwell and Pat Robertson were being heard on the national political scene. Perhaps sensing that significant shift in political leadership, Chief Justice Warren Burger struck a new chord in his opinion in *Lynch* v. *Donnelly* (1984),[1] tapping a seemingly less rigid reading of the First Amendment religion clauses on the part of

43

the justices. Chief Justice Burger became a champion of what has since frequently been termed "nonpreferentialism," offering a series of suggestions as to how the Court might revisit eighteenth-century history. Nonpreferentialism would exchange separation with a plural establishment of all "legitimate" religions.

In the *Lynch* case, Burger, addressing the placement of a creche on public property at Christmas, led a majority of five justices in affirming that the city of Pawtucket, Rhode Island, had acted appropriately by permitting the display since, in that situation "the city has a secular purpose for including the creche" along with many other symbols of the winter holiday season. Burger insisted that the Constitution "affirmatively mandates accommodation, not merely tolerance, of all religions, and forbids hostility toward any."[2]

In the following year, 1985, in *Wallace* v. *Jaffree*, a majority on the Court determined that the Alabama legislature's intent in its moment of silence law was "to return prayer to the public schools." Justice Sandra Day O'Connor, in her concurring opinion, suggested alternate language that might pass Court scrutiny.

On a distinctively strident note Justice William Rehnquist wrote a dissent in which he insisted that "nothing in the Establishment Clause requires government to be strictly neutral between religion and irreligion." Rehnquist thereby became the titular leader of a growing number of constitutional thinkers who currently wish to revisit the strict separation doctrine affirmed in *Everson*. Since the *Jaffree* case there has been a significant effort by many academics and Religious Right leaders to advance this alternative interpretation of historical events, insisting that the founders merely intended to prevent any single religious organization or doctrine from being established. Consequently, proponents argued that a plural establishment of religion was acceptable to the authors of the First Amendment. Going far beyond any historical evidence, Justice Rehnquist concluded that placing the lack of religion or "irreligion" on equal terms with religion itself is flawed history.

In order permanently to implement this alternative reading of the First Amendment it is apparent that proponents are desirous of replacing the "separation" metaphor with a different set of criteria for the Court. Again, Justice Rehnquist says in *Jaffree*: "The 'wall of separation between church and state' is a metaphor based on bad history, a metaphor which has proved useless as a guide to judging. It should be frankly and explicitly abandoned."

Within a year of that dissent William Rehnquist was named chief justice and an administration strongly linked to the Religious Right seemed poised to make the future of the separationist position grim indeed. However, history failed to follow the expected script. President George Bush appointed Justice David Souter who quickly and unexpectedly manifested staunch support for separation as defined in *Everson*. And Reagan appointee Justice Anthony Kennedy joined Souter in two Court decisions in 1992 that rebuffed twelve years of heavy-duty lobbying to return prayer to the public schools. President Bill Clinton then named Justices Ruth Ginsburg and Stephen Breyer to the Bench, both of whom have stood firmly on the same separationist tradition. Nevertheless, an election in November 1996 coupled with three possible vacancies (if Justices Sandra Day O'Connor, William Rehnquist, and John Paul Stevens were to resign) could alter the Supreme Court picture for the long term.

As the debate over alternative readings of the religion clauses of the First Amendment has continued, one of the most effective responses to the current willingness to accommodate nonpreferentialism has come in Justice Souter's concurring opinion in *Lee* v. *Weisman*. He wrote:

Whatever else may define the scope of accommodation permissible under the Establishment Clause, one requirement is clear: accommodation must lift a discernible burden on the free exercise of religion. Concern for the position of religious individuals in the modern regulatory state cannot justify official solicitude for a religious practice unburdened by general rules; such gratuitous largesse would effectively favor religion over disbelief. By these lights one easily sees that, in sponsoring the graduation prayers at issue here, the State has crossed the line from permissible accommodation to unconstitutional establishment. . . . Since Everson, we have consistently held the Clause applicable no less to governmental acts favoring religion generally than to acts favoring one religion over others. More recently, in *Wallace* v. *Jaffree* we held that an Alabama moment-of-silence statute passed for the sole purpose of "returning voluntary prayer to public schools," violated the Establishment Clause even though it did not encourage students to pray to any particular deity. We said that "when the underlying principle has been examined in the crucible of litigation, the Court has unambiguously concluded that the individual freedom of conscience protected by the First Amendment embraces the right to select any religious faith or none at all." This conclusion, we held, "derives support not only from the interest in respecting the individual's freedom of conscience, but also from the conviction that religious beliefs worthy of respect are the product of free and voluntary choice by the faithful, and from recognition of the fact that the political interest in forestalling intolerance extends beyond intolerance among Christian sects—or even intolerance among religions—to encompass intolerance of the disbeliever and the uncertain."[3]

Certainly the *Weisman* decision of 1992 was a setback for accommodationist theory, which argues that the First Amendment allows government accommodation in the form of religious institutions. But it has not deflected their ardor for recasting church/state jurisprudence along the Burger–Rehnquist line of thinking. The term "nonpreferentialism" sounds technical and is of recent vintage, but its ancestry includes Justice Joseph Story, who in 1815 wrote in *Terrett* v. *Taylor* that, "the free exercise of religion cannot be justly deemed to be restrained by aiding with equal attention the voteries of every sect to perform their own religious duties." In other words, legislating in favor of religion is acceptable as long as no one religion is preferred over another. In 1833 Justice Story noted in a letter to Jasper Adams, "My own private judgment has long been that government cannot long exist without an alliance with religion."[4]

Today the terms "accommodationism" and "nonpreferentialism" have been allied with a new minting of the word "toleration." The argument is deceptively simple. The majority has rights in the public schools. If the majority wants to practice religion under the auspices of the school, why should a minority not "tolerate" that simple desire? By employing the word in that fashion its meaning is distorted. It seems clear that when two people possessing, in equal measure, the rights of conscience engage each other in this democratic society, it is useful and productive for each to be tolerant of the other's convictions, no matter how strange and unreasonable they may seem. Good citizens do that in all walks of life. Individual tolerance is a good thing just because it requires that no one be forced against her or his will to accept or agree with those contrary views. The standard explanation is, "We get along in spite of our sharp differences." In a secular society that type of toleration is salutary.

The use of toleration by advocates of accommodationism in the schools to justify public school-sponsored religious activities is a prostitution of what organizations like the National Conference of Christians and Jews seek to foster. The latter's use of the term toleration is predicated upon the very fact that the government cannot enter into such a bargain with religion. The state makes laws and enforces them. It has no inherent right to judge, condone, or condemn religious sentiments in the name of toleration. When the government is "tolerant" it presumes a right to judge and define religion, thereby exercising preference in the name of majority rule to those who have the most votes. The state's inherent neutrality with respect to any religion is based upon its separation from all religious institutions.

But long before the language card was introduced, over the past fifty years there have been many efforts to rechart the separationist constitutional course. That becomes quite clear when we examine majority public opinion in response to individuals bringing legal challenges against local school districts that promote, endorse, or encourage religion in the schools. The stories stretch from the McCollum family in 1948 to the Herdahl family in 1996.

The movement toward accommodation chronicled here is now fueled by a sea change in congressional thought following the elections of 1994. In fact, county by county, state by state, the accommodationist viewpoint is practiced every day in hundreds of public schools. Emboldened by rash political rhetoric calling for changes to the First Amendment and defying Supreme Court decisions that have consistently blocked public school use as a means of religious teaching, prayer, and indoctrination, a growing number of communities simply choose to ignore High Court decisions as they implement majority rule to incorporate forms of religious expression in the school day. This behavior continues to adversely affect the fundamental, natural rights of a minority.

As the experiences described in this book attest, in practical terms, all functioning models of nonpreferentialism have contributed to a popular majoritarianism in which minorities have been castigated for refusal to accommodate or exercise tolerance for the dominant cultural patterns in a given community.

Establishment, Separation, and the Founders

Over time, as the arguments became more sophisticated, nonpreferentialism predicated its position on an alternate reading of constitutional origins and the founders' intentions. This is a type of historical revisionism. In stark contrast to the Supreme Court tradition begun in *Cantwell* (1940) and *Everson* (1947), nonpreferentialism argues that the First Amendment not only allows, but promotes some form of plural religious establishment. Distinguished Bill of Rights scholar Leonard Levy has identified it nicely: "The nonpreferentialists are innocent of history but quick to rely on a few historical facts which, when yanked out of context, seem to provide a patristic lineage to their views."[5] In sum, nonpreferentialists simply manipulate historical events to suit their arguments.

At this juncture it is useful to return to Justice Souter in *Weisman* (1992). He noted that some have read, ". . . the Establishment Clause to permit 'nonpreferential' state promotion of religion." These

> challengers argue that, as originally understood by the Framers, "the Establishment Clause did not require government neutrality between religion and irreligion nor did it prohibit the Federal Government from providing nondiscriminatory aid to religion." While a case has been made for this position, it is not so convincing as to warrant reconsideration of our settled law; indeed, I find in the history of the Clause's textual development a more powerful argument supporting the Court's jurisprudence following Everson.

> Implicit in the Framers' choice

> is the distinction between preferential and nonpreferential establishments, which the weight of evidence suggests the Framers appreciated. Of particular note, the Framers were vividly familiar with efforts in the colonies and, later, the States to impose general, nondenominational assessments and other incidents of ostensibly ecumenical establishments. The Virginia Statute for Religious Freedom . . . captured the separationist response to such measures. Condemning all establishments, however nonpreferentialist, the Statute broadly guaranteed that "no man shall be compelled to frequent or support any religious worship, place, or ministry whatsoever,"

including his own. Forcing a citizen to support even his own church would, among other things, deny "the ministry those temporary rewards, which proceeding from an approbation of their personal conduct, are an additional incitement to earnest and unremitting labours for the instruction of mankind." In general, Madison later added, "religion & Govt. will both exist in greater purity, the less they are mixed together."

What we thus know of the Framers' experience underscores the observation of one prominent commentator, that confining the Establishment Clause to a prohibition on preferential aid "requires a premise that the Framers were extraordinarily bad drafters—that they believed one thing but adopted language that said something substantially different, and that they did so after repeatedly attending to the choice of language." We must presume, since there is no conclusive evidence to the contrary, that the Framers embraced the significance of their textual judgment. Thus, on balance, history neither contradicts nor warrants reconsideration of the settled principle that the Establishment Clause forbids support for religion in general no less than support for one religion or some.

While these considerations are, for me, sufficient to reject the nonpreferentialist position, one further concern animates my judgment. In many contexts, including this one, nonpreferentialism requires some distinction between "sectarian" religious practices and those that would be, by some measure, ecumenical enough to pass Establishment Clause muster. Simply by requiring the enquiry, nonpreferentialists invite the courts to engage in comparative theology. I can hardly imagine a subject less amenable to the competence of the federal judiciary, or more deliberately to be avoided where possible.

This case is nicely in point. Since the nonpreferentiality of a prayer must be judged by its text, Justice [Harry] Blackmun pertinently observes that Rabbi Gutterman [the rabbi who gave the prayer at the Providence graduation] drew his exhortation "to do justly, to love mercy, to walk humbly" straight from the King James version of Micah, ch. 6, v. 8. At some undefinable point, the similarities between a state-sponsored prayer and the sacred text of a specific religion would so closely identify the former with the latter that even a nonpreferentialist would have to concede a breach of the Establishment Clause. And even if Micah's thought is sufficiently generic for most believers, it still embodies a straightforwardly Theistic premise, and so does the Rabbi's prayer. Many Americans who consider themselves religious are not Theistic; some, like several of

the Framers, are Deists who would question Rabbi Gutterman's plea
for divine advancement of the country's political and moral good.
Thus, a nonpreferentialist who would condemn subjecting public
school graduates to, say, the Anglican liturgy would still need to
explain why the government's preference for Theistic over non-The-
istic religion is constitutional.[6]

A Matter of Definition

Nonpreferentialism has a correlative thesis. As then Justice Rehnquist
put it in *Jaffree*, "The Establishment Clause did not require government neutrality between religion and irreligion nor did it prohibit the
federal government from providing nondiscriminatory aid to religion."[7] In so interpreting the nonestablishment provision Rehnquist
reverses history, returning to a concept of toleration. The justice
missed entirely the thrust of the Madisonian distinction between toleration and free exercise. In this regard, a petition by Jewish citizens
to the French National Assembly in 1790 put it well. "America, to
which politics will owe so many useful lessons, has rejected the word
toleration from its code, as a term tending to compromise individual
liberty and to sacrifice certain classes of men to other classes. To tolerate is, in fact, to suffer that which you could, if you wish, prevent and
prohibit."[8] Further, Rehnquist makes no allowance for a citizen's conscience to lead him or her to "irreligion."

In implementing this modern nonpreferentialism Justice Rehnquist would undoubtedly insist upon a much more inclusive concept
of religion than the Protestant model so popular in a previous century.
However, given the population of Virginia in 1784 and its religious
proclivities (few non-Protestants populated the state at that time), the
proposed Virginia Assessment Bill offered a broad interpretation.* It

---

*The Assessment Bill "Establishing a Provision for Teachers of the Christian
Religion" provided: "and be it further enacted, That the money to be raised by virtue
of this act, shall be by the Vestries, Elders, or Directors of each religious society,
appropriated to a provision for a Minister or Teacher of the Gospel of their denomination, or the providing of places of divine worship, and to none other use whatsoever, except in the denominations of Quakers and Menonists, who may receive what
is collected from their members, and place it in their general fund, to be disposed of
in a manner which they shall think best calculated to promote their particular mode
of worship." (*Everson* v. *Board of Education,* 330 US 1 [1947]).

is not clear how inclusive an interpretation the chief justice would employ today, but he clearly omits what he terms "irreligion" from it. But no matter how broad one makes the concept it inevitably leads to a restriction on freedom. Free exercise means that individual conscience is inviolate; it is beyond the power of the state to control. Working from the principle of natural right, the establishment clause must not be allowed to create a resident power enabling the government to select among creeds, endorsing some and merely tolerating others. Here nonpreferentialism arguments are threats to the rights of minorities and they suggest the creation of a tyranny of the majority.

Further, as noted earlier in remarks by Justice Souter, beyond the plural establishment question, another quite serious problem with non-preferentialism lies in its major premise, which inevitably results in requiring the federal government to "define" religion. One can hardly go about the task of plural establishment without definitions, which inevitably *include* and *exclude.* This problem is solved in the First Amendment by assigning to each citizen the responsibility of defining religion according to individual conscience. Hence, the government's judiciary should accept, without debate, as having equal worth all conscience claims by citizens. To be sure, practical implementation of some beliefs (snake handling, polygamy) have been restricted in the name of "compelling state interest."[9] In other words, the Court could not permit religious behavior that ran counter to the State's right to protect the health, safety, and welfare of the community. But the High Court, at the same time, was prepared to affirm that the beliefs that inspired such actions were unquestionably protected by the First Amendment.

Further, any effort to provide a "generalized endorsement of prayer" as Rehnquist says the establishment clause allows, necessitates a definition of prayer. But prayer, as many prominent religious leaders such as Bailey Smith, former president of the Southern Baptist Convention; Jerry Falwell; and Billy Graham have recently noted, is not generalizable. Falwell and Smith have publicly denied that prayer, other than in the name of Jesus, is prayer at all. What is the state's position to be on this matter? Did the Regents' Prayer of New York*

---

*The Regent's Prayer of New York, which was read at high school graduations in that state, was declared unconstitutional by the Supreme Court in *Engel* v. *Vitale* 370 US 421 (1962). The prayer stated, "Almighty God, we acknowledge our dependence upon Thee, and we beg Thy blessings upon us, our parents, our teachers, and our Country."

qualify as prayer? It did *not* for millions of Christians in this nation. Was the state of New York justified in affirming otherwise by endorsing a particular religious perspective, no matter how innocuous?

In sum, when the state takes sides with religion over the lack of religion it poses a fundamental dilemma: Who will define these terms? The Rehnquist strategy is merely a means of establishing "traditional" religions or it is a meaningless concept. If no definition of religion is forthcoming, then the argument is moot. If any definition is employed, no matter how broad, some belief systems will be excluded, which would be a clear violation of the establishment clause.

Some scholars suggest that the Court should "limit its interpretation of the First Amendment" to the "views of the majority" in the 1789 Congress. Let's examine that proposition. Many of the states had established religions at the time. Were we to be guided by their proclivities, the establishment clause would be devoid of content. Indeed, senators defeated Madison's proposal that the First Amendment apply to the states because they were protecting their home environment. The miracle of religious freedom as incorporated in the Bill of Rights is that freedom came in spite of a narrow, unenlightened sentiment that pervaded many of the new states. Many members of the 1789 Congress undoubtedly had as little sympathy for thoroughgoing separation in their states as they did for women's suffrage and emancipation.

Richard John Neuhaus, a current advocate of nonpreferentialism, insists that "the entire purpose of the religion clause of the First Amendment" is religious freedom. "Any use of 'no establishment' that restricts 'free exercise' is a misuse of 'no establishment.'"[10] This argument was employed by public school prayer advocates in several of the cases discussed in this book. It is contended that "no establishment" rulings that remove organized prayer from the schools are denials of free exercise to the majority that wanted such prayer.

Neuhaus hopes by this ploy to cure what he abhors: the "secular state in a secular society," "the naked public square," "secular humanism," "suppression of religion in the classroom." In other words, Neuhaus believes that neutrality toward religion is necessarily the endorsement of nonbelief, i.e., secularism. The argument is bogus. Yet, Justice Scalia's dissent, opposing the taxing of religious book sellers, in *Texas Monthly* v. *Bullock* (1989), is remarkably close to the language of Neuhaus:

It is not always easy to determine when accommodation slides over into promotion and neutrality into favoritism, but withholding of a tax upon the dissemination of religious materials is not even a close case. . . . If there is any close question it is not whether the [tax] exemption is permitted, but whether it is constitutionally compelled in order to avoid "interference with the dissemination of religious ideas."[11]

Here, in the words of Justice Scalia, we again encounter one of our three terms, accommodationism.

In a striking response to the Scalia position, Justice William Brennan, voting with the majority, noted, "Justice Scalia's opinion, conversely, would subordinate the Establishment Clause value. This position, it seems to me, runs afoul of the previously settled notion that government may not favor religious belief over disbelief."

The argument in the *Texas* case, advanced by Justice Scalia, is that free exercise mandates a tax exemption, no matter how such a practice might violate establishment. He believes, with Neuhaus, that the "no establishment" provision was intended only to support free exercise. Both argue that the founders had no intention of protecting the state from the church, but this point is badly reasoned and is clearly disputed by Madison's notes on the Virginia Declaration of Rights, his letter to Jasper Adams, and in his *Memorial and Remonstrance*.[12] Only by accepting the superiority of religion over irreligion can the Scalia position be seriously considered. But even given that assumption, the fact is that single *or* plural establishment as illustrated in the proposed Assessment Bill in 1784 impinges necessarily upon other citizens whose religious views differ from those receiving government approval. It would tilt the state toward one or more denominations or creeds and against others. Accommodationism becomes a demand laid upon the minority.

In arguing in the *Texas* case that the state may be mandated to extend tax exemption "to avoid interference with the dissemination of religious ideas," Scalia is creating for the state the responsibility to define religion. Justice Byron White recognized this problem in a 1989 Illinois case where he insisted that neither the Supreme Court nor Congress can place itself in the position of defining religion. The result, he noted, would be a clear violation of establishment. Justice John Paul Stevens addressed the problem directly in 1982:

There exists an overriding interest in keeping the government—whether it be the legislature or the courts—out of the business of evaluating the relative merits of differing religious claims. The risk that governmental approval of some and disapproval of others will be perceived as favoring one religion over another is an important risk the Establishment Clause was designed to preclude.[13]

Motives are hard to establish and frequently miss the mark, but in this instance the rhetoric of nonpreferentialism seems clearly aimed at creating a moral tone for the nation along specifically religious lines. It appears that an effort to "return" the country to a specific set of seventeenth- and eighteenth-century values is what the proponents of such an agenda find most satisfying. Those values are unmistakably identified as Christian in origin. Free exercise, then, would become a special largesse administered by the congressionally established religions. The inevitable result would be the creation of second-class believers, not to mention the irreligious, outside the realm of state-established truth who would be, at best, tolerated.

The genius of ideas cannot be captured in their historical context. The ideas concerning democracy and freedom espoused by Jefferson in the Declaration of Independence and by Madison in his constitution making were larger than the minds that gave them voice. Slavery, gender discrimination, and outrageous treatment of Native Americans marred that great beginning. The genius of the foundation principles inherent in the Constitution has, in spite of those narrow attitudes, consistently resulted in expanding rights while guarding against retrenchment and restriction. The concept of an ever more inclusive interpretation has most often answered Madison's fear that a Bill of Rights might, in future generations, become restrictive because an enumeration of such rights could omit others that later generations would require. Nonpreferentialism, with its flawed view of history, remains just such a threat to the notion of expanding rights.

Supreme Court precedents are crucial for an orderly democracy. To repeat, as new precedents have emerged in our history the Court has traditionally expanded on the rights of citizens. In *Brown* v. *Board of Education* (1954), an 1896 precedent was overturned. Today the *Plessey* v. *Ferguson* decision, which outlined the constitutionality of separate but equal facilities for blacks, is an antique, a reminder of a nation's blind past. Meanwhile, *Griswold* v. *State of Connecticut* (1965) on the question of access to birth control information and *Roe* v. *Wade* (1973) on the right to abortion as a privacy issue have provided access to the Ninth Amendment, which guarantees that rights enumerated in the Constitution shall not "deny or disparage other [rights] retained by the people."

Even as nonpreferentialist proponents speak of values and the student's right to pray in some organized fashion, there is a growing awareness that the diversity and factionalism, which Madison recognized as a protection of rights at the national level, have blossomed in vast numbers of communities across the land. Protestant hegemony is now fading in most hamlets, towns, and cities. That fact alone helps define the First Amendment in terms of which Madison would have approved in 1789. Any religious establishment, no matter how mild or bland, is patently unfair to existing minorities and politically destructive for the current majority. One recalls Madison's warning in the *Memorial and Remonstrance*: "Who does not see that the same authority which can establish Christianity, in exclusion of all other Religions, may establish with the same ease any particular sect of Christians, in exclusion of all other sects?"[14] Establishment in any form is a threat to the very democratic tradition we cherish.

Accommodationism: Give It a Rest

It is particularly disturbing to observe in 1996 the resurrection of the old prayer amendments of the 1980s. Negotiations among leaders of the religious and political right now appear aimed at yet another attack on nonestablishment. School vouchers* are an integral part of this strategy. As new proposals float and old rhetoric is refurbished, the simple reality is that school prayer in any form that extends beyond the protection of the individual student right to pray constitutes a direct or implied violation of the establishment clause of the First Amendment.

---

*The school voucher plan would allow parents to send their children to any school of the parents' choice. A voucher (whose value is derived from the parents' tax contribution to the public school system) would serve as a "credit memo" at any private or sectarian school. This plan is being promoted as a means of setting federal or state subsidies for nonpublic schools.

So then, as we turn to the cases that are the heart of this study, certain presuppositions are unapologetically set forth. First, and most important, the two religion clauses of the First Amendment are permanently joined in principle. *Only* complete separation of church and state, with absolutely no establishment, will guarantee free exercise of religion. To whatever degree a form of establishment, no matter how mild, enters the Constitution through the amending process, free exercise is dust. If free exercise is a natural right not conferred by any state, then any allowance for the control of conscience of any person or group, no matter how small, is a denial of the principle of free exercise for all others whatsoever. Indeed, there are degrees of establishment but there are no degrees of freedom of conscience: it's all or none.

Second, under any reasonable interpretation of the free exercise clause in its historical context, toleration was specifically rejected as a concept. As early as 1776 toleration was replaced by Madisonian phrasing: "all men are equally entitled to the free exercise of religion, according to the dictates of conscience."[15] That language replaced the words "all men should enjoy the fullest toleration in the exercise of religion" in the Virginia Declaration of Rights.

Third, the Constitution has indeed mandated a full accommodation to all persons respecting free exercise of religion. The First Amendment makes an ultimate accommodation to a free conscience. Any reasonable reading of the history of the free exercise clause makes it clear that all consciences, of whatever persuasion, are beyond government control. And even the "exercise" of conscience is protected save where compelling state interest is demonstrated. It is this "accommodation" to the human conscience that makes it absolutely necessary to forbid any and all establishments of religion that turn accommodation into selectivity. Any establishment is a violation of an ultimate accommodation that allows no other subset of accommodations. Madison phrased it properly when he pointed out that religion is removed from the "cognizance" of the state.

Fourth, any use of accommodation theory to amend the First Amendment is either redundant or destructive of the religion clauses included in the amendment. In late 1995 Representatives Henry Hyde (R-Ill.) and Ernest Istook (R-Okla.) introduced two proposed constitutional amendments, both of which sought to reverse the protection of free exercise secured by the establishment clause. The Hyde proposal would "accommodate" religious schools by providing funding; the Istook amendment would guarantee the right of the majority of students in any school district to establish religious practices in the classroom and in ceremonies. In both cases, if adopted, the amendments would eviscerate the establishment clause. At that point the "absolute" accommodation to a free conscience guaranteed in the First Amendment would be replaced with conditional accommodation based on a government definition of religion.

Finally, accommodation theory relies on Justice Rehnquist's words denying the need for the government to be "neutral between religion and irreligion." But what of the conscience of the citizen? If one's conscience produces "irreligion," then that citizen is at risk under the Rehnquist doctrine for following the dictates of her or his conscience. The debates of 1789 in Congress prove decisively, in spite of the Rehnquist argument, that the lawmakers recognized no such distinction. Indeed, if it were otherwise, the government, as we have argued above, would be in the business of defining what is and is not religion. Nothing would more clearly violate the no establishment provision.

As currently employed, the very concept of accommodation suggests the need of the state to define that to which it is making accommodation. And accommodate to what? Who is to accommodate whom? Which demands require accommodation? Which may be legitimately denied? Would it be so simple to substitute for "it's just a little prayer" the phrase, "it's just a little satan adoration"? The power to accommodate is the power to control and therefore to refuse accommodation.

The state has no right either to tolerate or accommodate in matters of religion. In either case a diminution of the natural right of free conscience, so graphically enunciated in Jefferson's Bill for Religious Freedom, is likely.

When the Anglican Church dominated the Virginia government's policy respecting religion in the 1760s, the colonial authorities did accommodate those religions that were prepared to keep the rules respecting Protestant religious dissent. In contrast, those dissenting Baptists in Virginia who, exercising their religious convictions, did not conform to official rules found themselves the victims of persecution and imprisonment. Why? Madison posed that question when he described them as "publishing their religious Sentiments which in the main are very orthodox."[16] Inevitably accommodation is a two-way street. Accommodation by the state alters the long-cherished tradition of a voluntary church in a free state. The First Amendment religion clauses remove accommodation from the table of legislative action by providing protection for what were deemed natural rights of conscience. Accommodationism and governmental tolerance based on a nonpreferentialist reading of the Constitution would perpetuate in the fabric of our judicial system the outrages described in the individual cases which shall be cited here.

Notes

1. *Lynch* v. *Donnelly* was decided in 1984 and the majority held, in the words of Chief Justice Warren Burger, that there is "an unbroken history of official acknowledgement by all three branches of government of the role of religion in American life from at least 1789." With his distaste for absolutes, Burger spoke for his four colleagues upholding the city of Pawtucket, Rhode Island, as not having violated the establishment clause, notwithstanding the religious significance of the creche displayed on public property.

2. Chief Justice Burger wrote these words following a citation from Justice Lewis Powell in which Powell wrote, "It has never been thought either possible or desirable to enforce a regimen of total separation." Burger failed to cite Powell's immediately preceding sentence which read: "Yet despite Madison's admonition and the 'sweep of the absolute prohibition' of the Clauses, this nation's history has not been one of entirely sanitized separation between Church and State." Powell was not talking about Constitutional requirements, but about history which, he said, raised such "perplexing questions." Nowhere does Powell suggest that his historical observations require some form of accommodation to religious institutions.

3. *Lee* v. *Weisman,* 505 US 577 (1992).

4. Robert S. Alley, ed., *James Madison on Religious Liberty* (Amherst, N.Y.: Prometheus Books, 1989), p. 87.

5. Leonard Levy, *The Establishment Clause* (New York: Macmillan, 1994), pp. 83–93.

6. See Justice Souter's concurring opinion in *Lee* v. *Weisman,* 90–1014, June 24, 1992.

7. Robert S. Alley, *The Supreme Court on Church and State* (New York: Oxford University Press, 1988), p. 247.

8. Quoted in Edward F. Humphrey, *Nationalism and Religion in America, 1774–1789* (New York: Russell & Russell, 1965), p. 404.

9. Jefferson made this point in a letter to Madison: "The declaration that religious faith shall be unpunished, does not give impunity to criminal acts dictated by religious error. . . ." *JMPapers*, vol. 11, p. 213.

10. Richard John Neuhaus, "Contending for the Future: Overcoming the Pfefferian Inversion" (paper presented at the National Symposium on the First Amendment Religious Liberty Clauses and American Public Life, Charlottesville, Va., April 11–13, 1988), p. 186.

11. *Texas Monthly* v. *Bullock,* 480 US 1 (1989).

12. In his letter to Jasper Adams, Madison pointedly stated that, "it will scarcely be contended that Government has suffered by the exemption of Religion from its cognizance, or its pecuniary aid." (Gallard Hunt, ed., *The Writings of James Madison,* vol. 9 [New York: G. P. Putnam, 1910], p. 487).

13. *United States* v. *Lee*, 455 US 25 (1982).

14. "On Behalf of Religious Liberty: James Madison's *Memorial and Remonstrance*," *This Constitution,* no. 12 (Fall 1986): 26–33.

15. Virginia Declaration of Rights, *JMPapers*, vol. 1, p. 174.

16. *JMPapers,* vol. 1, p. 107.

3

Fundamentalism and the Court

In recent history there have been two powerful forces at work resisting the creation and/or continued existence of secular states which have voluntary religion and no establishment: religious institutions and certain political leaders.

Religious organizations, with amazing frequency, have sought to turn the state to their advantage. Throughout hundreds of centuries religious institutions have demonstrated an ability to manipulate the political system to their advantage. By the same token, political leaders have coveted the clout that religious organizations possess over the population of the kingdom or state in question. When this competition evolves into conflict, each party turns to its particular strengths. Confrontations occur when the power of one closely matches that of the other. One of the most famous examples of this is the encounter between Pope Gregory VII and Henry IV at the castle of Canosa in 1077. The pope claimed that he alone could invest bishops of the Church. Henry defied the pope and appointed the archbishop of Milan in 1075. Gregory excommunicated Henry in 1076 and the confrontation at Canosa pitted miter against scepter. The pope reinstated Henry on a promise of obedience to Rome. It was a political victory for Henry, as the pope had lost his advantage while Henry continued to ignore future papal claims. The goal then, and in hundreds of similar encounters since, was to attain possession of superior power without losing the viability of the opposing force. Domination without destruction was the object. In the long run each combatant needed the other in the struggle for power. Each sought to bend the other to do his bidding.

Many other examples of church–state conflict are evident throughout history. Henry VIII's failure to force the papacy in Rome to bend to his request for annulment of his marriage to Catherine of Aragon led to the creation of the Church of England in 1631. In Germany, faced with a powerful Roman Church, the monarchy found satisfaction in a local cleric, Martin Luther, whose loyalty was to Germany. In contrast, French theologian John Calvin championed a theory of statecraft in which the true church was intended to dominate the state. His success implementing such a system in Geneva served as a model for sixteenth-century Europe. These examples, and many others, were a part of the history of colonial settlers that began in 1607.

It was such conflicts and resolutions, many of which generated war and persecution, that prompted most eighteenth-century founders of the new United States of America to seek a buffer between church and state. While many of our seventeenth-century forebears preferred an alliance between Protestantism and the state, European memories were sufficiently vivid that slowly the penchant for establishment was curtailed. Beginning at the national level in 1787, a secular state emerged from Philadelphia, created by men who were, for the most part, devout Christians. The result was a new kind of religious institution, driven by the principle of voluntary association.

This outcome appeared salutary for Protestants, so long as they represented the vast majority of the population. In 1996 the luxury of that majority status is all but a memory at the national level. Still, there remain large numbers of communities where Protestants, Catholics, or some other group (such as Mormons) are dominant. In the case of Protestants, the dominant denomination locally may represent only a small part of the huge variety in the entire tradition. Nevertheless, where there is a working religious majority, its leaders frequently seek advantages for their faith from local political leaders, who in turn envision a powerful political base stemming from the membership of the religious majority in the community.

As noted previously, the first European settlers in North America quickly established the Protestant religion in several forms, dependent upon the proclivities of the majority in any given colony. By 1607, when the first American colony was established at Jamestown, conditions in England had reached a crisis stage. In the fifty-three years following that date, the Anglican Church was disestablished and reestablished; a king, Charles I, was executed; the King James Version of the Bible appeared; religious wars gripped England; Oliver Cromwell ruled briefly over a new commonwealth which in turn unraveled, reigniting loyalty to a crown that returned to power in 1660; religious debate highlighted sessions of a rancorous Parliament as it sought to replace one established religion with another; and many seeds of later bitterness between Ireland and England were sown. By 1689, a mere thirty years after the return of the monarchy, the single Anglican Church supremacy was replaced by that institution's "most favored church" status, and dissenting Protestants enjoyed a wide range of toleration.

This religious-political cauldron affected every English settlement in seventeenth-century North America and these effects were expressed differently in the various geographical sections of the colonies. Three degrees of tolerance can be ascertained. The crosscurrents in England created a natural environment for the growth and expansion of the single Anglican Church in Virginia and the other southern colonies. However, to Plymouth in New England first came a dissenting lot of Separatists, Plymouth Colony followed, within less than ten years, by Puritans intent upon establishing the "true" Protestant Church in Massachusetts as a beacon for the world. In accordance with this outlook, all non-Puritan groups were persecuted and frequently driven from the borders of the Massachusetts Bay Colony. As the climate changed in England, a more generous establishment policy became the practice in the middle colonies, including New Jersey and Pennsylvania. However, with the exception of the brief experiment with complete church–state separation in Rhode Island under the guidance of Roger Williams, John Clarke, Anne Hutchinson, and others, the model was for an established Protestant faith exhibiting more (Pennsylvania) or less (Virginia) toleration to other brands of Christianity.

England does not and did not have a federal system whereby individual counties or shires can legislate for themselves, apart from Parliament and the British government. Further, when Christianity became dominant in England in the Middle Ages, the result was the establishment of the Roman Catholic Church. After Henry VIII broke

with Rome over his failed marriage, that English establishment continued under its new name, Anglicanism. In truth each of the thirteen
English colonies was a microcosm of the English establishment system, albeit with a different establishment from colony to colony. The
central government for the colonies, until 1776, was the English king
and Parliament with its unquestioned devotion to Anglicanism.

Creation of the United States, first under the Articles of Confeder-
ation and then under the Constitution in 1789, presented each colony
with a challenge because there was no history of a state church in the
new federal republic. There was a blank slate on that issue. The Constitution of 1787 created a genuinely secular republic, as it made
absolutely no mention of a state religion. The single mention of religion had to do with prohibition of religious tests for public office.
Many of the thirteen states had not been transformed accordingly
when the first Congress met in 1789.

Reluctantly the members of Congress accepted Madison's plea for
consideration of a bill of rights when they met in New York in 1789.
What was to become the First Amendment offered sixteen words of
regulation respecting religious matters. The very first clause, "Congress shall make no law respecting an establishment of religion," broke
once and for all with the English tradition and mandated voluntary
religion in a free state.

Nevertheless, the roots of establishment were buried deep in the
English tradition and its many faces of Protestantism. Thus, when
modern evangels call for some form of virtue in the body politic, it is
natural for them to use colonial history with its establishment traditions to back up their claims. For example, President Ronald Reagan
was fond of quoting John Winthrop concerning a city on a hill in
Massachusetts Bay Colony. That, however, was a vision of a Christian
state which was rejected by the founders in 1789 and by the Commonwealth of Massachusetts in 1833. Even so, throughout the nineteenth century the de facto reality was a Protestant hegemony in most
states in political and social matters. The result was conflicts similar
to that between Catholics and Protestants in Philadelphia, the city of
"brotherly love," in 1844, leading to death and destruction perpetrated by the Protestant majority.

Old habits seldom die easily and in spite of more than fifty years
of Supreme Court decisions (beginning in 1940), the prerevolutionary

establishment mentality is continually laid upon the national agenda. Before we examine the heroic struggles for liberty and justice in public schools across the nation, it is essential to understand the power behind the antagonism that erupted after 1962 toward the Supreme Court's decisions regarding establishment of religion.

One of the first attacks by a religious leader on the Court's *Engel* decision came from evangelist Billy Graham. It was a high profile, olympian denunciation which was taken to heart by many members of the Congress and therefore was effective in galvanizing a political movement to amend the First Amendment. But Graham did not testify before any committees. He contented himself with offering to his flock, the media, and interested politicians what he considered God's view on the subject. Graham operated without political organization or agenda; consequently, his influence was seldom felt with great intensity at the grassroots level. In marked contrast, Pat Robertson and Jerry Falwell have built political careers out of their proclaimed outrage over Court decisions. We want to examine both strategies in an effort to clarify the power centers that so vigorously denounce the Court's separationist tradition.

Billy Graham: The Religious Politics of Fame

Billy Graham is a man who loves the spotlight and craves celebrity status. He is a person generally uninterested in political and social causes, with little talent for or proclivity toward issue-driven organizations. Beginning in the 1950s his has been a solitary witness as God's man with a message. His books and his crusades manifest a single-minded attention to the personal dimension of the Christian faith and its ultimate impact on the future of the United States. But in Graham's opinion, you didn't organize a movement to obtain legislation and action, you spoke the "word of God," and if enough hearers made decisions for Christ, then God would do the right thing and reward the United States. Graham genuinely seemed to believe that on occasion.

Graham's love of the limelight, which certainly does not exceed the same penchant in Robertson and Falwell, led him to seek out celebrities and political leaders as a means to get his own message out. After twenty years of advocating religion as deeply personal and associating "decisions for Christ" with the nation's future, Graham became a member of President Richard Nixon's "kitchen cabinet" just as the fumes of Watergate overwhelmed the chefs. But few knew the extent of Graham's political activities. In contrast, who doesn't know about the political goals and actions of Pat Robertson? In the past fifty years we have witnessed two markedly different styles of religious public address that together have aided the unrelenting attack on the First Amendment now in evidence.

My first encounter with Billy Graham was in the mid-1950s while I was a student at Southern Baptist Seminary in Louisville, Kentucky. Graham spoke to our student body one evening and openly asserted his regret that he had no scholarly theological or biblical instruction. He urged the seminarians to pursue their studies with diligence, using appropriate scholarly tools with which to study biblical texts. In fact he seemed to approve biblical criticism. My first up-close impression of this exploding television religious phenomenon was quickly obliterated by a sermon in that same chapel the next morning when Graham, pumping his Bible relentlessly, served up a plate of emotional appeals to the Bible as the unerring Word of God that left reason in the dust. Suddenly, as if in a stupor, nearly the entire student body of some one thousand people rose as Graham gave the altar call for all to rise who would commit themselves to *his* Gospel. As I sat staring at my classmates I was certain that I was the only person there not standing. I learned later that perhaps a dozen of us had "embarrassed" the school by our behavior. In later years, when I read a description by Reinhold Niebuhr (a distinguished theologian and Protestant scholar) of Graham as "a domesticated and tailored leftover from the wild and woolly frontier evangelistic campaigns," it rang true.

Throughout his entire career Graham has sought to incorporate mainstream Protestant America with all-inclusive crusades across the land. He is a master of salesmanship. When Graham inaugurated White House religious services for President Nixon, Niebuhr described it as "The King's Chapel and the King's Court." With typical insight, Niebuhr went on to observe that Nixon, at the urging of Billy Graham, "has established a conforming religion by semiofficially inviting representatives of all the disestablished religions. . . ."

Graham was no stealth evangel. His crusades, widely displayed by the new medium of television, provided ample evidence as to what he was about. Graham was a natural ally for the simplistic religious thoughts of President Dwight Eisenhower. And it was during Eisenhower's presidency that Graham appears to have become a friend of Richard Nixon. Throughout the 1950s and 1960s Graham tried to maintain his nonpartisan, "above politics" image. While John Kennedy, we are told by White House insider Ted Sorenson, cringed when he was informed that Graham wanted to see him, the evangelist had ample access to Lyndon Johnson. Johnson must have loved it. After all, Graham was ecstatic over communist containment theory as practiced in the Vietnam War. He declared that God was now using the United States in a grand design in which China slowly replaced the Soviets as the atheistic menace. Still and all, Graham argued that America could only hope to prevail if it "turned to God." This turning was specific and individual in character. Believers, one by one, must make a difference in American life so that God would bless our military efforts.

Graham's style did not include the creation of a formal political organization, either hidden or overt. To achieve his vision for Christianity it would be necessary for Graham personally to be at the right hand of power, something he achieved early in his career. He had few legislative projects of his own and generally confined himself to proclaiming the menace of ungodly communism.

I recall as if it were only a few days ago my attendance at a Southern Baptist Convention meeting in Atlantic City in 1964. It was a celebration of the One Hundred Fiftieth anniversary of the Triennial Convention, the first nationally organized Baptist movement in the United States. The speaker for the session was Billy Graham. Bible in hand, the timbre of his voice never better, Graham mesmerized the audience of perhaps fifteen thousand with the biblical-cold war rhetoric that had become his hallmark. As his audience warmed to his frightening words, he assaulted the moral decadence of the United States and "authoritatively" warned that unless America turned to God, God would punish the failure of the church in this nation with Soviet atomic bombs and bullets. God was planning to use this atheist enclave to purge the sin from America, to lay judgment upon a nation that had failed to heed God's calling as the chosen nation. Only a great revival could save us. It was a puzzle to me at the time why God was punishing the United States with Russian military might when, by Graham's own admission, the church in the Soviet Union was in shambles. But logic was not the order of the day. Graham intended to the living hell out of his audience, calling for "decisions for Christ," as he built his ark with the souls he saved during his crusades.

So effective was the preacher with his dramatic turns that you could almost hear the roar of missiles and exploding bombs even as the cadence of Graham's voice rocked the microphone on the platform. And for once Graham had been given a single domestic issue to buttress his grand global design. The Supreme Court decisions of 1962 and 1963 concerning prayer and Bible reading in public schools were all the evidence that Graham and God needed to demonstrate our nation's failure. High on God's list of sins in America was this perceived removal of prayer from the public schools by the Supreme Court. For that we would surely pay dearly.

The interlocking of history and divine initiative in the historical continuum was the trademark of Graham's message. His God was a hands-on kind of deity. There was no freedom except the freedom to embrace Graham's style of Christianity. In the cosmic drama unfolding in Graham's mind, there was no room for life, liberty, and the pursuit of happiness. Equality was a myth. Free inquiry was an evil. Truth was revealed by God to Graham through the Bible. He was never quite clear as to how one knew that *Graham's* vision of biblical truth was the correct one. He just said it. He became, intentionally, the religious authority for millions of Americans. Self-government, constitutional democracy, and human rights were set aside on behalf of a deity committed to mass conflagrations and hideous last days for the unsaved. According to a book Graham wrote on miracles, during the height of World War II God surrounded a young Christian girl with a ring of angels to protect her modesty in a Nazi prison camp. What an interesting view of a "loving" God who apparently in every other instance *ignored* prison camps where millions of Jews were systematically slaughtered.

True to his style, Graham never resorted to the formation of a political organization. He depended upon the power of his personality and public popularity to affect policy. In the minds of the majority of citizens he undoubtedly was the voice of Protestant America. Having co-opted the main line clergy in nearly every city in the nation, few critics were heard as he offered his version of Christianity to the high and mighty.

When the debate over school prayer was first on the front pages of the nation's newspapers, Graham castigated the Supreme Court for its bad judgment and urged corrective measures. But when Senate and House committees held hearings on the subject, Graham stood above the fray. He did not testify. In contrast, mainline Protestant and Jewish leaders inundated the committees with arguments favorable to the Court decisions. The National Association of Evangelicals did urge a constitutional amendment to correct the Court, but the grassroots organizations so carefully planned by the Christian Coalition in the 1990s had no counterpart in the 1960s. Graham's influence was seen more in the efforts made by members of Congress, many of whom were lay communicants of churches, to pass a constitutional amendment. Graham may have failed his constituents by speaking from Olympus in the belief that something would happen in Congress. It did not.

By 1965 both Pat Robertson and Jerry Falwell were proclaiming their nonpolitical religious messages through the use of television. When in the 1970s they adopted a political strategy, they surely recognized what must have seemed a lost opportunity by Graham. They would not make the same mistake. But what they were able to accomplish in 1980 was built solidly upon a mood generated by Graham which had, for millions of followers, eviscerated the intellectual content of the Christian religion so effectively voiced in the 1930s, 1940s, and 1950s by persons such as Harry Emerson Fosdick, the most popular radio preacher of the 1930s and '40s; George Buttrick, a distinguished Presbyterian minister in New York City and popular lecturer on a national circuit in the 1950s; and Reinhold Niebuhr.

In the 1960s most so-called fundamentalists were largely apolitical. Many did not vote. Graham wanted to deliver the fundamentalist vote to Richard Nixon, but he knew better than to become openly partisan. While most observers knew by 1969 that Graham was Nixon's ally, the evangelist went to great lengths publicly to distance himself from partisan politics.

The Christian Right: From Moral Majority to Christian Coalition

The graying of Graham was completed with the demise of Nixon. Thus, when the political operatives for the extreme right began their search for fresh votes to stimulate a new wave of conservative power in the nation, they latched on to the religion of television. And as the new breed of religious television personalities were assessed, the clear choice of the right wing politicos was Jerry Falwell.

The *Roe* v. *Wade* decision of 1973 appears to have triggered the political interests of Jerry Falwell, a Baptist preacher from Lynchburg, Virginia. His "Old Time Gospel Hour," which appeared on a weekly basis, had its television debut in 1956. For over fifteen years Falwell preached a standard fundamentalist, biblical, literalist message to his Baptist church and his extended congregation. Slowly, his show grew to a nationally syndicated program. According to Falwell, he came to the conclusion that he must find a way to influence the nation to reject *Roe*. That impetus led him to political activism in the name of a moral cause. In 1980 Falwell was, for most Americans, a fringe figure, the latest edition of religion hawking on the tube. That set him and his colleagues apart from Billy Graham's use of television, which avoided, as much as possible, association with gross fund raising.

When Ronald Reagan was nominated by the Republican party in 1980, Falwell's stock rose rapidly. Selected to head the Moral Majority by a small collection of right-leaning political pros, Falwell moved quickly to solidify his leadership among religious broadcasters. In the fall of 1980, at a regional gathering of those broadcasters in Lynchburg, Virginia, Falwell's college hosted Reagan, greeting him with bumper stickers reading "Christians for Reagan."

As I sat quietly in the Holiday Inn, the hotel headquarters for the broadcasters' convention, a group of four men, obviously ministers, entered the lobby with a national magazine in hand.[1] Beaming from the cover was Jerry Falwell. One of the men observed, "We've finally made it!" Another added, "They can't ignore us anymore." Both men were correct, but there was a sense of pathos in their voices, suggesting a long winter since the Scopes trial of 1925.*

Fundamentalists had never been particularly active politically, but

---

*John T. Scopes was arrested and tried for teaching Darwin's theory of evolution in his Dayton, Tennessee, classroom. Scopes was defended by Clarence Darrow while William Jennings Bryan represented the state. Scopes was convicted and fined $100, but the case was overturned on technical grounds when it was appealed to the Tennessee supreme court. And for most of the nation Bryan's testimony about biblical inerrancy made his efforts appear ridiculous.

after 1925 they seemed to disappear from the landscape. Radio was the medium which brought to the public ear a dozen moderate to liberal ministers such as Ralph Sockman and Harry Emerson Fosdick, who wore the label "modernist" with pride and some humor. Those men dominated Sunday from their pulpits via the radio. In 1929 NBC provided Fosdick a weekly national forum called "National Vespers." CBS unveiled the "Lutheran Hour" in 1930. By 1945 almost all of the Protestant denominations were in the radio market, as was the highly successful Mormon Tabernacle choir. Few fundamentalists competed in this electronic awakening, a major exception being Charles E. Fuller, whose "Old Fashioned Revival Hour" began in 1934 as one of the few syndicated programs for which it was possible to find an audience and raise money.[2]

The 1950s saw the beginning, with Graham and Bishop Sheen, of a phenomenon that reached its zenith that fall of 1980 in Lynchburg. Fundamentalists had "arrived." The motel lobby crowd quickly moved to lunch, where Jerry Falwell addressed an overflow crowd that anticipated the arrival of Reagan later in the week. It was one of the last times that Falwell would publicly state that if you do not pray in the name of Jesus, God will not answer. This is one of the few adjustments he has made over the years in the name of good taste.

As we have noted, Graham's ideology was circumscribed by his awareness that his larger public was not as committed to fundamentalism as he was himself. Graham was no advocate of a fundamentalist theocracy; his substitute was a simplistic civil religion more acceptable to a wider audience. The dual standard that was evident in his appearance at Southern Baptist Seminary in 1954 and his lack of purity often offended those who read their own calling as setting forth a national agenda of foreign and domestic policy. These were persons unprepared to accept a secular state and unwilling to act in cautious ways for achieving some moderate compromise. They were "true believers."

Falwell's targets included the prayer decisions of the Supreme Court. He wrote in his magazine, *Fundamentalist Journal,* in 1985, "Secular Humanism has eliminated the teaching of Judeo-Christian values from our public schools. We must lobby for freedom of religion. We need to mobilize and deluge our congressmen with mail urging the passing of a prayer amendment."[3] Jerry Falwell finally entered the power elite in 1980 through hard work and a clearly defined political goal. His celebrity status grew out of his political actions, in direct contrast with Graham, whose political actions were shaped by his celebrity status.

It is a sign of the religious rift between fundamentalists and non-fundamentalist American Protestants that the president who preceded Reagan, Jimmy Carter, was perhaps the most dedicated Christian man ever to hold the office. Carter required no religious front man to interpret his thoughts on prayer. He articulated them for himself. Falwell surely sensed that fellow Baptist Carter was not an ally in his battle over *Roe* and school prayer. In fact, Carter and Falwell held opposing views on those issues. In the election of 1980, the Religious Right turned to nontheological Ronald Reagan instead.

The leaders of the various facets of the Religious Right began to come together for the first time in the election of 1980, and this confluence can directly be linked to the growing power and effectiveness of television. This new breed of evangel was politically charged and ready made for exploitation by right wing political operatives such as Ed McAteer, Paul Weyrich, and Howard Phillips. For example, a religious-political rally in Texas was the occasion for the recruitment of Jerry Falwell to head the Moral Majority.

Jerry Falwell had begun to assert his political concerns after the 1973 *Roe* decision. After his selection to head the Moral Majority, Falwell campaigned for President Reagan and pressed vigorously for the adoption of a school prayer amendment to the Constitution. He was a frequent visitor to the Reagan White House and became something of a religious mentor for the president and his cabinet. Reagan himself was quoted widely when he noted that he had been looking at the biblical prophesies and thought they might well indicate the end was near. Falwell's influence was obvious.

Falwell's commitment to George Bush in 1988 was not helpful to the evangelist, and his star began to decline. Falwell began to experience financial setbacks with his projects and became involved in the ill-fated effort to bail out Jim Bakker's empire in North Carolina after Bakker was convicted of crimes and sent to jail. Neither Bakker's Pentecostal followers nor the Falwell fundamentalist troop took kindly to that. The theological gulf between the two systems is wide and deep, something Falwell should have known.

With the Bush defeat in 1992, Falwell lost all access to power in

Washington and, having abandoned the Moral Majority, he sought to regain national attention by selling a videotape implying that President Clinton was implicated in a murder in Arkansas. He pushed the tape over his "Old Time Gospel Hour" television show. It would be a mistake to dismiss Falwell as ancient history, but his prospects are not bright in 1996.

Pat Robertson, who first appeared on the air with his "700 Club" in the mid-1960s, began moving into a political action stance nearly simultaneously to Falwell, in the late 1970s.

Marion Gordon "Pat" Robertson was born in 1930, two years prior to the election of his father, A. Willis Robertson, to the U.S. House of Representatives. Willis was a Democrat, but an extremely conservative politician, completely loyal to his patron, Senator Harry F. Byrd. Pat graduated from Washington and Lee University where he majored in history, and in 1952, after service in Korea with the Marines, he entered Yale Law School. After graduation, unable to pass the bar exam, he went into business in New York. Failure in those ventures led to severe depression.

Robertson's mother, Gladys, was an intensely religious woman who left the Baptist church in Lexington, Virginia, where the family lived, to join a charismatic group. In 1956 she introduced her son to some of her charismatic friends and he subsequently enrolled in New York Theological Seminary, from which he graduated in 1959. He moved to Virginia Beach and was ordained as a Southern Baptist minister although his beliefs concerning speaking in tongues, faith healing, and spiritual gifts were at odds with that denomination.

In 1960 Pat Robertson purchased a struggling UHF television station for the sum of $37,000 and got a charter for his Christian Broadcasting Network (CBN). With financial assistance from friends he went on the air. In 1963 he asked 700 viewers to pledge $10 each per month to defray expenses at the station. The givers became known as the 700 Club.

In 1965 Robertson hired Jim and Tammy Bakker and their 1966 on-air floodgate of tears brought large contributions to the station. This resulted in the launching of a nightly program hosted by Jim Bakker. The audience, small at first, grew quickly with the expansion of cable television. During this phase Robertson became a popular faith healer and began to predict that the end of the world would occur prior to the year 2000, a concept that infected the Reagan administration.

In 1981 Robertson formed his first political group, the Freedom Council, designed to encourage people to become involved in politics. After Ronald Reagan's inauguration, many of the highest officials in the president's administration made frequent appearances on the "700 Club." Robertson used the program to push his political agenda, which more and more seemed focused on his own ambitions. He called for an amendment to repeal *Roe* v. *Wade,* he demanded an amendment to authorize public school prayer, and he urged support for funding of private religious schools. Particularly harsh were his attacks on the public schools, which he felt should be abandoned. When it came to foreign policy, Robertson used his peculiar brand of biblical inerrancy to predict events in the Near East. The public took particular notice of him when he claimed to have convinced God to divert a hurricane from the Virginia coast.

Robertson, abandoning his ordination, ran for president in 1988. This failed campaign caused him to reevaluate his strategy, and led to the founding of the Christian Coalition. Using his constant access to the public on television, he continued to perform faith healing, to attack President Clinton, and to encourage laws to "correct" the Bill of Rights. Robertson is extremely wealthy. He presides over Regent University in Virginia Beach, Virginia, and he recently purchased the television production company MTM.

Pat Robertson seems genuinely deluded into thinking that he is God's man with God's message and uses his charismatic "gifts" to convince his viewers of his heavenly connections.

Falwell, Robertson, and other televangelist leaders carefully developed, although not always in concert, a full-blown political agenda for Christians which culminated in the presidential run by Robertson in 1988 and the founding of the Christian Coalition in 1993 to assume the reins from Falwell's Moral Majority, by then defunct.

Since 1981 public education itself has become a target of mounting criticism by Religious Right leadership. The consequence is that public schools are, more than ever, in jeopardy, a target of vicious attacks upon thousands of school teachers in classrooms across the land. Robertson, Falwell, and the Christian Coalition argue that public schools without prayer become value free, relativistic bastions of immorality. This scurrilous and dishonest assertion is aimed at teachers, underpaid and overworked, who dedicate themselves daily to the welfare of the nation's children. These maligned public servants, our neighbors and our friends who value the welfare and education of our children, deserve better.

In a recent discussion in which I participated, sponsored by the National Humanities Center, twenty-five public high school teachers, all but one active in a church or synagogue, identified values upon which they focus in their classrooms. Their list included honesty, integrity, fairness, responsibility, dependability, generosity, compassion, independence, tolerance, cooperation, and kindness. Further, they noted, their respect and love for the children will not allow them to impose their own singular definitions of faith upon their students. That very regard for fragile and precious relationships in class is now being attacked by dogma-driven citizens bent upon destroying public education. In the process, what messages are transmitted to students who regularly hear from self-styled moralists that their classrooms are devoid of values and that their teachers preside over a moral cesspool?

In 1994 Speaker of the House Newt Gingrich once again dramatically injected the prayer issue into the public discourse on education. A year later there had been no action, only a couple of House hearings that asked those testifying to react to legislation that had not been formulated. It was a farce. Then, toward the end of 1995, two constitutional amendments were introduced. One, filed by Representative Istook, was innocuous. The Istook amendment reads, "Nothing in this Constitution shall prohibit acknowledgements of the religious heritage, beliefs, or traditions of the people, or prohibit student-sponsored prayer in public schools. Neither the United States nor any State shall compose any official prayer or compel joining in prayer, or discriminate against religious expression or belief." With the possible exception of "student-sponsored prayer," which may be interpreted several ways, the strictest interpretation of the content of the amendment would find it in accord with Supreme Court decisions. Indeed, Rep. Istook has conceded in his wording that the *Engel*, *Schempp*, and *Weisman* decisions are acceptable to him. If, for sake of argument, public schools were in fact bastions of barbarism, as Pat Robertson seems to believe, this amendment is a pointless pretense of a response which barely qualifies as legislation.

In point of fact, that the authors of this bill have an agenda is patently clear. Their sole purpose is to disrupt Supreme Court jurisprudence running back to 1940, and passage of the bill will be tantamount to malicious mischief. Altering the First Amendment so very slightly with vague language about "student-sponsored prayer" would certainly bring much confusion to school administrators while setting a precedent of amending the Bill of Rights. By bringing in through the back door what the framers specifically rejected—a state authorization of religion—the proposed amendment could easily require that the Court re-examine its whole church/state history. The Istook amendment is a piece of fluff designed to confuse the Court precedents of some fifty-six years. Fortunately it seems doomed from the beginning.

So where is the real action for the Christian Coalition? It lies in the new Henry Hyde-Orrin Hatch amendment also introduced into the Congress in 1995. The Hyde-Hatch amendment reads: "Neither the United States nor any State shall deny benefits to or otherwise discriminate against any private person or group on account of religious expression, belief, or identity; nor shall the prohibition on laws respecting an establishment of religion be construed to require such discrimination." With one phrase, "Neither the United States nor any State shall *deny benefits*," their strategy is clear. The Coalition, consistent with the fifteen-year pounding message of Robertson and Falwell, abandons the public schools to perdition and asks for equal funding of religious schools. No one should say Americans were not warned. In 1994 Regent University education professor Wally Cox wrote that since public schools teach beliefs like evolution, contrary to his Christian views, either public schools should cease receiving tax dollars or religious schools should be funded by taxes. He went on to say, "This issue of discriminatory tax money distribution may be a far more central pursuit than the school prayer amendment."[4] That is precisely the Robertson agenda—vouchers.

Vouchers, providing state and federal funds to pay for attendance at private schools, are a frontal attack on the First Amendment and nonestablishment. The ploy of the Religious Right is to so smear public education that the claim can be made that what is being taught there violates free exercise. By this logic free exercise inevitably wins out over establishment, a point quite congenial with the insupportable position that the founders meant to subordinate establishment to free exercise. Unfortunately for the Religious Right, nothing in the record supports such a reading.

In this game, driven by the goal of funding private religious schools and home schools, the vast majority of students in elementary and secondary schools are eagerly sacrificed. Robertson and Falwell know that vouchers will be of no help to most present public school students: the meager sum provided will not come near paying the tuition of private schools; the schools would be able to discriminate on any basis they chose; and before any funds are dispensed to public school students, every student currently in a private school would automatically receive a voucher. Robertson and Falwell know their plan will further balkanize public education. Yet, by using the prayer game they also encourage untold numbers of students to tyrannize the minority by voting for graduation prayer. That is something advocates of a voucher program have admitted would be unconstitutional for adults to do. They tell us, "Let the children do it. Let the children break the law. What court will prosecute? So ignore the Constitution and the Bill of Rights. And while you are at it ignore the rights of minorities—Jews, Muslims, atheists, agnostics, Buddhists, Hindus."*

In the long run we know that even if every public school in the nation suddenly had legal authority to mandate some sort of prayer it would not affect the Religious Right in the least. Their complaints about public schools extend to philosophy, textbooks, science, and sex education, and those objections will in no way be erased by student-initiated prayers. But they know that if one dedicated and principled citizen like Lisa Herdahl, whose story will be detailed shortly, can be publicly maligned as antireligious and local sentiments can be mounted against her and her family, the public may come to see her as an agent of the American Civil Liberties Union (ACLU) attempting to destroy religion. If the Christian Coalition can sell that image and the courts generally side with Herdahl, then their case against public education is made. Their hearts are in their own religious enclaves.

The fundamentalist movement has not too subtly moved from pressing for school prayer as their top agenda item to advocating vouchers for religious schools. But before they totally abandon the public schools they are leaving in their wake a nationwide hatred of the Supreme Court prayer decisions by millions of their followers. In small towns and counties across the nation, dominated by variations of

---

*The quotation marks are for emphasis and do not denote attribution.

religious fundamentalism, there are majority movements in defense of local mores and patterns acting with a holy zeal encouraged by the extreme rhetoric of Robertson and Falwell. The stories of some of those victimized by that zeal is the purpose and the focus of this book.

When Dwight Eisenhower or Richard Nixon turned to Billy Graham for advice or assistance, it was as one celebrity to another. Rubbing shoulders with the evangelist was the key to improving one's reputation. Graham received the same rush. With the new collection of religious types the tables are turned, however. Most politicians of both parties really don't want to be seen with Pat Robertson or Jerry Falwell. Instead, the politicians now go to Ralph Reed, executive director of the Christian Coalition, hat in hand. Robertson keeps his distance. His celebrity quotient does not easily translate into votes; it is his organization that presumably delivers those. And that delivery system becomes highly suspect when Robertson goes on the air claiming a Christian Coalition membership of 1.7 million while the post office statistics reveal that the membership magazine is currently mailed monthly only to about 300,000.[5] It seems rather suspect that 1.4 million "members" of the Christian Coalition do not receive the magazine which is the organization's primary means of communicating with its adherents.

Billy Graham represents no lobby. He is himself. Identification with Billy Graham does not automatically translate into assumptions about political philosophy. Graham is at home with politicians like the Johnsons and the Nixons, persons with widely diverging foreign and domestic agendas. Graham may have political preferences, but they do not control his crusade message. The modern evangels and faith healers are altogether different.

Notes

1. I attended this October 1980 meeting in Lynchburg as an observer. I have an audio recording in my possession of the Falwell luncheon speech.

2. Robert S. Alley, "The Television Church," in *TV Genres,* Brian Rose, ed. (Westport, Conn.: Greenwood Press, 1985), p. 398.

3. Jerry Falwell, *Fundamentalist Journal* (January 1985): 10.

4. Joe Taylor, "Prayer Opponents Found in Unlikely Places," *Richmond* (Virginia) *Times Dispatch*, 10 December 1994, p. B8.

5. See *Church and State* magazine, January 1996, published by Americans United for the Separation of Church and State.

4

The Early Years:
Salutes, Prayers, Religion, and Rage

"You have managed to uncover a phrase in our constitution which
no doubt would have gone unnoticed throughout the centuries!"

Children at Risk

In this and the succeeding chapters we will be listening to parents and
children. We will meet children abused by angry communities in the
name of a deity whose existence, for many people, is hard to imagine.
We will experience the offense against the tender consciences of the
nation's greatest treasure. The examination of the harsh treatment
these children and their families received will provide the answer to
the question, "What's wrong with a little prayer?"

I begin with a personal memoir. There are no footnotes, no newspaper accounts. But the events are no less real for all that. In the fall of
1940 I was in fourth grade in a Richmond public school. Early in the
year my teacher distributed a permission slip to be taken home. I duti-
fully delivered the note to my parents. It was necessary for my father or
mother to sign in order for me to take the religion course being taught
in a classroom in Westhampton School. Since it was the early 1940s,
there was no *McCollum* (1948) decision upon which to rely, and religious
instruction often took place during school hours. My father was a Bap-

tist minister who edited a denominational newspaper in Virginia. He quoted James Madison frequently and referred to Roger Williams's belief that righteousness does not give people the right to impose their own definitions upon others. My father believed that the public school class, sponsored by the Virginia Council for Religious Education, later the Virginia Council of Churches, was a violation of the establishment clause. He would not sign. Three years later, in 1944, my dad wrote the following editorial for a Baptist journal in Virginia: "Unfortunately one part of the Christian community frequently expends much of its energy in promoting methods which do violence to the fundamental convictions of another part of the Christian community which is compelled to use its efforts in the defense of spiritual freedom."[1] Four years later, immediately following the *McCollum* opinion, he wrote, "We hold that the state is not an agent which may be used to propagate religion."[2]

Without a signature, I returned to school the following day, gave the teacher the note, and was ushered out into the hall to sit on the steps during the time for the religion class. There I saw my friend, Alvin Lehman, already seated. His parents had refused to sign as well. Now, I must say that we probably enjoyed ourselves more than our classmates and it certainly cemented a lifelong friendship. But it was also a clear example of what such policies do to children. By the end of the second day our classmates were calling Alvin "the Jew." It was the first instance of that happening to him at school. This was clearly a reflection of explanations offered at home the previous night by many parents as their children asked about why Alvin was on the steps. It is interesting that apparently no explanation was offered for my failure to take the class. As I recall, no names were assigned to me. The evening after the first class Alvin's mother phoned my dad and they talked at length. I still recall sitting in his study trying to absorb what was being discussed. At the close of the call my father told me that Mrs. Lehman wanted to rear Alvin as a conservative Jew and did not want him to be subjected to Christian witnessing. As best he could my father tried to explain this to me, pointing out that Alvin's religion was as important to him as mine was to me. I do recall him commenting that each person must approach God according to the claim of his or her conscience. There was no resolution and Alvin and I were left to sit on the steps for the remainder of the year. Neither of us appear scarred by the experience, but it affected both of us deeply.

Last year a reporter heard about the story and asked us to join him at the old Westhampton School for a picture. We arrived only to be told by the acting principal for the day that we probably could not have permission to have the picture taken because it was a controversial subject. We told him we were alumni back for a visit but that did not help. Finally he got in touch with the principal by phone and she gladly authorized the photograph. Without consulting we both moved directly to the same flight of stairs and the same step, where we sat again after fifty some years. "How do you remember so vividly those events?" asked the reporter. I responded that my memory had been reinforced by my parents over the years. Quickly, Alvin responded, "Not me. I was 'the Jew.' I remember on my own."

As we shared those times on the steps long ago we were not aware that the early 1940s were marking a dramatic change in church/state litigation in this country.

In 1940 the Supreme Court, in *Cantwell* v. *Connecticut*, applied the religion clauses to state and local laws for the first time. As noted earlier, Madison had urged the first Congress to make such an application. It was the Fourteenth Amendment (1868) that provided an opportunity to do just that. It read, "No state shall make or enforce any law which shall abridge the privileges or immunities of citizens of the United States nor shall any State deprive any person of life, liberty, or property without due process of law." Justice Owen Roberts, writing for the Court in *Cantwell*, stated: "The fundamental concept of liberty embodied in that [Fourteenth] Amendment embraces the liberties guaranteed by the First Amendment."

Later in 1940, the Court decided a free exercise case that pitted local mores and customs against the rights of a minority. As the Court began to feel its way toward a coherent set of precedents on the religion clauses, victimization of children became a matter of public record. Federal court cases that confronted the discrimination encountered by children in public schools, harassed for holding views at odds with the majority in a given locale, began with Jehovah's Witness Lillian Gobitis and her family in Pennsylvania. In 1935 Walter Gobitis sued the school board of Minersville, Pennsylvania, for expelling his children, Lillian and William, for their refusal to salute the flag and recite the pledge of allegiance. Peter Irons, in his excellent study *The Courage of Their Convictions*, relates that struggle from its inception to the Supreme Court decision of 1940 that found in favor of the school board.[3] On June 3, 1940, Justice Felix Frankfurter, writing the majority opinion of the Supreme Court, which decided *Minersville School District* v. *Gobitis* in an 8 to 1 vote, argued that the state of Pennsylvania had a right to provide for gestures of "respect for the symbol of our national life."[4] Justice Stone dissented, insisting that "by this law the state seeks to coerce these children to express a sentiment which violates their deepest religious convictions." From the distance of fifty-five years it is important to recall that it was not until 1954 that the phrase "under God" was added to the pledge. Therefore, those words had nothing to do with the complaint of the Gobitis family.

Irons published an account of the Gobitis struggle written by Lillian. She faced the torment of the community after becoming the focus of the pledge issue in 1935. Lillian and her brother, Bill, had learned from the president of the Watchtower Society of Jehovah's Witnesses that he would not salute the flag because the Bible tells one not to worship an image. Bill decided he would stop pledging allegiance in his fifth grade class. Lillian followed suit. After a brief period the children were expelled for insubordination and began to attend another school in a neighboring town. "After we had been expelled, one of the Catholic churches in Minersville announced a boycott of our store." When the Court decision was announced in 1940 Lillian remembers "it was like open season on Jehovah's Witnesses." In spite of the mounting attacks, Lillian recalls, "I was driving to pick up Daddy, and a group came and started to let the air out of the tires and surround the car. I stepped on the gas and my father said, 'Don't you *ever* do that again! You could have hurt someone.' "[5]

Nationwide, the reaction to the Gobitis decision was appalling. Irons notes, "Within two weeks of the Court's decision, two federal officials later wrote, 'hundreds of attacks upon the [Jehovah's] Witnesses were reported to the Department of Justice.' "[6] The list of horrors includes much of the population of Litchfield, Illinois, mobbing a group of some sixty Witnesses and only the call up of State Police ultimately protected them; another community forcing a group of Witnesses to drink large doses of castor oil; and the kidnapping, beating, and castration of a Nebraska Witness. Irons observed that according to federal officials these acts can all be traced directly to the Gobitis decision. He wrote, "In the two years following the decision the files of the Department of Justice reflect an uninterrupted record of violence and persecution of the Witnesses. Almost without exception, according to those files, the flag and the flag salute can be found as the percussion cap that set off these acts."[7]

The abuse of the Witnesses is well documented and a sad commentary on the citizens who perpetrated the actions. The Gobitis family was an easy target because its members were so different from their neighbors. Somehow a mob could feel doubly justified because deep down they didn't like these people anyway. That very difference on the part of the Witnesses required of them a more severe standard of conformity in order to have a chance of being accepted by their neighbors.

By 1943 the Supreme Court atmosphere was different: President Roosevelt's appointees dramatically changed its character. Eleanor Roosevelt spoke out on behalf of the Witnesses.

As distressed as Lillian Gobitis was in 1940, she was delighted when on Flag Day, June 14, 1943, the Court decided a case in West Virginia involving the Barnette family. The *West Virginia State Board of Education* v. *Barnette* decision overturned the Gobitis decision and the worst was left behind for that family. In the midst of what were the darkest days of World War II for the United States, the Supreme Court, with two new appointees and a change of position on the part of three who had voted with the majority in 1940, reversed itself. In one of the most memorable statements to emerge from the Court on the subject, Justice Robert Jackson, appointed by President Roosevelt in 1941, wrote for the majority concerning the First Amendment: "If there is any fixed star in our constitutional constellation, it is that no official, high or petty, can prescribe what shall be orthodox in politics, nationalism, religion, or other matters of opinion or force citizens to confess by word or act their faith therein. If there are any circumstances which permit an exception, they do not now occur to us."[8]

Within four years the Court would complement those words with the sentiments expressed by Justice Hugo Black in his opinion for the majority in *Everson* v. *Board of Education* (1947). In this narrowly decided case (5–4) the Court upheld the State of New Jersey's right to fund transportation to parochial schools. The justices made it clear, however, that the issue revolved not around a child's right to education, but around his right to safety. Turning to the first clause on religion in the First Amendment, Black wrote:

The "establishment of religion" clause of the First Amendment means at least this: Neither a state nor the Federal Government can set up a church. Neither can pass laws which aid one religion, aid all religions, or prefer one religion over another. Neither can force nor influence a person to go to or remain away from church against his will or force him to profess a belief or disbelief in any religion. No person can be punished for entertaining or professing religious beliefs or disbeliefs, for church attendance or nonattendance. No tax in any amount, large or small, can be levied to support any religious activities or institutions, whatever they may be called, or whatever form they may adopt to teach or practice religion. . . . In the words of Jefferson, the clause against establishment of religion by law was intended to erect "a wall of separation between Church and State."[9]

In dissent, the remaining four justices made it clear that they agreed fully with those sentiments. They simply rejected the majority's contention that parochial school bus transportation in New Jersey fell under the definition of child benefits. All nine justices gave full weight to the ideas and words of Madison and Jefferson in their opinions. Justice Black knew that President Jefferson had weighed carefully the words he wrote to the Danbury Baptists in 1802. And he was conscious that Madison had used separation in an identical fashion when describing the religion clauses. Indeed, in one of his final comments on the principle of nonestablishment, Jefferson described it as, "separation between the authority of human laws, and the natural rights of Man."[10] In a similar style he wrote concerning, "the line of separation between the rights of religion and the Civil authority. . . ."[11]

The Court found occasion in the next few years to address the issue that plagued Alvin Lehman in 1940. In *McCollum* v. *Board of Education* (1948) the Court observed: "Here not only are the state's tax supported public school buildings used for the dissemination of religious doctrines. The State also affords sectarian groups an invaluable aid in that it helps to provide pupils for their religious classes through the use of the state's compulsory public school machinery. This is not separation of Church and State."[12]

Jim McCollum and Public School Religion Classes

"Poor pagan pussy cat."

"You slimy bastard, may your filthy rotten soul roast in hell."

I first met Vashti and Jim McCollum in the fall of 1995. No case before the Supreme Court was closer to me than the one affecting their school situation. When I heard the decision announced in 1948 I was a junior at Thomas Jefferson High School. My classmate Alvin Lehman and I could not have been more pleased with the Court's opinion. My father and Alvin's mother had been right all along: it was unconstitutional to do what the Virginia Council for Religious Education had been doing when we were in Westhampton School.

One Woman's Fight by Vashti McCollum (published in 1951) provides a personal account of the trials and the tribulation of the McCollum family in the three-year battle with the public schools of Champaign, Illinois. Her memories, flavored with current reflections by Jim McCollum, are the sources of the account that follows.[13]

Vashti McCollum describes herself as a humanist, in no way antireligious. As she undertakes to tell her story she stresses that fact. She was married, with children, when religion became a part of the public school curriculum in Champaign, Illinois, in 1940.

James Terry is the oldest son of Vashti and John McCollum. He entered the fourth grade at South Side School in Champaign, where he encountered the classes in religious instruction sponsored by the Council of Religious Education. Attendance was not compulsory, but there was social pressure. Jim came home "with a slip I was to sign permitting him to take the course." In this case he was also to indicate on the paper whether he was to receive Catholic, Protestant, or Jewish instruction. (In my own case in Richmond the choice was Protestant or nothing.) Vashti refused to sign, but Jim wanted to enroll and his mother finally consented for the second semester. Quickly she discovered it was, in her view, a course of indoctrination. Faced with a program she felt was unconstitutional, she told Jim she could never again grant permission.

Jim recalls that he moved to another school for the fifth grade,* a

---

*The McCollums lived on the line dividing the two school districts, so he was free to attend either school.

school much less sympathetic to the kind of protest his mother was making. The teachers were hostile to him. The homeroom teacher "put me in the punishment seat in the hall where I was ridiculed by other children. I occasionally got into fights."

In February 1945, Jim came home in tears because he had had to sit in the hall alone during the religious instruction period. Other children saw him there and teased him. His mother's protest of this treatment received no action by the school and a visit to the superintendent of the city schools was unsatisfactory. Faced with this administrative refusal to take action to halt the religious instruction, Vashti determined to file suit in the state court. In order to pursue that course she needed more information about the religious instruction, so she went to see Methodist minister Clifford Northcutt, who had started the religious instruction program. Vashti told him she thought the program was unconstitutional. At that point Northcutt became "terribly angry." He said he would fight for the program even if it were unconstitutional.

McCollum then moved to request the school board to discontinue the program. Failing to achieve her goal, she filed a suit in court. At that point a sense of fear of the future began to affect her. "To understand this fear, I suppose one has to know something about the small, tightly knit social structure of a small college town in the heart of the Midwest Bible belt."[14] As calls and letters demonstrated both antagonism and support for the McCollums, the situation in the schools became quite tense.

Not all the grade levels had the Jewish instruction as an option. In fact, as Jim recalls, the Jews were included in the program only briefly and then the reformed rabbi "realized the folly of his participating" and withdrew. In any event, in one fifth grade where there was no Jewish option the teacher interrogated all the children who did not have signed permission slips. One child responded that he did not receive permission "because I'm Jewish." That child had never previously had any problems in the school. He was adopted and his parents were anxious to see him happy and productive. "The next day one of the other little girls pointed him out to her older brother in junior high, and the brother beat up the little boy with accompanying anti-Semitic remarks."[15] As Jim remembers, the teachers in the fourth and fifth grades were militant about enrolling children in the religion classes. The "teachers were rewarded for having 100% of their children in the religion program."

Vashti McCollum sought occasion to try and make her case to the public. In one such meeting she was angrily attacked by speakers from the other side. Finally a young scholar from the University of Illinois rose and commented, "One side seems to have all the support, all the money, all the respectability. The other side seems to have nothing but sincerity. Now what I can't figure out is why the side with all the advantages should stoop to name calling. I think the gentleman who just spoke owes the young lady [Vashti] an apology."[16]

The case opened in the state circuit court in 1945 and in the fall Jim changed schools, choosing to go back to the one near the University of Illinois, which he had attended for fourth grade. There were more students there who didn't take the religion classes. At the school Jim had attended for fifth grade "black eyes, bloody noses, and welts had been all in a day's routine, but at South Side he was beaten up only once."[17] The trial ended and there was a four-month wait for the decision. In the meantime mob violence aimed at the McCollum home on Halloween night frightened them. "I didn't dare open the door but waited out the storm, and eventually they left after piling trash and leaves two feet high on our front doorstep. Our pet kitten disappeared, too, that night. Poor pagan pussy cat, even she had to pay for belonging to a family of nonconformists."[18] In spite of this treatment, not one denunciation of community violence was reported to have been heard from a Christian pulpit.

In the fall of 1945 letters arrived by the hundreds. Excerpts include the following: "You slimy bastard, may your filthy rotten soul roast in hell"; "Rats like you should be put on the firing line to be shot"; "We will make some lovely incisions in your filthy bellies and pull out those nervy Guts one by one, slow and easy"; "Go to hell! . . . Viva Jesu!" and, finally, "You have managed to uncover a phrase in our constitution which no doubt would have gone unnoticed throughout the centuries!"[19]

The McCollums lost in the state circuit court and appealed quickly to the state supreme court, which in March 1947 upheld the circuit decision. Vashti had lost again. Prior to that, in the fall of 1946, Jim had entered junior high school. "That was the worst time of all," he relates. Harassment was far more severe. There were physical encounters, although he does not recall being beaten up. He had no friends there, but "two teachers were supportive." Vashti remembers

that the harassment and cruelty were daily occurrences. Jim was phys-
ically attacked on the city streets. The last straw for Vashti took place
when a new child in the community befriended him. Jim told his
mother, with tears in his eyes, "He's a nice boy. He just moved to town
and I like him. He's my friend. But in another week he won't be. The
others will turn him against me."[20] Within days Jim was enrolled in a
private boarding school in Rochester, New York.* It was quite expensive and the family funds were depleting, but Jim stayed in Rochester
for a year and a half before returning to enroll in the University High
School in Champaign. "All the time he was there [Rochester] both faculty and students did their best to make him feel wanted. It turned
out to be a wise and fortunate move for us."[21]

On June 2, 1947, the United States Supreme Court noted "proba-
ble jurisdiction" on the McCollum case, meaning the Court would
entertain an appeal. By that time several religious groups had joined
to support the McCollum appeal, including Baptists, Seventh-Day
Adventists, Unitarians, and Jews. Argument of the case before the
Court took place on December 8, 1947. On March 8, 1948, the
Supreme Court, by an 8 to 1 margin, found for the plaintiffs, the
McCollums. Justice Hugo Black, writing for the majority, concluded,
"Here not only are the State's tax-supported public school buildings
used for the dissemination of religious doctrine, the State also affords
sectarian groups an invaluable aid in that it helps to provide pupils for
their religious classes through the use of the State's compulsory public
school machinery. This is not separation of church and state."[22]

Jim McCollum, now a successful attorney living in Arkansas, is not
quite sure when he became conscious of the issues with which his parents had become involved. He clearly did not understand much of it
while he was in the fourth grade. Slowly he found himself seeking information, and during the trial "I became familiar with the mechanics of
the courtroom." He also remembers that his father was most helpful in
suggesting ways to engage the other children in conversation when they
began to taunt him with charges of atheism. He never had any doubts
about the suit and he affirmed that his mother "never looked for a
fight." But, once she had undertaken a task, she was a formidable oppo-

---

*Jim's two brothers remained in the school system, thereby retaining the
McCollums' standing in court.

nent. Jim is particularly pleased that his brother, Errol, is now in his third term as mayor of Champaign. "The Republicans used the Court case against him in the first election and it did them no good."

One of the most memorable moments in Jim's life was an opportunity to meet with Justice Hugo Black in 1966, just after Jim had passed the Bar and been admitted to practice in the Supreme Court. "Justice Black told me he wished he had not voted as he did in the Everson case [i.e., in favor of the state's right to fund transportation to parochial schools]. If he had it to do over again he would have voted the other way." That is an intriguing thought. Because of the narrow margin of the decision, 5 to 4, the outcome would have been reversed, but Black likely would have still written the majority opinion and with essentially the same arguments for strict separation.

The McCollum case is alive today in Lisa Herdahl's fight in Ecru, Mississippi, where the state and local officials are continuing to violate the 1948 decision. And the primary strength of the Herdahl case flows still from *Illinois ex Rel. McCollum* v. *Board of Education of School District No. 71, Champaign County, Illinois, et al.*

Four years later, in *Zorach* v. *Clauson* (1952), the Court adopted a position of support for what came to be described as "released time," a device by which students desiring to receive religious instruction would be transported off the campus to a nearby church building. In his majority opinion Justice William O. Douglas contended that to extend the McCollum decision, applying it to and thereby denying the legality of released time, might be seen as "hostility to religion." Justices Black, Frankfurter, and Jackson saw it differently.

In 1961 the Court upheld as constitutional state laws requiring that businesses remain closed on Sunday because the laws in question had transformed the earlier "religious character" of Sunday into something altogether different.[23] In the Court's mind Sunday took on a secular tone as it was set apart "as a day of rest, repose, recreation, and tranquility." In that same year the Court unanimously ruled that a Maryland law denying a notary commission to a man because he would not declare his belief in God was a religious test for public office and invaded, "the appellant's freedom of belief and religion."[24]

Through these cases the stage was set for the major battles to come over First Amendment interpretations. From 1940 to 1962 there had been abuse of dissenting citizens who claimed rights under the religion clauses of the First Amendment. This was markedly so in the pledge of allegiance cases. But nothing in the recent history of the nation prepared it for the venom that spewed forth with the *Engel* decision of 1962. In the nineteenth century there had been serious violations of citizen rights respecting the public schools and religion,[25] but by 1945 even Hollywood was at work to incorporate into the public mind sentiments of tolerance that had emerged from World War II. Catholic/Protestant conflicts, prominent in the 1928 presidential election, began to ebb and, by 1960, an environment was generated that enabled a Roman Catholic, John F. Kennedy, to be elected president. The horrors of the Holocaust kept under wraps the more extreme anti-Semitism in the country. And the film *Gentleman's Agreement,* starring Gregory Peck, took aim at what was becoming genteel anti-Semitism, identifying the insidious character of such discrimination. However, as Jewish and Christian leaders were creating avenues of conversation, the public awareness of other religious traditions, so obvious today, was only vaguely on the horizon of more enlightened minds.

Ellery Schempp: Prayer and the Bible in Schools

"Since the statute requires the reading of the 'Holy Bible,' a Christian document, the practice . . . prefers the Christian religion."

"I cited the First Amendment and was soon on my way to the guidance counselor."

In 1962 the first of three "prayer" cases, *Engel* v. *Vitale,* was decided by the Supreme Court. Two more decisions focusing on similar circumstances, *Murray* v. *Curlett* and *Abington* v. *Schempp,* followed in 1963. The consistent message from *Engel* to *Murray* to *Schempp* was the same: state-mandated prayer and/or Bible reading in public schools is unconstitutional. There was an immediate, high profile reaction by Congress against the Court rulings, resulting in hundreds of efforts to amend the First Amendment to allow prayer in public schools.[26] It is now the summer of 1996 and no such amendment has yet emerged from the Congress, although there have been two new proposals brought before the House and one before the Senate as the research on this volume concluded.[27]

The thirty-four year debate on this subject has witnessed several

Court decisions since 1963, the most significant of which is *Lee* v. *Weisman* in 1992. The particulars of that case are discussed in chapter 6.

Since the cases of 1962–1963 are the fountainhead for most of the interaction and conflict described in succeeding chapters, it seems appropriate to examine one of those decisions both from the point of view of the Supreme Court and, with the advantage of historical perspective, from the memory of one of the participants. Because the specific issues addressed in *Abington* v. *Schempp* closely parallel the succeeding thirty-odd years of public debate over religion in the public schools, we begin with the Court's statement of the "facts" followed by Ellery Schempp's reflections as he was interviewed in 1996.[28]

Writing for the majority, Justice Tom Clark set forth the history of the *Schempp* complaint. He noted that the Commonwealth of Pennsylvania required that "At least ten verses from the Holy Bible shall be read, without comment, at the opening of each public school on each school day."[29] The Schempp family, husband and wife and two of their three children,

> brought suit to enjoin enforcement of the statute, contending that their rights under the Fourteenth Amendment to the Constitution of the United States are, have been, and will continue to be violated unless this statute be declared unconstitutional as violative of these provisions of the First Amendment. They sought to enjoin the appellant school district, wherein the Schempp children attend school, and its officers and the Superintendent of Public Instruction of the Commonwealth from continuing to conduct such readings and recitation of the Lord's Prayer in the public schools of the district pursuant to the statute. A three-judge statutory District Court for the Eastern District of Pennsylvania held that the statute is violative of the Establishment Clause of the First Amendment as applied to the States by the Due Process Clause of the Fourteenth Amendment and directed that appropriate injunctive relief issue. . . .
>
> The appellees Edward Lewis Schempp, his wife, Sidney, and their children, Roger and Donna, are of the Unitarian faith and are members of the Unitarian Church in Germantown, Philadelphia, Pennsylvania, where they, as well as another son, Ellery, regularly attend religious services. The latter was originally a party but having graduated from the school system *pendente lite* [*] was voluntar-

---

*during litigation

ily dismissed from the action. The other children attend the Abington Senior High School, which is a public school operated by [the] appellant district.

On each school day at the Abington Senior High School between 8:15 and 8:30 A.M., while the pupils are attending their home rooms or advisory sections, opening exercises are conducted pursuant to the statute. The exercises are broadcast into each room in the school building through an intercommunications system and are conducted under the supervision of a teacher by students attending the school's radio and television workshop. Selected students from this course gather each morning in the school's workshop studio for the exercises, which include readings by one of the students of 10 verses of the Holy Bible, broadcast to each room in the building. This is followed by the recitation of the Lord's Prayer, likewise over the intercommunications system, but also by the students in the various classrooms, who are asked to stand and join in repeating the prayer in unison. The exercises are closed with the flag salute and such pertinent announcements as are of interest to the students. Participation in the opening exercises, as directed by the statute, is voluntary. The student reading the verses from the Bible may select the passages and read from any version he chooses, although the only copies furnished by the school are the King James version, copies of which were circulated to each teacher by the school district. During the period in which the exercises have been conducted the King James, the Douay and the Revised Standard versions of the Bible have been used, as well as the Jewish Holy Scriptures. There are no prefatory statements, no questions asked or solicited, no comments or explanations made and no interpretations given at or during the exercises. The students and parents are advised that the student may absent himself from the classroom or, should he elect to remain, not participate in the exercises.

It appears from the record that in schools not having an intercommunications system the Bible reading and the recitation of the Lord's Prayer were conducted by the home room teacher, who chose the text of the verses and read them herself or had students read them in rotation or by volunteers. This was followed by a standing recitation of the Lord's Prayer, together with the Pledge of Allegiance to the Flag by the class in unison and a closing announcement of routine school items of interest.

At the first trial Edward Schempp and the children testified as to specific religious doctrines purveyed by a literal reading of the

Bible which were contrary to the religious beliefs which they held and to their familial teaching.[30]

The children testified that all of the doctrines to which they referred during their testimony were read to them at various times as part of the morning exercises. Edward Schempp testified at the second trial that he had considered having Roger and Donna excused from attendance at the exercises but decided against it for several reasons, including his belief that the children's relationships with their teachers and classmates would be adversely affected.

The trial court summarized his testimony as follows:

Edward Schempp, the children's father, testified that after careful consideration he had decided that he should not have Roger or Donna excused from attendance at these morning ceremonies. Among his reasons were the following. He said that he thought his children would be labeled as "odd balls" before their teachers and classmates every school day; that children, like Roger's and Donna's classmates, were liable "to lump all particular religious difference[s] or religious objections" [together] as "atheism" and that today the word "atheism" is often connected with "atheistic communism," and has "very bad" connotations, such as "un-American" . . . with overtones of possible immorality. Mr. Schempp pointed out that due to the events of the morning exercises following in rapid succession, the Bible reading, the Lord's Prayer, the Flag Salute, and the announcements, excusing his children from the Bible reading would mean that probably they would miss hearing the announcements so important to children. He testified also that if Roger and Donna were excused from Bible reading they would have to stand in the hall outside their "home room" and that this carried with it the imputation of punishment for bad conduct.[31]

The trial court, in striking down the practices and the statute requiring them, made specific findings of fact that the children's attendance at Abington Senior High School is compulsory and that the practice of reading ten verses from the Bible is also compelled by law. It also found that:

The reading of the verses, even without comment, possesses a devotional and religious character and constitutes in effect a religious

observance. The devotional and religious nature of the morning exercises is made all the more apparent by the fact that the Bible reading
is followed immediately by a recital in unison by the pupils of the
Lord's Prayer. The fact that some pupils, or theoretically all pupils,
might be excused from attendance at the exercises does not mitigate
the obligatory nature of the ceremony for ... [it] unequivocally
requires the exercises to be held every school day in every school in
the Commonwealth. The exercises are held in the school buildings
and perforce are conducted by and under the authority of the local
school authorities and during school sessions. Since the statute
requires the reading of the "Holy Bible," a Christian document, the
practice ... prefers the Christian religion. The record demonstrates
that it was the intention of ... the Commonwealth ... to introduce
a religious ceremony into the public schools of the Commonwealth.[32]

The language of the Court cannot convey the full measure of the
story in any way comparable to that offered by Ellery Schempp. Two
extended conversations with Dr. Schempp have brought the background of this extraordinarily important decision fully into focus.
Today Ellery has his own consulting firm, Harvard Consulting Group,
in Massachusetts. After leaving high school he attended Tufts University where he graduated with Phi Beta Kappa honors and a degree in
physics and geology. He earned his Ph.D. at Brown University.

Ellery is the eldest child of Sidney and Ed Schempp. He says that
he was "raised in a family that believed in free inquiry"; his parents
encouraged the challenging of ideas. They belonged to the local Unitarian Church. Because he was an excellent student at Abington Senior
High School, as a junior in the 1957–1958 school year, he was enrolled
in advanced classes in science, math, and history. Students in these
classes were "encouraged to think and to write in an expository fashion." Even today he remembers the most influential teacher in his life
at the school, Allan Gladhorn. Gladhorn invited his students to his
home each Thursday evening for a discussion of ideas and current
events. During that fall Ellery explored history and government,
examining the Bill of Rights. As he compared the First Amendment
with the prayer and Bible reading required each morning, he concluded "there was a genuine issue here." Some of his fellow students
agreed and Ellery and two or three others decided to protest. "They all
chickened out when they thought of the principal calling their par-

ents. I determined that if I believed the prayer to be unconstitutional I had to do something." It was Thanksgiving and

> I was riding with my family in the car when I told them what I planned to do. . . . My parents had no strong reaction but they offered no opposition.
>
> The next week I decided I would not participate in the prayer. My friend George lent me a copy of the Koran and the next morning as the Bible was read and the Lord's Prayer was recited by all the students standing I sat, opened the Koran and read to myself. When they said the flag pledge I stood up and joined in.

The reaction was very quick. "My home room teacher asked what was going on. He said he noticed I had not participated in morning devotions and that in the future I was to stand up and pay attention. I said to him that in good conscience I don't believe I can do that any longer." Ellery was then sent to the vice-principal who was "flabbergasted by my behavior." He told Ellery he had a lot of friends in the Unitarian Church and none of them would ever do this. He said it was a matter of respect. "Eleven hundred others show respect," the vice-principal said. "I cited the First Amendment and was soon on my way to the guidance counselor." Ellery was to become well acquainted with Evelyn Brehm over the next few months. She asked a lot of questions in her role as school psychologist. After about an hour she apparently was satisfied that he was sane and "hinted that she was sympathetic with my actions."

Ellery went home and told his family about it. They supported him and told him he was right but they "left it up to me." His father was an ACLU member, so Ellery found the address and wrote for help. When he returned to school the next day, Ms. Brehm had arranged for Ellery to come in each morning and sign in as being in attendance and then go to her office during the devotions. "We had many conversations over that year and she soon ceased trying to talk me out of my stand."

> Sometime in January or February of 1958 the ACLU came to our home and interviewed me and my parents. Dad and mother said we wanted to pursue the case. From the beginning it was understood that the case would be filed in the name of Edward Schempp and his children. The ACLU attorney, Spencer Coxe, made it clear that we would be entering at least a five-year period of litigation. The fact

that my sister Donna was five years younger than I meant we could maintain standing in court long enough to see the matter through.

When the news came out that the suit was filed Ellery saw little change in his daily routine at school. "One teacher attacked my position in the classroom, but those of us in advanced placement were somewhat isolated from the rest of the school. We had the best teachers and most were sympathetic."

It was at that time that Ellery recalls a rare meeting with Norman Thomas, the legendary Socialist party leader who in 1920 had helped found the ACLU and had several times run for president of the United States. The Unitarian Church the Schempps attended had a regular schedule of guest lecturers on Sundays during the year. The resident minister of the church was seldom in the pulpit.

> I can remember Norman Thomas as a powerful speaker with a ringing voice and a hugely intellectual speech. In the spring of 1958 we had the honor to meet him, just our family, for an extended conversation. He had become my idol. He was a highly regarded political leader whose ideas often were incorporated in President Roosevelt's platform. He said he was thoroughly in agreement with our complaint, but he feared that the suit, if successful, would raise such a backlash that we could lose everything. For that reason he urged us not to do it.

After careful consideration of Thomas's arguments, "we decided to go on with the suit. As I entered school for my senior year the ACLU filed suit."

In the fall of 1958 the school refused to allow Ellery to miss morning "devotions" any longer. The Pennsylvania law made no provision for such excuse. The family and the ACLU determined that rather than make a stand on "civil disobedience" Ellery should remain in the class with everyone and participate in the prayer and listen to the Bible reading. This would show the coercive nature of the law. So he went through the exercises.

Ellery graduated in the spring of 1959 and was no longer a plaintiff, although he did testify in the Pennsylvania State District Court on August 5, 1959. The Schempps' attorneys had requested a three judge panel so that the case could be appealed directly to the U.S. Supreme Court. The district court found for the Schempp family and the school appealed to the U.S. Supreme Court. At that point the Pennsylvania legislature, on December 17, 1959, changed the law to allow students to be excused from the "devotions." As noted by the 1963 Supreme Court opinion in the case, "Pending appeal to this Court by the school district, the statute was so amended, and we vacated the judgment and remanded for further proceedings. The same three-judge court granted appellees' motion to amend the pleadings, held a hearing on the amended pleadings and rendered the judgment from which appeal is now taken." In other words, the law was amended while the school district was appealing the lower court's decision, so the Supreme Court chose to nullify the lower court ruling and ask the lower court to rehear the case now that the law had changed. But even after the law had been changed, the three-judge court still considered it in violation of the Constitution. The Schempps had won again in the district court in 1960 and once again the school district appealed.

Ellery was, by then, enrolled at Tufts University in Boston. CBS News decided to do a story on television and invited Ellery to be on the program. In preparation for that appearance Ellery spoke with the admissions officer at Tufts to discover whether his participation in the suit in any way affected the decision to admit him. The admissions officer smiled and commented, "You don't know, do you?" He related the following story: Principal Eugene Stuhl had taken the authority away from the school registrar to send any information concerning Ellery Schempp to any college. Stuhl assumed that responsibility and ordered all matters pertaining to Ellery be sent to his desk. Stuhl called the admissions office at Tufts, told them they had made a terrible mistake in accepting Ellery, who was perhaps a communist or worse, and that Tufts should rescind the admission. Obviously that did not occur and the admissions officer told Ellery, "We put it in context" and that he was certain the admissions office was right in their decision. Oddly, Mr. Stuhl's career paralleled Ellery's. From elementary school through junior high to high school Stuhl was the principal for Ellery's entire career in the public schools. As fate would have it, he was moved up every time Ellery was.

Ellery has a vivid memory of attending the oral arguments at the Supreme Court in February 1963. He sat in the front row and marvelled at the informality of the justices as they posed questions. He was also deeply impressed by the family's attorney, Henry W. Sawyer. When the Court handed down its opinion on June 17, 1963, Ellery had graduated from Tufts and was on his honeymoon. After a long and highly successful career as a scientist and scholar he is comfortable with everything that transpired and feels pleased to have been a part of a critically important moment in First Amendment jurisprudence.

Under the same title another case, *Murray* v. *Curlett*, was decided that day in 1963. It involved Madalyn Murray and her son. Murray became quite famous in later years as an advocate of atheism and her son attracted attention when he converted to Christian fundamentalism. Indeed, the son has become a poster child for the Religious Right since that conversion. In fact, in 1995 he was in Mississippi condemning both his mother and Lisa Herdahl for their evil ways.

The Supreme Court detailed the following facts before finding in favor of Murray. The Code of Maryland

> provided for the holding of opening exercises in the schools of the city of Baltimore, consisting primarily of the "reading, without comment, of a chapter in the Holy Bible and/or the use of the Lord's Prayer." The petitioners, Mrs. Madalyn Murray and her son, William J. Murray III, are both professed atheists.
>
> Following unsuccessful attempts to have the respondent school board rescind the rule, this suit was filed for mandamus [an order] to compel its rescission and cancellation.

William was a student in a public school of the city and Mrs. Murray, his mother, was a taxpayer therein. They argued

> that it was the practice under the rule to have a reading on each school morning from the King James version of the Bible; that at petitioners' insistence the rule was amended to permit children to be excused from the exercise on request of the parent and that William had been excused pursuant thereto; that nevertheless the rule as amended was in violation of the petitioners' rights "to freedom of religion under the First and Fourteenth Amendments" and in violation of "the principle of separation between church and state, contained therein. . . ." [The Murrays] stated that the rule, as practiced, violated their rights "in that it threatens their religious liberty by placing a premium on belief as against nonbelief and subjects their freedom of conscience to the rule of the majority; it pronounces belief in God as the source of all moral and spiritual values, equating these

values with religious values, and thereby renders sinister, alien and suspect the beliefs and ideals of your Petitioners, promoting doubt and question of their morality, good citizenship and good faith.

The Court agreed with Murray. The Murrays were badly treated and threatened in their neighborhood. The degree of abuse was probably exacerbated by the fact that they were atheists, which was in the minds of many citizens at that time the equivalent of communism. The Murrays were subjected to an excessive amount of hatred. Madalyn Murray (O'Hair) disappeared in the late summer of 1995 and all attempts to find her to arrange an interview failed. However, Ellery Schempp had two long conversations with her and he recalls that "Baltimore turned against her, including the newspapers." The Murray children "were beaten on the way home from school, teachers harassed the[m], and when their house was firebombed, the fire department refused to respond. When [Murray's] father died in the late 1960s, she could not find a local Presbyterian minister to conduct the funeral, although the father was a faithful [member of that church]. The mother and sons were finally forced to leave the city."

Forgetting that the formative years of William Murray's life were filled with religious vituperation, or perhaps because of that fact, the Religious Right exults in his decision to become a Christian. They parade him on every opportunity so that he can bash his mother and prove, in their minds, that her atheism was a disease that led to attacks on religion in the schools and then destroyed the Murray family. It never appears to occur to Religious Right leaders that *Christians* maligned Murray for her conscientious stand and made life a living hell for William.

As noted, these cases led to a massive movement to retain government-sanctioned prayer in public schools. Leadership for this movement has been supplied by persons who insist that with removal of prayer the nation's youth are left awash in immorality and secularism. In the past twenty years people like David Barton* and Pat Robertson

---

*A Christian Coalition activist, David Barton is the author of two books, *The Myth of Separation* and *America: To Pray or Not to Pray.* Both are Religious Right propaganda aimed at destroying the separation of church and state and "proving" that the United States was founded to be a Christian nation. Barton is the founder of Wallbuilders, Inc., a business (not a nonprofit organization) which sells videotapes based on his books.

have asserted that the Scholastic Assessment Test (SAT) scores of American youth began to decline in 1962 as a direct result of *Engel* and its progeny.[33] (Of course, this begs the question as to why the scores began to climb in 1982 even as the Congress refused in that year and in years following to pass a constitutional amendment to alter the First Amendment and allow prayer.) The stated premise of most vigorous advocates of public school prayer is a moral one. And yet, as the following chapters will make abundantly clear, on most occasions, when such prayers were objected to by a minority in a community, the "good citizens" in power ridiculed, threatened, abused, and terrorized fellow citizens in the name of prayer.

This abuse took both personal and political forms. While we will be looking closely at the personal attacks on fellow citizens, it should not be forgotten that such disturbing behavior is part of a coherent political strategy. Demonizing persons who invoke the First Amendment is certainly not new. In the late 1940s seeking protection under that amendment was interpreted as evidencing disloyalty, perhaps even communist leanings. Today citizens who challenge government sponsorship of religion are quickly characterized as atheists, moral laggards, and troublemakers. They are perceived as giving minorities a bad name since minorities, according to leaders of the Religious Right, are supposed to be subservient to the majority even in the area of civil and human rights. (This will be discussed further in chapter 10.)

With such a premise, which presumes political privilege for a particular brand of Christianity, it is a short step to blame those of other convictions as causing moral rot in the nation. Thus begins the politicizing of claims for Bill of Rights protections. The ever recurring claim is that public morality has declined, along with SAT scores, since organized prayer was removed from the public schools. The Christian Coalition appears to believe that those who challenge religious establishments are enemies of God. Jerry Falwell equated Supreme Court decisions favoring minority religious rights in schools with "kicking God out of the schools." And who put the Court up to those decisions? It was citizens the reader will meet in the succeeding chapters.

When newly elected Rep. Wicker (R-Miss.) told a crowd in Ecru, Mississippi, that the Constitution does not guarantee anybody the right not to be offended, he was making a point he failed to understand. Prayer that offends anyone is surely an offense to a loving deity.

Such a position was enunciated by Roger Williams when, as governor of Rhode Island, he welcomed believers and nonbelievers alike as equal citizens in the colony. State-established religion offends the Constitution and every citizen of a nation that espouses the principles of justice, freedom, and equality. It is doubly tragic when a claim made in the name of religious freedom becomes the target of hate. In the chapters that follow we will explore when and in what manner prayer has become a destructive weapon in the hands of angry and bitter citizens, first against individuals and then against political institutions.

James Madison reminded his readers that, "The free men of America did not wait til [*sic*] usurped power had strengthened itself by exercise, and entangled the question in precedents. They saw all the consequences in the principle, and they avoided the consequences by denying the principle."[34] The presumption that one possesses a corner on truth, religious or otherwise, when translated into political action, provides a most dangerous threat to our traditions of equality and freedom. Ours is a government that has made possible the development of the most religious population among the nations just because we are a nation of laws, not sins. Religion in the United States is what it is because of respect for diversity and commitment to the rights of minorities. The Constitution gives Rep. Wicker the right to offend whomever he chooses in the body politic. It gives him no right to use government as an offending tool against the consciences of fellow citizens, particularly children.

Notes

1. "Religion in Public Schools" (editorial), *The Religious Herald* 117, no. 47 (November 30, 1944): 10.

2. "Bible Teaching in Virginia Public Schools" (editorial), *The Religious Herald* 121, no. 25 (June 24, 1948): 10.

3. Peter Irons, *The Courage of Their Convictions* (New York: Penguin Books, 1990), pp. 13–35.

4. Cited in Robert S. Alley, *The Supreme Court on Church and State* (New York: Oxford University Press, 1988), pp. 365–76. See also the original source, *Minersville School District* v. *Gobitis* 310 US 586 (1940).

5. Irons, *The Courage of Their Convictions,* p. 31.

6. Ibid.

7. Ibid., p. 23.

8. Alley, *The Supreme Court on Church and State*, p. 385. Quotation from *West Virginia State Board of Education* v. *Barnette* 319 US 624 (1943).

9. Alley, *The Supreme Court on Church and State*, pp. 44–45.

10. In the "Detached Memoranda," ed. by Elizabeth Fleet (*William & Mary Quarterly* 111 [October 1946]: 554), Madison expanded on several concerns having to do with religion and state including chaplains and presidential proclamations. The writing likely began a few years after leaving the presidency and was completed by 1832.

11. Gaillard Hunt, ed., *The Writings of James Madison* (New York: G. P. Putnam, 1910), p. 487 (letter to Rev. Adams). Internal evidence would place the date of this letter in 1834 or later.

12. Alley, *The Supreme Court on Church and State*, p. 177.

13. Vashti McCollum, *One Woman's Fight* (New York: Doubleday, 1951), p, 11. Further information included in this account was obtained in February 1996, when the author had a lengthy conversation with Jim McCollum, the tape of which is in the author's possession.

14. McCollum, *One Woman's Fight,* p. 45.

15. Ibid., p. 48.

16. Ibid., p. 58.

17. Ibid., p. 73.

18. Ibid., p. 87.

19. Ibid., p. 163.

20. Ibid.

21. Ibid., p. 165.

22. *McCollum* v. *Board of Education* 333 US 203 (1948).

23. *McGowan et al.* v. *Maryland* 366 US 420 (1961).

24. *Torcaso* v. *Watkins* 367 US 488 (1961).

25. In 1842 Roman Catholic Bishop Hughes of Philadelphia addressed a letter to public school officials complaining that the Protestant Bible was being read to Catholic children and that religious exercises were being made a part of the instruction. The Bishop asked that Catholic children be allowed to use their own version of the Bible. In 1843 the school board complied with the request. This event caused a rising anger of Protestants towards Catholics. This "nativist" movement took hold of large parts of the population and in 1844 riots began and St. Michael's and St. Augustine's Catholic churches were burned. See Ray Allen Billington, *The Protestant Crusade, 1800–1860: A Study of the Origins of American Nativism* (Chicago: Quadrangle Books, 1964).

26. Robert S. Alley, *School Prayer: The Court, the Congress, and the First Amendment* (Amherst, N.Y.: Prometheus Books, 1994), pp. 107–26.

27. As was discussed in chapter 3, in the House, Representative Istook offered an amendment to the Constitution, "To secure the people's right to

acknowledge God according to the dictates of conscience: Nothing in this Constitution shall prohibit acknowledgments of the religious heritage, beliefs, or traditions of the people, or prohibit student-sponsored prayer in public schools. Neither the United States nor any State shall compose any official prayer or compel joining in prayer, or discriminate against religious expression or belief."

House Joint Resolution 121 offered by Representative Henry Hyde (R-Ill.) proposed a constitutional amendment which reads: "Neither the United States nor any State shall deny benefits to or otherwise discriminate against any private person or group on account of religious expression, belief, or identity; nor shall the prohibition on laws respecting an establishment of religion be construed to require such discrimination." This resolution was introduced into the Senate by Senator Orrin Hatch (R-Utah).

28. Personal interview with Ellery Schempp by the author, February and July 1996.

29. See the opinion in *School District of Abington Township, Pennsylvania, et al.* v. *Schempp et al.* 374 US 203 (1963).

30. Ibid.

31. Ibid.

32. Alley, *The Supreme Court on Church and State*, pp. 204–23.

33. *America's Godly Heritage,* videotape produced by Wallbuilders, Inc., Aledo, Texas, 1994. Narrated by David Barton. See Appendix A for the district court decision in the Herdahl case. The judge ordered that this tape *not* be shown in the Pontotoc School history classes.

34. Ibid.

5

Joann Bell and Lucille McCord:
Where Have All the Christians Gone?

"There's a place for prayin', and a place for learnin', and school ain't the place for prayin'."

"How does it feel to have a mother who doesn't believe in God?"

"When my child's rights are violated, my rights are violated."

Joann Bell and her family moved to Little Axe, Oklahoma, in 1976. The town has a single school which serves grades one through nine. As each of the four Bell children reached school age they were enrolled there.

In the fall of 1980 the parents of several children, including Bell and Lucille McCord, became concerned over the distribution of Bibles by the Gideon Society, as well as religious meetings being held on the school premises.[1] The organizer and sponsor of the meetings was an English teacher, Kitty Blackwell, who asserted that her God had appeared to her in her classroom and charged her to save the school for Jesus. The meetings of the Son Shine Club took place in Blackwell's classroom before school began. She and a colleague, Becky Ernest, led the group. When Blackwell first began the club she had sought permission from an assistant superintendent. He declined and sent her to the superintendent, who did give permission.

Joann Bell had been deeply involved in the life of the Little Axe school since her arrival in the town, and never missed a school board meeting. For six months Bell and the other parents worked quietly to reach an agreement respecting the two main areas of contention. In a lengthy interview in January 1996, Joann Bell observed that the school never negotiated in good faith and finally made the dispute public in a school board meeting in the spring of 1981. The board chairperson, Elizabeth Butts, sarcastically commented that the complaining parents could bring on the American Civil Liberties Union. Even before that dramatic turn, however, Bell was aware of extraordinary pressure on her children. Immediately following the first voicing of concern in the fall of 1980, some teachers, apparently fighting back, resorted to giving fundamentalist-oriented quizzes to their students. When Carlee McGuire's fifth-grade daughter refused to take a test that was based on the King James Version of the Bible she was given a failing grade. The McGuires were Roman Catholic and their concerns were similar to those of Catholics in Philadelphia in 1844 which led to the previously discussed riots in that city. In the Little Axe school, children of "the troublemaking parents" were singled out by teachers and asked, "How does it feel to have a mother who doesn't believe in God?"

Harassment was not confined to the students. Hate mail was received in abundance at the families' homes, as were threatening phone calls suggesting something might happen to the children. Parents were warned that their homes would be burned.

Even as parents like the McCords and Bells sought to meet and discuss matters with school officials, they continued to hear reports about the religious meetings being held each Thursday before class began. Many students asked the McCord and Bell children why they did not attend the meetings; some suggesting that their parents must not believe in God. Advertisements for the Son Shine Club appeared on posters in the halls of the school. Speakers were invited by students and/or teachers, including ministers and athletes who spoke about how God and Christianity had been beneficial to them. The club's name, Son Shine, was an obvious play on the word "sunshine," with the clear intention of using the word "son" to refer to Jesus, believed by most Christians to be the "Son of God." The posters advertising the club frequently depicted religious themes, including one that presented a Little Axe teacher saying that she "had seen a vision of Jesus Christ and had been anointed by him to lead the students of Little Axe to him."

In the spring of 1981, once the conflict was widely known, the Son Shine Club became the focus of noisy arguments. Bell notes, "I went twice to see what was going on." It was obvious that religious doctrine was a source of often angry debate among the children. The students were arguing over who was going to hell and who to heaven. Leaders of the club were urging members to go out and bring in other students for conversion. Children who refused to attend because their parents went to another kind of church were told they were going to hell. Bell noted, "Our children were coming home with different religious ideas from those we were teaching."

The school board meetings became more and more acrimonious by late spring. They were "packed and dangerous. When some of us who were objecting to the Club attended the meeting and were using the women's rest room, parents and board members held the door so we couldn't get out. 'We are going to do what we want to out here,' they screamed." The vice president of the school board, Bill Scott, pulled his truck up to the school door and distributed signs reading, "Atheists Go Home" and "Go to Russia." Oklahoma State Representative Cal Hobson (D) tried to reason with the school officials but they told him to go away. This was an arrogant disregard of reasonable advice, a blatant exhibition of a type of "Christian" thought that consistently rejected all appeals to consider the rights of the minorities. The religious commitments of many teachers, staff, and administrators were so ingrained with exclusivistic claims that they apparently were unable to recognize why anyone would consider their actions as anything but reasonable and fair.

When Elizabeth Butts threw down the gauntlet of the ACLU, there was no longer room for negotiations. To be sure, the ACLU attorneys tried to open dialogue, but all they got for their efforts was a contamination of their automobile gas line while they were meeting with school officials.

On May 7, 1981, the American Civil Liberties Union filed a lawsuit in the federal district court in Little Axe, Oklahoma, on behalf of Joann Bell and Lucille McCord. The suit sought an injunction against the Little Axe Independent School District thereby stopping religious meetings from being held on school premises and from permitting the distribution of Gideon Bibles on school grounds. They also asked that the Oklahoma voluntary prayer statute be declared unconstitutional. Under pressure, the school administration arranged to change the Son

Shine Club name to the nondescriptive phrase "sharing sessions."
Nothing else changed.

Whatever the name, the sessions clearly took the form of prayer
meetings. A physical education teacher, Les Roberts, who played the
guitar for the gatherings, insisted, "We're just trying to have some
fun." He described a typical meeting in which a few songs were sung
and then "a young man or woman will come in and talk about their
lives before they accepted Christ and after." Roberts said no one had
ever complained before.

Bell and McCord were devout Christians, members respectively of
the Church of the Nazarene and the Church of Christ. But whatever
their faith, they were perceived as troublemakers and outsiders by the
predominant, largely Baptist, Christian majority in Little Axe. Lucille
McCord recalls that their chief antagonist was the minister of the
nearby First Baptist Church of Del City, Oklahoma. He came to Little
Axe and condemned Bell and McCord for their evil ways. Finally, on
the fateful evening of Butts's ACLU remark, the school board, meeting "before an agitated crowd," voted four to one to permit the club
meetings to continue until such time as they were declared unlawful.

The local response to the Bells and McCords was immediate. More
threatening phone calls were received by both families. The children
were called "devil worshippers." An upside-down cross was hung on
thirteen-year-old Robert McCord's locker. At the school sports banquet, the McCord and Bell children, who had played football, basket-
ball, and baseball, were the only two who were not recognized by name
as being Little Axe athletes. "The children who had participated in
athletics with my son Robbie and were his friends began to tell him
he didn't believe in God." Others told him he was "going to hell."
Lucille recalls, "Robbie was a quiet child and he let most of this roll
off of him. He knew we all believed in God. And he had the love of
his family and faith in God." For him the wise and good course was to
ignore them.

The Bell children were subjected to similar treatment. Marc Bell
(age fourteen) had won all but one of the ninth grade academic prizes.
The school officials refused to give them to him at the annual banquet
and he received them after the graduation ceremony, in private. This
was the case with every award the children won, Lucille remembered.

"The real friends of the children talked to them on the phone and a few of their closest friends stuck with them. My middle son, Jesse," Lucille commented, "was headstrong and got into fights." Robert McCord had had a perfect attendance record in the school up to the ninth grade. In 1981 he and some classmates went on a one-day trip to an adjoining town, an excused absence since it was a school-sponsored event. Upon his return, the school officials counted it as an absence for Robbie, thereby denying him the perfect attendance record he had won. "Jared was in kindergarten the year the suit was filed," Lucille remembers. "At the end of the year the school told me they were holding him back because he was not able to be taught." In fact, the school ignored him, made no effort to teach him, and had him sit in the corner. We moved out in 1981 and sent the three children to Harrah [school, which was eleven miles away, in another county]."

Lucille remembers that they were welcomed at the Church of Christ in Tecumseh, some two miles from Little Axe, although some of the older members had questions. There was no problem with the younger members and "as we talked to individuals they came to understand and put aside their earlier, distorted view of what had happened in Little Axe."

Lucille also recalled that there was one minister who publicly supported them in Little Axe and for that they were most grateful. There was also Harold Watts, another parent with children in the school, who "supported us all the way and quite publicly." Watts was a devout member of an Assembly of God church and did not want his child involved in the school religious activities.

As the record of the Federal Court of Appeals for the Tenth Circuit makes clear, the prayer meetings continued and in November 1981 the board adopted an equal access policy "purporting" to regulate student use of facilities.[2] Teachers were not permitted to participate and the school claimed it was not sponsoring the meetings. But the format of the club sessions remained unchanged. "Shortly thereafter, plaintiffs amended their complaint to challenge the new policy and to seek damages for the alleged unconstitutional acts of the district. The harassment persisted. The meetings continued until October 1982, when the school district agreed to suspend them until after the trial."[3]

Conditions continued to deteriorate. Bell remembers hate calls and phoned threats that seemed always to come when her husband was at work. "The phone never stopped ringing." More than once a caller said he (most calls were from men) was going to break in the house, tie up the children, rape their mother in front of them, and then "bring her to Jesus." "Threats were made to burn my house. When I got an unlisted number I had to supply it to the school and someone there immediately gave the number to our detractors. Only this year [1996] do I have a listed number again."

Events got progressively worse. Only now, fifteen years later, is Joann able to talk about the next incident with some objectivity.

> In September 1981, they burned my house. We were warned, but I could not believe people would do that. . . . Within days of the fire, school board lawyers filed a motion in federal court seeking to have the suit dismissed because I no longer had a home there. The federal judge told the school lawyers that he would not let vigilante justice prevail and he ruled that we did have standing in court.

And of course the Bells still owned the land and paid taxes. With the house in shambles, the family moved in with Joann's mother and father.

In a documentary film made several years ago, Joann made the following remarks about the emotional impact of the fire:

> Unless you've ever had a fire, the devastation is something you cannot even begin to describe. To lose everything you've ever had. And with four children you really accumulate a lot of things—the trophies, everything that you saved, your baby pictures, the little things—your marriage license. You lose everything. There's nothing hardly that can be saved. One of the things, the very few things that survived the fire was the christening dress of my daughter. We have three sons and we have a daughter that we're very proud of and this was her christening dress. It's one of the things that you'd like to pass on and let them use it for their children. This is just an example of things that were ruined and what our family lost in the fire. Because we essentially lost everything we had.[4]

Joann Bell also discussed the burning at the 1982 trial, showing a picture of the mobile home that was destroyed in September 1981, and stating, "People, I think, were ready to kill me if they could have gotten away with it." Bell said the fire was set by someone who took literally a remark by school board member Elizabeth Butts to the effect that "People who play with fire get burned." Butts said she meant the remark only as "a proverb."

At the time, the FBI and local fire investigators said they found no evidence of arson. Much later, according to Bell, after the trial, the FBI admitted that the material collected at the Bell home strongly suggested arson.

Anger apparently was the primary ingredient in the school's curriculum after the filing of the lawsuit.

> One day when I arrived home my husband told me that our friend Carlee McGuire had called, quite hysterical, saying someone had called her saying there was a bomb at the school and all the children were going to be killed. My husband and I rushed to the school, and as we drove up we could see that the children had been evacuated. The minute we pulled into the parking lot our car was surrounded. Many school employees were there, including the head cook, Corine Spurlock. She is a big, strapping woman and she began trying to get me out of the car. She succeeded in battering my head and my shoulder against the right door frame. She got hold of my hair and arm. She pulled out quite a bit of my hair, broke my glasses and tore my blouse. As my husband tried to hold me in the car the cook screamed "I'm going get you out of this car and kill you." I believed her. But not one time did I say a word to her. As a federal plaintiff I was certain that fighting back was not the thing to do. Just then Larry Garner, elementary principal, who was standing observing the struggle finally said "Corine, I think she's had enough." Garner was the person responsible for the distribution of Bibles and he was angry.

The cook later pled guilty to assault and was fined by a local court.

But the final act of hate and aggression would occur as the school year was winding down in 1982. Joann spoke carefully, but with feeling, as she recounted the story to me in 1996:

> Jason [a fifth grader] had the hardest time of the four. He was shy and he had a vision disability. In the spring of 1982 he was swinging on a swing on the playground at morning recess when the superintendent, Paul Pettigrew, who had been very hostile to us, came out of his office, which overlooked the playground, and called the teacher who was on playground duty into his office, leaving all the children

unattended. While she was away someone pushed Jason out of the swing from behind. Jason said it was big hands. That's all he could say. He didn't see who did it but he felt like it was a big person who pushed him from the swing. The resulting fall caused what was later found to be a compound fracture of his arm. Mr. Pettigrew reappeared and took Jason to his office. He kept him there in the office all day without a nurse and without calling me. He would pick up Jason's arm and say, "Oh why are you crying? It's not broken. You just bruised it."

Mr. Pettigrew did not let me know about the incident and the injury until I picked up my child. Jason had to have emergency surgery on his arm that night. I can tell you that's the one time out of all of this that I lost my cool. I went to that school the next day. I nearly tore that man up. I had the doctor bills and hospital bill in front of me since Jason and I were in the emergency room all night because of the severe pain. I told the superintendent, "I want a check by 3 P.M. this afternoon to pay for every one of my son's medical conditions. I can't guarantee your safety once my husband hears what you have done to my son." I lost it. I was so angry. That's when I decided that there was no one at that school who was going to protect my children and I had to get them out. Jason was greatly affected. But he is fine now.

And so she transferred her children after school closed in 1982. In December of that year Joann Bell and Lucille McCord appeared for the opening of the trial in federal district court. The women were represented by the ACLU and the school board had as its lawyer, State Representative William Graves, the man who authored the 1980 Oklahoma prayer bill. It was reported that the Moral Majority was assisting the Little Axe school with funding. The Moral Majority field director, Clyde Rollins, had reportedly told school board members that if the ACLU won, communism would be taught for an hour each day in Little Axe schools.

The judge in the case was U.S. District Judge Ralph Thompson. At the opening of the trial Judge Thompson told attorneys for both sides, "the issue in this case is not whether there should be prayer" in public schools, but whether prayer is "permitted under the Constitution." Further, he told them he was not going to overturn any U.S. Supreme Court decisions or create any new law."

The record of the trial, reported by United Press International (UPI), offers a journalist's view of the arguments that consumed the Court for some six days. What follows is an account woven together from the UPI material.[5]

On opening day, December 2, 1982, on behalf of Bell and McCord, their attorney offered the testimony of a father, Harold Watts, who stated that his grade-school children were forced to stand outside in the cold while other students attended the prayer session. He said: "I felt like my child was being punished because I would not let my child attend the prayer sessions." Watts also stated that he saw a box of Gideon Bibles in the principal's office. When Watts asked why they were being passed out, Larry R. Garner said it was a good practice and it would be continued. Watts noted, "I didn't like that, the way they were distributed in the classrooms during class time." Watts was the son of an ordained Assembly of God minister. In his testimony he said he didn't like the idea of religion in a public school. "There's a place for prayin', and a place for learnin', and school ain't the place for prayin'."

Three children of the plaintiffs testified that they were called devil worshippers and were taunted by classmates because they refused to attend school-sponsored prayer sessions. Robert McCord, age fifteen, said people came up to him and asked why he wasn't attending. "They accused me of devil worship . . . and put an upside-down cross on my locker," he said. Robert's brother, Jason, age twelve, told the Court that he also had been accused of devil worship because he decided himself not to go to the weekly sessions.

On the second day of the trial there was testimony from an Oklahoma clinical psychologist, Dr. R. Vernon Enlow, that "the children are experiencing emotional disturbance because of what's going on. . . . They feel like they are being persecuted." Enlow had interviewed the children and found each to be upset by the abuse he received from classmates before and after the lawsuit was filed. He argued that "When you set up a prayer session like this at school, you automatically create a 'right or wrong' situation." He further argued that the four children who refused to attend the prayer sessions suffered emotional damage. A second psychologist, Professor Thomas J. Berndt of the University of Oklahoma said a conflict would be established in the child's mind if the child was told one thing at home and another by teachers at school.

That day during the court session, the former school district superintendent, Charles Holleyman, said he was unaware of the sessions
prior to hearing about them from the ACLU attorney. (Recall, however, that Kitty Blackwell, the teacher who began the club, sought
permission from him to hold the pre-school meetings.) He said he
ordered the sessions stopped until the school board could consider the
matter. Further, he noted that he felt the "Little Axe school board lived
under the threat of being legally out of bounds all along."

The third day of testimony took place on Monday, December 6.
Professor Tom Boyd, who taught religion at the University of Oklahoma, said he would find "profoundly inappropriate" any kind of religious activity on public school grounds. Regarding the distribution of
Gideon Bibles, he said: "To hand these out in a public school setting
is implying an espousal of a religion."

As the day progressed, more disturbing testimony was elicited
from Carlee McGuire. She stated that an anonymous caller threatened
"to get my daughter" unless she stopped her opposition to religious
activities in the Little Axe school. McGuire, a Catholic mother of six
children, said she had received more than fifty harassing phone calls
since she began making known her objections to the religious activities at the school. When asked by the attorney for the school, William
Graves, why she had not joined Bell and McCord in the suit, she
replied it was because she was afraid of what would happen. "I had a
feeling about what was coming. I am not strong enough to face that."

A sixth-grade teacher stated that while the sessions were religious
in nature, she did not know whether they advanced any particular
belief. Rebecca Ernest, one of the leaders of the prayer group, also
stated that she received approval from the administration to help organize weekly prayer sessions, all of which had religious overtones.

As the court entered its fourth day, Lucille McCord told the judge
that she moved from the school district because she received her own
obituary in the mail and was concerned for her family's safety. Someone with the name McCord had died, and whoever sent a copy to her
had scratched out the first name and put Lucille in its place. She stated
that her children had been harassed and abused. Asked by Mr. Graves
if her constitutional rights had been violated, she replied: "No, but it
violated my child's constitutional rights and when my child's rights
are violated, my rights are violated." She noted that she tried on sev-

eral occasions to get officials to change the policy and was told nothing would be done.

As the court turned to the arguments on behalf of the school, one witness stated that he thought American public education was "declining into fascism" because of the lack of religion in the schools. A former teacher at Little Axe said she held devotionals in her classroom and she urged the court to let the children pray. "It doesn't hurt anybody to pray," she said.

Elizabeth Butts, the Little Axe School Board member who had dared the McCords and Bells to call in the ACLU, told the judge she called the landlady of Mrs. McCord merely to find out when she rented the house. McCord insisted that the calls upset the landlady and that Butts had said derogatory things about McCord. At that point the school district's attorney, William Graves, said he might have suggested that Mrs. Butts make the call.

During this fifth day of the trial, Dr. Paul Schmidt, a clinical psychologist and member of a group of Christian psychologists, contended that moral principles taught in church were becoming irrelevant because religious teaching was not allowed in the nation's public schools. He argued that unless religious activity was permitted in public schools, "God would be seen as an impotent, irrelevant figure. He doesn't have the power to come to school." Schmidt insisted that people who attend church regularly have a higher moral standard than those who did not. It should be obvious, then, that it is necessary to keep religion in the public schools in order to instill that "higher moral standard" in our youth.

In the final day of testimony a thirteen-year-old boy stated that he attended the weekly prayer sessions because it made him feel good. As several students recounted their impressions, the contention of the defense that the sessions were not specifically religious became ever more suspect. One student said she didn't go to church often so she attended the sessions. Others affirmed that students and teachers often discussed religious ideas. "People come in and share experiences, and give their testimony and all kinds of different things." A Church of Christ minister confirmed that the sessions included prayer, hymn singing, and testimony. Finally, a student who had fled Romania in 1979 stated that the sessions were "tilted in favor of Christianity."

Little Axe was a classic case of a majority simply unwilling to consider the rights of those offended by unconstitutional behavior. Joann Bell stated:

> The reaction that we got when we complained was this is what everyone wants—we've been having things like this for years. It doesn't matter what a few people think. This is the way we're going to do it. In fact the school board themselves gave me the idea to call the ACLU because I had never had any contact with the ACLU. The school board president actually said so sue us—bring in the ACLU.

Lucille McCord had similar thoughts.

> My first reaction when I was told that probably the only people that could help us was the ACLU was I almost threw my hands up and screamed because everything I had heard about the ACLU was just totally against my whole religious upbringing. I had been led down the path that the ACLU really were the bad people of the world.

A devout Nazarene, Bell was concerned that if the majority religion "could be practiced in Little Axe schools then maybe some other religions that I was leery of could also be brought in." In the final analysis it was the fear generated by the community that so astounded both McCord and Bell. Looking back on the experience, Bell reflected, "[Like Lucille McCord,] I got my own obituary in the mail. My kids were threatened constantly. I was told my kids were not going to survive."

Addressing the horror of those experiences, Lucille McCord noted: "Every day something happens that brings back the memories—something that happens, something the kids will say, something they do, something that I see. It was a devastating experience. For anyone. And I can understand why people don't want to get involved with it."

No court action could repair the damage meted out to these two families in Little Axe. They experienced up close the terror and horror of religious fanaticism. One would certainly be justified in inquiring about the efficacy of prayers that would result in intimidation, hate, and destruction. Nevertheless, the United States Tenth Circuit Court did provide a modicum of relief to the McCords and Bells in June 1985. Five years after the first confrontation over the activities of the Little Axe School District in Cleveland County, Oklahoma, the judges went to the root of the problem.

The school district, seeking to defend itself against the charges made by Bell and McCord, had adopted a ten-point policy concerning use of school facilities. Using those guidelines, the school district declared it was merely providing equal access. The circuit court determined that the school district's "policy was actually adopted to conceal a pre-eminent religious purpose." After months of contention with McCord and Bell, the school officials had absorbed nothing remotely related to an understanding of the First Amendment. The judges put it well:

> In October 1983, seven months after the district court enjoined the meetings [which were being protested by McCord and Bell], the school administration required the junior high classes to attend a religious assembly at approximately 1:00 P.M. At the assembly, a local minister introduced an evangelist known as "Yo-Yo" Collins who spoke to the assembled students. After he and his wife led the students in a variety of modern religious songs, Mr. Collins "testified" about an accident that had physically disabled him and about how God had loved him and helped him. He then invited the students to attend an ongoing revival that evening at the Little Axe Baptist Church. He also offered them autographed pictures, literature, and records which were handed out during and after his speech.[6]

When the prayer meetings were challenged by the plaintiffs, the school officials insisted that the assembly was a cultural activity. Its justification of this interpretation was caught with all its absurdity in the words of the circuit court decision. It is a classic:

> Most preposterously, the [school] District argued that the assembly was not the same type of activity encompassed by the injunction [the district court decision on behalf of McCord and Bell], asserting the following distinctions. First, the meetings of the Son Shine Club occurred before classes actually started whereas the assembly was held in the middle of the school day. Second, the meetings were directed by the students themselves, while the assembly was initiated by the administration. Third, the meetings were voluntary and no classes or extracurricular activities were cancelled for the purpose of facilitating attendance; in contrast, classes were cancelled to compel student attendance at the assembly. The district court correctly characterized the District's contention as "so patently absurd, that it

is unworthy of further comment," and held the "religious meeting" to constitute an act prohibited by the injunction.

The circuit court then expressed the following sentiment: "The District's blatant disregard for the clear import of the court's injunction convinces us that the District's 'pre-eminent purpose' in permitting these meetings to be held was religious in nature and that the policy was adopted to conceal that purpose."

Concluding, the court forbade the meetings of the Son Shine Club or

any concerted religious activity held on the school grounds during school hours. . . . We reverse the denial of compensatory and punitive damages that is reasonable in light of the nature and extent of the particular invasion of Bell's and McCord's rights under the First Amendment. The court should also consider whether the actions of the individual defendants manifested a reckless or callous indifference for those rights. Finally, the court should determine and enter an award of appropriate attorneys' fees to the Oklahoma ACLU for this appeal. The costs of this appeal will be borne by the District.[7]

Looking back after fifteen years, both Lucille McCord and Joann Bell reflect a reasoned analysis of their experiences, but they remain scarred by the events. Interviews with the two women clearly demonstrated how prayer was employed as a weapon to seek their removal from the community.

In 1983 the two mothers were invited to Washington, D.C., to be honored at a banquet hosted by Americans United for Separation of Church and State, an organization which monitors civil rights and the Religious Right's attempts to infringe upon them. Neither Joann nor Lucille knew much about the organization, but they accepted the invitation.

When we arrived in Washington and went to the . . . meeting almost all the people were men and it seemed like they were mostly Southern Baptists. We were shocked and scared. What had we gotten ourselves into, we wondered. Had they invited us to Washington to ridicule [us]? That night when we went to the banquet and heard what they had to say about us we were very pleased and quite relieved.

Before leaving this Oklahoma scene (which, as we were informed over and over again on television after the April 1995 bombing of the Murrah federal building in Oklahoma City, is a kind and loving place where terrorism does not happen) listen again to Joann Bell's description of the abuse of her son Jason and how the horror perpetrated by "righteous" people against those who challenged local mores in the name of childhood, democratic freedom, and justice affected them: "That's when I decided that there was no one at that school who was going to protect my children and I had to get them out. Jason was greatly affected. But he is fine now."

Notes

1. The citations in this chapter are drawn from contemporary newspaper accounts, comments by Lucille McCord and Joann Bell on an ACLU video entitled *America's Constitutional Heritage,* Video Presentation of the ACLU, New York (1993), the decision of the United States Court of Appeals for the Tenth Circuit (*Bell* v. *Little Axe Independent School District* 766 F2d 1391 [1985]), and extended taped interviews with each by the author in January and February 1996.

2. *Bell* v. *Little Axe Independent School District,* 1397.

3. Ibid.

4. *America's Constitutional Heritage.*

5. United Press International issued daily releases concerning this case from December 2, 1982, through December 8, 1982. Several of the articles carried the byline of Rocky Scott and were all datelined from Oklahoma City. Excerpts herein come from the original releases rather than from any edited newspaper account.

6. *Bell* v. *Little Axe Independent School District,* 1403.

7. Ibid.

6

The Bible:
Now You See It. Now You Don't

"Here was a situation where the school superintendent was deciding which religions were appropriate for the students to be exposed to, [and] which religions were inappropriate."

"Did you know that since the Bible and prayer have left our public schools, we went from problems such as chewing gum and talking in class to students concealing weapons, murder, and drugs . . . ?"

The Gideon Bible is so ubiquitous that it is almost like background music in an elevator, although not as intrusive. Anyone who has spent the night in a hotel or motel from Pontotoc County, Mississippi, to New York City has found a Bible on a table or lurking in a drawer. It is perhaps the single most predictable object in any overnight accommodation. The inscription in these books is always the same: "Placed Here by the Gideon Bible Society." There is no constitutional issue raised by this type of distribution as long as the owner of the hotel agrees to the placement of the Bibles. It stands to reason that an organization which goes to the expense of placing a Bible in every hotel and motel room in the United States must care about that activity. Indeed, the Gideons are evangelical in their single-minded commitment to get out the "word."

Less known is the fact that for some thirty-five years the Gideons

118

have been distributing, on a selective basis, Bibles in public schools. From Mississippi to New Jersey to Indiana to Oklahoma the actions of the Gideons have drawn attention. (You will recall that this activity was partly the basis of Joann Bell and Lucille McCord's complaint, discussed in chapter 5.) Gideon International, with its headquarters located in Tennessee, is a religious organization devoted to the promotion of the Gospel of Christ. Over the years there have been numerous suits to halt public school distributions, but none of the cases had nationwide application—until Allen and Rebecca Berger.

Allen Berger is a professor at St. Joseph's College in Rensselaer, Indiana. His two children attended the public school operated by the Central School Corporation. When Berger learned in the fall of 1989 that the school policy permitted the Gideons to distribute Bibles, he sent a letter to the superintendent, Roberta Dinsmore, asking that the policy be halted. According to a newspaper interview with Dinsmore, she tabled the 1990 Gideon request after the letter from Berger arrived. Berger's attorney contended that, on the contrary, the Rensselaer school system reaffirmed their authorization of Bible distribution. In any event, the Berger suit concerned an ongoing policy that had been in place for over a quarter century. While Berger's letter did not convince the school board, it scared off the Gideons, who withdrew from a thirty-five-year association with the schools and temporarily ended the Bible distribution.[1]

When the Gideons distributed Bibles in Rensselaer, they sent two representatives who came once a year after clearing a date with the principal. There was no set method of distribution. However, the men usually went to each of five classrooms of fifth graders, always during regular school hours. They spoke for a minute or two about their organization. The Bibles handed out by the Gideons contained the entire New Testament but only the books of Psalms and Proverbs from the Hebrew Scriptures. At least some of the Bibles had the statement "My Decision to Receive Christ as My Savior" printed on them, with a place to sign one's name. Most of the Bibles had no such statement, only the name and address of the Gideons.

Isabel Wilkerson, writing for the *New York Times*, described the community of Rensselaer in January 1992. She pictured the community as "a quiet, insular town of 5,045 people, just off a remote stretch of highway between Chicago and Indianapolis. This is Bible country and flag-waving farm country where the local newspaper is the *Republican.*"

Wilkerson's thorough look at the community included "a survey by the local Methodist church" which

> found that almost 9 out of every 10 residents were regular churchgoers, and some think that may be an undercount. No one in town knows when the first Gideon arrived for the annual giveaway. The ritual went like this: After getting clearance from the school, two men from Gideons International, an organization of volunteer Bible distributors, would show up at a classroom, sometimes at the end of school, sometimes in the middle of a lesson. The men would introduce themselves to the children and place a box full of little red Bibles on a table by the blackboard or in a hallway outside the principal's office. The men would say something catchy like, "The Bibles are red and meant to be read." Then children would line up for their Bibles. "This town is just full of those little Bibles," said Virginia Houston, a longtime resident. "We never really thought about it. It was a way of life." Her fifty-two-year-old son, Herbert Arihood, still has his Bible, tucked away in a bookcase in his first-floor hallway at home. "It was the first time you had a Bible that was yours," Mr. Arihood said in his tire store. "It meant you were growing up a little."

The *Times* article closes with this assessment of the mood in the town:

> In Rensselaer, people are now blaming the absence of Bibles for every social ill in town. "Did you know that since the Bible and prayer have left our public schools," wrote an exasperated Phyllis Stamper in a recent letter to the *Republican,* "we went from problems such as chewing gum and talking in class to students concealing weapons, murder and drugs in such a short time since the Bible has left?"[2]

The Bergers were convinced that the distribution constituted a violation of the establishment clause of the First Amendment. And, like many other persons whom we have met, it was this constitutional argument that led them to the Indiana ACLU, and a suit was filed in April 1990. The chief federal judge in the northern district of Indiana, Allen Sharp, gave a summary judgment on May 7, 1991, dismissing the Berger suit. He argued "that the Gideons' passing out Bibles was no different from baseball coaches' passing out Little League brochures."[3]

The Bergers appealed to the United States Court of Appeals for the Seventh Circuit, in Chicago, on October 21, 1992. Franklin Morse, representing the Bergers, argued before the judges that "the school district was proselytizing when it allowed Gideon representatives to make short presentations and distribute the Bibles." Morse went on to say, "The involvement of the school was paramount. . . . The obligatory nature of the ceremony leaves a 10-year-old student with no alternative than to submit." Jay Sekulow, chief counsel for the American Center for Law and Justice (the legal arm of the Christian Coalition), who had joined the case representing the school district, said children were not forced to accept the gift.

On January 5, 1993, the appeals court reversed the district court and ordered the Bible distribution to cease. The three-judge panel said that the school district's policy subjected fifth graders to annual presentations from a religious group in violation of constitutional principles requiring the separation of church and state.

The opinion continued by stating that the assistance provided to the Gideons by the Rensselaer Central School Corporation was "a far more glaring offense to First Amendment principles" than the offering of nondenominational prayers at a graduation ceremony, an obvious reference to *Lee* v. *Weisman*, which had been decided by the Supreme Court the previous summer. The Appeals Court made it clear, however, that its decision would have been the same without the *Weisman* decision (this case is detailed in chapter 7).

In a strongly worded critique of the district court reasoning, Judge Walter Cummings, writing for the three-member Appellate Court panel wrote,

> The district judge opined that permitting the Gideons to distribute Bibles was no more offensive than allowing the Little League into classrooms to talk up the National Pastime. . . . Such a conclusion is tone deaf to the Constitution's mandate that the government must not establish a state religion, and is utterly insensitive to the special concern about coercive influences on impressionable public school children.[4]

Jay Sekulow argued that the case was about the free-speech rights of the Gideons. The point was made that once the school district allowed other groups such as the Boy Scouts or 4-H Clubs to talk to pupils, it could not exclude the Gideons without discriminating against them.

The court of appeals totally rejected that argument, stating that it ignored the involvement of school officials in providing the Gideons with what was essentially a captive audience. "At no point in the record does any school official suggest that students were free to leave the room during the Gideons' talk or to skip the school assemblies at which Bibles were distributed," Cummings wrote.

The school officials took the case to the United States Supreme Court which, on May 17, 1993, denied a petition for hearing on appeal. The public school doors closed on the Gideons. Of course they will be back, seeking school administrators ignorant of the Berger case or officials who appear to relish defiance of Supreme Court decisions, characterizing such decisions as interfering in the freedom of the people to operate their own schools without interference from Washington.

The story of Becky and Allen Berger reflects positively on the community of Rensselaer, Indiana. As Professor Berger notes, "it is a fairly conservative community. It's a rural community, it's a fairly homogeneous community. It's a church-going community." Describing the early stages of their conflict with the public school, Allen Berger recalls,

> It didn't really start as any kind of crusade. It started simply as a letter of complaint to the school corporation when I found out from a young woman who had been a student of mine at St. Joseph's College that Bibles were being distributed by the Gideons each year to the fifth-grade students in the classrooms in the schools.

Becky commented, "In some ways it seemed like a very small issue to a lot of people but I think that the ramifications are more far-reaching." Her husband continued, "Here was a situation where the school superintendent was deciding which religions were appropriate for the students to be exposed to, [and] which religions were inappropriate. We are a multi-faith family. I am Jewish, Becky is Protestant. We feel the religious formation of our children is a personal matter."[5]

Some months after the Supreme Court decision, Allen Berger wrote an extended op-ed piece for the *Chicago Tribune*. Commenting on the article. David V. Kahn of the American Jewish Congress stated,

Perhaps his words will lead to greater understanding that the First Amendment's establishment clause requires that religion be kept out of government and that free exercise of religion is also a First Amendment principle.

These two cherished constitutional bulwarks enable all of us to practice and express our religious beliefs. This protection is extended to the very people who, often with the best intentions, endanger our constitutional heritage by endeavoring to force their religious ideas into the public schools.[6]

A limited audience read Allen Berger's remarks in the summer of 1993. I offer it here as an example of the tenacity, integrity, and understanding that is so much a part of all the persons described in these pages:

Given the contemporary "culture wars" over school prayer, abortion, homosexuality, etc., activists from all sides appear to have concluded that rational debate and the search for a common ground are impossible. Whether we are Christians warning about "secular humanists" or liberals warning about "fundamentalists," we imagine ourselves divided by contradictory moral visions. Compromise appears unthinkable. Engagement in the public arena seems a zero-sum game [when someone wins, someone else must lose].

The news media, according to many critics, exacerbate these divisions by sensationalizing and simplifying the arguments of the competing sides. As a result, public discourse is reduced to shouting and sloganeering. Dialogue is replaced by rhetorical excess.

Though there is much truth to this vision of the contemporary situation, I think there are possible ways out if we understand the ways we got in. My own experiences as a veteran of the "culture war"—I was the plaintiff in *Berger* v. *Rensselaer* (Ind.), a recent case in which the distribution of Gideon Bibles in public schools was ruled unconstitutional—have led me to reflect on the battleground and the possibility of reconstructing a common life. Certainly we can learn from our mistakes.

In the fall of 1989 when I first learned of Gideon proselytizing and Bible distribution in the fifth grade classrooms of the Rensselaer schools, I was shocked. My son, a fifth grader at the time, was and still is working out his own religious identity and beliefs in the context of a multi-faith, Christian and Jewish heritage. With government sponsorship, the Gideons were interfering with what we felt was a family prerogative—the religious formation of children. This couldn't possibly be happening in an America where public school-sponsored prayer had been ruled unconstitutional almost 30 years before. What kind of time warp did my rural, small-town neighbors live in? I was determined to bring them up to date.

My mistake? I assumed the Gideon practice was simply a product of ignorance (on the part of school administrators) and over-zealousness (on the part of a local religious majority). Even though by profession I am a cultural anthropologist, I failed adequately to understand the sacred and symbolic aspects of this tradition. I failed to recognize how delicately I would need to tread.

In October of 1989 I wrote a letter of complaint to each school board member and to the superintendent. I requested an opportunity to discuss the issue, but afraid that my complaint would not be taken seriously by a non-elected board reputed to be insensitive to patron criticisms, I mentioned that I might seek legal counsel for the purpose of bringing suit in federal court if the matter were not resolved to my satisfaction.

My mistake? I failed to recognize that the legal card, once played, even if only tentatively, can only provoke polarization.

I never received a reply to my letter. Instead, the school superintendent, who had informed me that the issue could not be discussed for a couple of months, gave a photocopy of my letter to the local press. The next day, the headline in our local newspaper, the *Rensselaer Republican,* read, "Parent Threatens Suit Over Bible Distribution." Conveniently, I was "unavailable for comment."

The school board's mistake? They opted to reach out to what would obviously be a sympathetic mass audience, but did so in a manner guaranteed to incite people's passions, not engage their reason. The nuances of my moral position could not be captured in a headline or even a standard-length news article. Furthermore, small-town newspapers routinely rely upon inexperienced, poorly paid staff. The reporter in this instance later confessed that he had never heard of the establishment clause of the First Amendment to the Constitution. As a result, the public perception was simply that I wished to "ban the Bible." Community-wide polarization was now inevitable.

Reasoned discourse and compromise were virtually impossible after this point. An onslaught of letters-to-the-editor portrayed me as an outsider (though I had lived in Rensselaer for eight years), as anti-Christian, or simply as evil. During this time, however, the school board was receiving advice from local attorneys and the state school board association that legally I was on solid ground. Caught between the public and their own lawyers, the board escaped their bind by seeking out the advice they wanted to hear. It was provided by two conservative religious organizations in Virginia, the National Legal Foundation and the American Center for Law and Justice.

The school board's mistake? They permitted themselves to be used as pawns by outside groups whose religio-political-fundraising agendas are advanced by public litigation and national publicity, not by quiet discussion and local resolutions. At this point, if I wished to pursue my complaint, my only option was to go to court.

In the end, I won, as the lawyers had always predicted. However, it took more than three and a half painful years, until May 1993, when the Supreme Court declined to hear the school's appeal. The school board (i.e., the taxpayers) will now be stuck with substantial legal fees—their own and mine.

I am convinced that the principle (government neutrality and non-involvement in religious, especially sectarian, affairs) was worth the struggle. However, the struggle itself was probably unnecessary.

Had there been an opportunity for dialogue at the beginning, each side might have discovered that the other felt that sacred principles were at stake. The spirit of neighborliness might have pushed us toward compromise—perhaps Gideon access to the sidewalks outside school or Gideon-sponsored events in the schools outside normal class hours. In the process we might even have discovered a common ground—a belief in religious freedom, in religious voluntarism (the notion that the advancement of a religious sect should come from the voluntary efforts of its members), and in the value of religion. Unfortunately, that common ground is now more obscured than ever.

But there is also cause for optimism. Over the course of the litigation, I only had one opportunity to engage a school board member in extended discussion. We spent more than an hour together in the back seat of a limousine as we traveled to and from a network television interview. He and I solidified an endangered friendship. We listened to one another. Most importantly, our discourse was phrased in personal, moral—not sterile, not legal—terms. We talked about our pasts, how [while] growing up in New Jersey I came to one set of beliefs and [how while] growing up in Rensselaer he came to another, and we talked about our kids, the main reason we both cared so much about the Bible issue.

Perhaps, then, if we could just share our stories, we might quit arguing so much. Minimally, we might understand our differences.[7]

The Bergers received thanks for their actions from parents who are themselves among religious minorities: parents of Seventh-Day Adventist children, parents of Jehovah's Witness children.

Berger did not believe the matter belonged in court, and never expected it to end up there.

I was naive. I thought a simple letter of complaint to the school corporation would settle the issue. Once the issue hit the press there was tremendous polarization in town. There was little dialogue after that. And that's tragic because these issues ought to be settled without lawsuits. There's no reason this ever had to become a lawsuit.

Of course, such belief may cause a slight problem. If the Constitution's meaning were self-evident to all citizens then the Supreme Court would largely become a relic. Because that is not the case, the courts become the greatest protection we possess against anarchy. That requires public respect for Supreme Court decisions, no matter how little they may conform to one's personal interpretation of the law.

Allen Berger quickly answered his own musings when he stated:

I think for us the broader ramifications for this case mainly have to do with a renewed faith, a renewed faith number one that the system works. A renewed faith secondly in our neighbors and in our friends. We did not lose friends. Our neighbors did not turn on us. We did not have crosses burned on our lawn. We received nasty hate mail over the three-and-a-half years, but very little of it came locally. And to me, that says something about the value and the goodness that exists in many small towns in America like Rensselaer.

Notes

1. Information for this chapter was garnered from the district and circuit court opinions (*Berger* v. *Rensselaer Central School District,* 766 FSupp 686 [1991] and *Berger* v. *Rensselaer Central School District,* 982 F2d 1160 [1993] US App., respectively), an ACLU videotape (*America's Constitutional Heritage,* 1993), numerous newspaper reports over a three-year period, and a letter from Allen Berger addressed to the *Chicago Tribune.*

2. Isabel Wilkerson, "Bible Giveaway Is a Rural Ritual to Some, an Offense to Others," *New York Times,* 12 January 1992, Sect. 1, p. 12.

3. *Berger* v. *Rensselaer,* 776 FSupp.

4. *Berger* v. *Rensselaer,* 982 F2d.

5. *America's Constitutional Heritage.*

6. David V. Kahn, "Culture Wars," *Chicago Tribune,* 19 August 1993, p. 22.

7. Allen Berger, "Calling a Cease Fire in Culture Wars," *Chicago Tribune,* 3 August 1993, p. 17.

7

And a Rabbi Shall Not Lead Them

"Prayer exercises in elementary and secondary schools carry a particular risk of indirect coercion."

"Our friends reminded us that after all we wouldn't be offended, we got a rabbi. We tried to point out [that] that was not the issue."

"We also had the support of many friends who provided a 'safe' environment."

While there have been dozens of church/state cases decided by the Supreme Court since 1963, none seemed so clearly to revisit the tumultuous days which followed the early decisions as the *Weisman* case of 1992. It was a genuine, unembellished, organized public school "prayer" lawsuit. But now a graduation ceremony replaced the classroom setting.

The beginnings of this confrontation were simple enough. The elder Weisman daughter, Merith, attended Nathan Bishop Middle School in the city of Providence, Rhode Island, where principals "were permitted to invite members of the clergy to give invocations and benedictions at their schools' graduation ceremonies." Principal Robert E. Lee did just that, inviting a Baptist minister to officiate over such ceremonies as Merith's graduation in 1986. The minister thanked Jesus

Christ for the students' accomplishments. As her parents recall, it was a most upsetting experience for their daughter, a young Jewish girl, to be forced to listen to a narrowly sectarian message which thanked the Christian God for the success of the graduates. Daniel and Vivian Weisman complained to the school superintendent the next day.

Principal Robert E. Lee remembered that complaint quite clearly as the time approached for Merith's sister, Deborah, to graduate. Indeed, he called the Weismans to inform them that this time they had no cause to worry because he had arranged to have a rabbi give the invocation and benediction. Daniel responded by saying to Lee that he obviously didn't understand the problem. If it was wrong to have a Baptist minister, then it was wrong to have a rabbi. He and Vivian said "the prayers could be offensive to some non-Jewish students at the school."[1] Shortly before the ceremony, the district court denied a motion by Daniel Weisman "for a temporary restraining order to prohibit school officials from including the prayers in the ceremony. Deborah and her family attended the ceremony, and the prayers were recited."[2] The occasion was not without humor. Deborah was called to the stage to receive an award for having the "best school spirit."

Quickly thereafter the Weismans filed a suit against the school district seeking a permanent injunction to prevent the inclusion of invocations and benedictions in the form of prayer in the promotion and graduation ceremonies of the Providence public schools, including Classical High School where Deborah was then enrolled.

In hearing the case, the U.S. District Court noted,

> The ceremony was planned by two teachers from the school, and was to be held on the school grounds. Part of the program for that day included an invocation and benediction delivered by Rabbi Leslie Gutterman of the Temple Beth El of Providence. . . . The principal of the school, Robert E. Lee, had received the "Guidelines for Civic Occasions" pamphlet from the Assistant Superintendent of Schools, and provided Rabbi Gutterman with a copy of the guidelines. Mr. Lee also spoke to Rabbi Gutterman to advise him that any prayers delivered at the ceremonies should be nonsectarian. Rabbi Gutterman was not told that he could not appeal to a deity.

This incident is remarkable. The school invited a clergyman, presumably because of his special expertise, to pray. Then the school officials gave him a canned prayer and guidelines. To his credit, the rabbi didn't follow the script.

The Weismans won in the district court and in the circuit court of appeals. Providence schools appealed to the U.S. Supreme Court which, in its 1992 opinion, detailed the history of the case, noting, "It appears likely that such prayers will be conducted at Deborah's high school graduation."[3]

The U.S. Justice Department, which entered the case on the side of the school district in Rhode Island, went to great lengths to make clear that location was "everything." As Solicitor General Kenneth Starr argued the merits of his position, he was at pains to assure the justices that if attendance at the graduation ceremony were required, then the school officials *would* be in violation of the First Amendment restriction on establishment. Because attendance was voluntary, he argued, then no violation had occurred. In order to make his point, Starr agreed that school-sponsored prayer in the classroom was and always had been coercive. In making that plea, Starr not only accepted the precedent set by *Engel* and *Schempp*, he endorsed the principle upon which the two cases were resolved. Starr cut the ground out from under thirty years of argument on behalf of prayer in public school classroom. In that time, almost all of the advocates of amendments of the First Amendment's religion clauses sought to overturn *Engel* and *Schempp* by providing for school-sponsored prayers in the classroom. Starr's position would have denied the constitutionality of all such efforts.

It is only fair to give Starr the benefit of the doubt and assume that he sincerely believed that the Court had decided correctly in 1962 and 1963. But it is also true that by switching to the coercion argument he hoped to avoid the probable reticence of the Court to revisit the classroom-sponsored prayer decisions of the past. In short, he believed he had a winner. In order to secure that victory, Starr had to demonstrate that graduation was distinct, different, and unrelated to the classroom. It proved to be a hard sell for a majority of the justices.

It is also possible that Starr's co-counsel undermined the newly minted coercion argument with his unique interpretation. Charles J. Cooper was the Washington attorney hired by the school. As Vivian Weisman noted, there was no question in the minds of the school officials that they were going to prevail. They did not seek someone with expertise in church litigation. Indeed, they chose a young, high-profile lawyer. This deficiency was painfully obvious in Cooper's part in the oral argument before the Court, when he ran afoul of established precedents. Responding to questioning from Justice Sandra Day O'Connor, Cooper affirmed that if a state legislature were to go so far as to adopt a particular religion, as long as no one was coerced into that religion, it would satisfy the First Amendment. It was no different than adopting an official state bow tie. Justice O'Connor suggested there was a wide gulf between these two examples. Perhaps sensing that Cooper was in deep water, Justice Antonin Scalia tried to bail him out. Scalia suggested that while it is acceptable to have "In God We Trust" on the currency, surely Cooper would not insist that it would be proper to inscribe "In Jesus Christ We Trust" on the money. He must have been somewhat astonished when Cooper saw no problem with the latter slogan.

Both Cooper and Starr emphasized the need to abandon the three-part formula developed by Justice Warren Burger in his *Lemon* v. *Kurtzman* opinion in 1971 that established the criteria by which to judge the constitutionality of statutes and laws in the church/state establishment arena. Burger phrased it thus: "First, the statute must have a secular legislative purpose; second, its principle or primary effect must be one that neither advances nor inhibits religion; finally, the statute must not foster 'an excessive government entanglement with religion.' "[4]

The decision to attack *Lemon* appeared necessary to Cooper's and Starr's case since for twenty years the opinion rendered in *Lemon* had proved an almost insurmountable obstacle to wedging any kind of religion into the public schools and, far more important, that test seemed a permanent block to all efforts to build on the accommodationist theory advanced by Justices Burger and Rehnquist. A government victory in *Weisman* would have aided the opponents of a strict separationist view. Starr and Cooper appeared to have reasoned that the Supreme Court would reject any coercion of young children in a public school, but if it could be shown that prayer, in an appropriate setting, was not coercive, even if sponsored by school officials, then a panorama of other options would likely follow. In the wake of a government victory, some form of prayer and religion in schools might be construed as legitimate. By such a narrow reading of the term "coercion," school officials could possibly begin to cooperate in promoting the religious interests of a majority of students, as long as the term "voluntary" could be attached. Likewise, freed from the restrictive *Lemon* criteria, aid to religious schools could be advanced as another form of cooperation, accommodation, and nonpreferentialism.

The Weismans' attorney, Sandra Blanding, was on target in arguing that "there was no magical difference from the daily classroom prayer cases here, because the graduation also involves an element of continuity; the middle school students were moving from one public school to another." She continued, "The mere fact that this case is removed from the classroom doesn't change its essential nature." She doubted that it was possible to compose a nonsectarian prayer in the first place, but concluded that "it is virtually impossible to devise a nonsectarian prayer that covers all the diverse religious beliefs of U.S. citizens."[5]

An examination of the word "coercion" in relation to the cases discussed in this volume suggests a most elusive term. All too often the prevailing religious sentiment in a given community has been imposed in public schools with apparent failure on the part of school officials or citizens to imagine how such religious activities, when providing each student the right to choose not to participate, could possibly be coercive. Frequently there is a failure to comprehend that forcing a choice between participation in the majority's religious or cultural rites and volunteering to leave is the height of coercion. And the reason is apparent. Such plans and programs carry the unmistakable mark of endorsement by the school authorities. This is particularly true in the case of elementary school student perceptions. No amount of free "choice" can change that fact. There is only one choice that places the child in agreement with the teacher. Suggesting that choice removes coercion is folly. If the school plans and directs religious observance or activity in any way, it remains an establishment of religion no matter how many choices are offered. That is why the *Weisman* decision was so critically important.

Because of that importance, *Lee* v. *Weisman* was a case that many strict separationists dreaded because they feared that an altered Court, with new justices, could easily accept Starr's arguments and set aside the *Lemon* test. The Supreme Court was being viewed as growing ever more hostile to the *Everson* tradition. Not only had Chief Justice William Rehnquist openly challenged the separation metaphor, he was joined in that opinion by Justices Antonin Scalia, Byron White, and the then newest appointee, Clarence Thomas. These were four "sure" votes against the Weismans. Justice David Souter was at the time untested, Justice Antony M. Kennedy had already voiced concerns about the *Lemon* test, and based on her past decisions, Justice O'Connor was far from predictable on this issue. At best, separationists could depend on Justices Harry Blackmun and John Paul Stevens. The departure of Justices William Brennan and Thurgood Marshall from the bench had removed two of the most gifted advocates of strict separation.

In light of the "untested" new Court, it was reasonable for the Bush administration to anticipate a productive summer in 1992. There is little doubt that the religious right and the Department of Justice expected to win not only *Weisman*, but the Pennsylvania abortion case* as well. Had that occurred, President Bush would have taken credit for accomplishing two tasks assigned to him by the Moral Majority. Abortion and school prayer were the hot button items of the 1980s, but neither issue had been resolved to the satisfaction of President Bush's most conservative supporters. Success in the two cases would have propelled him from Desert Storm, the military action in the Middle East which resulted from an Iraqi invasion of Kuwait, through the summer to a likely vigorous campaign for a second term in the fall.

The failed opportunity of the Republicans to capitalize on twelve years in office and six Supreme Court appointments as a means to return the abortion issue to the states and establish religious exercises in public schools was one of the most surprising results of the twelve chaotic years which comprised the presidencies of Ronald Reagan and George Bush. Within a week in June 1992, both the abortion and school prayer issues were decided by the High Court in five-to-four votes. In the Pennsylvania case the Court refused to abandon *Roe* v. *Wade*, although it did permit some state restrictions, and the government simply lost outright in *Weisman*.

It is beyond the purview of this study to examine the Pennsylva-

---

Planned Parenthood of Southeastern Pennsylvania v. *Robert P. Casey* addressed the right of states to place restrictions on the exercise of the right to abortion, such as waiting periods and parental consent for minors.

nia decision which failed to overturn *Roe*, but what of the Weisman case? Why did the government attorneys lose that one? Looking back, it seems astounding that after twelve years of Republican control of the White House, a Supreme Court with only one Democratic appointee out of nine on the bench (Justice White, who consistently voted with Rehnquist and Scalia on church/state cases), decided on behalf of the Weismans. Presidents Reagan and Bush together appointed three of the five justices who voted in the majority in Weisman—Kennedy, O'Connor, and Souter. So much for litmus tests. And President Clinton has now added Justices Ruth Ginsburg and Stephen Breyer (replacing Justices Harry Blackmun and Byron White) providing the new majority.

Looking back to the Senate confirmation hearings regarding then Judge Robert Bork, the importance of the extended dialogue between Senator Joseph Biden (D-Del.) and Bork takes on major significance. Biden argued vigorously for a constitutional right of privacy. Judge Bork, using the slogan "original intent," found no such right. As Leonard Levy has written, "What Bork's theory of jurisprudence adds up to is that in his opinion, any right with which he disagrees is not a right derived from original intent."[6] If Bork had been appointed instead of Kennedy, both the right of a woman to choose and the right of citizens to be protected from a religious establishment might well have been seriously crippled at the federal level. In light of these facts, it is not an idle warning to bear in mind that once again a presidential election (that of 1996) may hold the key to the future direction of the Supreme Court.

Returning to the *Weisman* case, in the opening synopsis which precedes the decision written by Justice Kennedy, the following observation appears: "The Establishment Clause was inspired by the lesson that in the hands of government what might begin as a tolerant expression of religious views may end in a policy to indoctrinate and coerce. Prayer exercises in elementary and secondary schools carry a particular risk of indirect coercion." The justices found that no amount of good intentions could prevent such coercion. A review of the Bell/McCord experience merely suggests the lengths some persons may go to indoctrinate. And the Court recognized the clear, unmistakable distinction between individuals being tolerant of other views and a government institution presuming the right to tolerate.

With all this information in the public domain, I sought out the Weisman family in the spring of 1995 to explore their memories and their feelings about the case.[7] Daniel and Vivian live in a Providence residential area close to the college where Daniel teaches. During our visit the family was preparing for the Memorial Day weekend. It was a busy time as the home was being prepared for the holiday. Yet, Vivian and David graciously sat and talked with my wife, Norma, and me for nearly two hours. Family members moved about the house and the phone rang frequently as we explored *Lee* v. *Weisman*. Both parents were animated as they reflected on their involvement in the case. They generally spoke as one, and for that reason most of the following observations are attributable to both.

"It was not the strongest case on the subject. Our friends reminded us that after all we wouldn't be offended, we got a rabbi. We tried to point out [that] that was not the issue." Indeed, the school principal had assumed, as was mentioned previously, that obtaining Rabbi Gutterman would squash the anticipated reaction from the family.

> We were warned to be ready for hate stuff. Of course, we thought we would win as a complaint but the court did not step in because of the timing. We started the protest to stop a specific act, not to deal with an overall policy. We thought they would pull back. Of course they didn't, and we had to decide whether to go forward with a suit.

Meanwhile, the family determined to attend the graduation although they were unhappy about the circumstances. "It was a special time for Deborah. She had had good experiences at school and we were determined to celebrate that."

Daniel continued,

> There was a full range of reactions to our suit. While perhaps 70 percent of Rhode Island's population is Roman Catholic, there were a large number of supporters from that tradition. The Jewish community was divided with the Orthodox Jews offering a typical fundamentalist response. People who were our friends and whom we really cared about were supporters from the beginning. Many commented that what we did they could never have done, but "it was such a relief to be at our son's graduation and not have to worry about a prayer."

As for the local school board, they made their decision to defend their policy. We had some strong support in the religious community, including the minister of the First Baptist Church of Providence, Roger Williams's church. We also discovered that some very religious people didn't like the idea of a nonsectarian prayer because it did not address their religious convictions.

When asked about Rabbi Gutterman, the Weismans responded:

The school thought choosing him would satisfy us. Mr. Lee is a nice, gentle, caring man who runs a good school. He cares about the community and the kids. He was trying to solve a problem the best way he knew. As for the rabbi, he is involved in community service and outreach. But he just did not understand how a little religion could be dangerous. We knew the prayer had been a committee project, but it came out sounding very much like a typical Jewish family blessing. When the rabbi, departing from the "script," quoted from [the Hebrew Scripture's Book of] Micah, the prayer became clearly sectarian.

Vivian Weisman was out of the city on the day they were to file the suit in court. Daniel handled the press and the publicity. He sent Deborah to stay with friends and went home to hear his phone ring constantly until 1 A.M.

The calls for the next few days were . . . a little abusive. People wanted to argue. I put on the answering machine and stopped taking calls. The police warned us of persons known to be anti-Semitic in the community. With harassment on the rise we were pleased that our address was not listed in the phone book. People had to work to reach us but a good bit of hate mail arrived either at home, at work, or at Deborah's school. Finally the night calls ended in 1993, a year after the Supreme Court ruled.

During the time while the case was in the courts, some persons tried to get us both fired. But our jobs were secure and our colleagues supported us, even those who disagreed with us. We also had the support of many friends who provided a "safe" environment. Of course there were the bad times such as when one of Deborah's teachers publicly commented [that] "this problem between me and you has nothing to do with your parents." Gratuitous comments like that are unsettling. Deborah knew what was happening. We did this as a family. She knew why there was a problem and why she resisted the graduation policy. But we did not anticipate how much this would take over our life. It became a priority.

We got less hate mail than we expected. There were some serious threats and we have two cartons of angry letters. And, again, even our neighbors who opposed our position were for the most part quite friendly. When our daughter Merith had to stay in the house alone when the rest of us, out of necessity, were away from the city, a neighbor who absolutely disagreed with our stand volunteered to look out for her and the house while we were away.

This thing affected both of our daughters. In a positive way it helped sharpen their ability at public speaking, rare in young women. We sued without knowing the consequences and so our daughters learned to deal with whatever happened. And we had a community that stood by us. Deborah found it was easier to deal with her time in school when she explained why she did what she did. Nobody turned on her. She wasn't excluded. . . .

After the 1992 decision the Providence school complied with the order. There was more media attention after the decision. It was an adventure when the phone rang.

In one community near Providence a Roman Catholic priest called on parishioners to contact school board members and insist that prayer not be removed there. A girl from that area called the Weismans, in tears, upset with herself because she felt she needed to say something but she was scared.

> We told her . . . one of the main reasons we did speak up and go to court was for children in situations like [hers]. The child was torn up because of what would happen if she did what she believed was the right thing. It was too hard for her and we tried to assure her that . . . we could make things better for children like her by doing what we did. I think we helped her to understand.

The Weisman story brought out the best in most Rhode Island citizens even as they battled over a fundamental issue. What began as a simple protest of one event expanded quickly until it became a historic moment for the Supreme Court, for religious freedom, and for all parents and children who did not have the luxury of a nest of support. It is the kind of story one wants to believe that Rhode Island's liberal founders, Roger Williams and John Clarke, would have relished.

As one might expect, having lost a seeming sure thing, the advocates of accommodation regrouped and quickly sought to find loopholes in the *Weisman* decision. What if, instead of a principal or other administrator, one or more students voluntarily elected to have prayer at graduation? What would happen if the graduation prayer were "student-initiated"? Of course that is a hard game to play in elementary schools, but it has some chance in high schools. Thus far there have been three high-profile challenges to the *Weisman* conclusion, all focused on student initiation of prayer in other-than-mandated situations. One of those three is the case to which we now turn.

Notes

1. *New York Times*, 19 March 1991, p. A16.
2. *Lee* v. *Weisman*, 505 US 595 (1992).
3. Ibid.
4. *Lemon* v. *Kurtzman, Superintendent of Public Instruction of Pennsylvania et al.* 403 US 602 (1971).
5. "Supreme Court Proceedings," *The United States Law Week* 60, no. 19 (November 12, 1991): 3351–53.
6. Leonard Levy, *Original Intent and the Framers' Constitution* (New York: Macmillan, 1988), p. 383.
7. The material for this chapter comes from the author's taped interviews with the Weisman family in Providence, Rhode Island, in the summer of 1995. Extended interviews broadcast by the C-SPAN television network with the participating attorneys following oral arguments were most helpful. Additionally, the Supreme Court decision of 1992 and several amicus briefs (a friend of the court argument offered by interested parties on either side of a case) have been employed to relate the details.

8

Harris and Doe in Idaho

"Elected officials cannot avoid constitutional mandates by putting them to a majority vote. . . . The notion that a person's constitutional rights may be subject to a majority vote is anathema."

"It's too important an issue and far too few people are willing to fight for a world in which my children and grandchildren will experience the blessings of liberty."

"I say if they don't like it here, they have the free agency to move away. There are plenty of places where they can find the godless society they want. They have no right to deny us our right to freedom of religion and of speech."

"We are expected to believe that the Constitution is designed to protect the rights of the minority. These claims are all nonsense."

In 1994 Phyllis Harris brought suit in the Federal Appeals Court for the Ninth Circuit on behalf of her children, Beverly and Samuel, regarding the issue of prayer at graduation ceremonies.[1] Grangeville High School in Idaho had had an invocation and a benediction at graduation every year since 1981. However, the school district immediately made efforts to distance itself from the religious ceremonies in question: they decided to make the prayer a matter of student vote. It was argued by school officials that whether to have a prayer, who is to say it, and how it is to be said lie with a majority vote of the senior class. Thus, school officials argued that "In this case it is the senior students themselves, not the principal, who determine every element of their graduations, including whether or not prayer will be part of the ceremony, and if so, who will say it." In 1991 fifty-two seniors voted for prayer, twelve against. Only one or two students were willing to admit publicly that they had voted against the prayer.

Based on those facts, the federal district court concluded that there was "little or no state involvement." Harris appealed on grounds used to decide the *Weisman* case of 1992, that what might begin as "tolerance" for various religious expressions can easily become indoctrination. The court of appeals reversed the district court, noting, "we find state involvement in this case pervasive enough to offend Establishment Clause concerns." The primary argument was that the "school ultimately controls the event" and that "the school underwrites the event." In a reasoned explanation the court found "that school officials cannot divest themselves of constitutional responsibility by allowing the students to make crucial decisions. . . . Elected officials cannot avoid constitutional mandates by putting them to a majority vote." The court relied on a district court decision in eastern Virginia, *Gearon* v. *Loudoun County*, which found student-initiated graduation prayer unconstitutional, for the wording of its most basic complaint with the situation in Idaho: "One's . . . fundamental rights may not be submitted to vote; they depend on the outcome of no elections. The notion that a person's constitutional rights may be subject to a majority vote is anathema." The circuit court concluded "the school delegated its authority to make decisions . . . to the Student Council. We cannot allow the school district's delegate to make decisions that the school district cannot make. . . . A decision to the contrary could allow students to vote daily prayers and the Ten Commandments back into the classroom."[2]

The victory at the circuit court level by Harris led to an appeal to the U.S. Supreme Court on the part of the school district. In the spring of 1995, only days after Samuel Harris, the youngest child, had graduated from high school, the Supreme Court refused to hear the case, declaring it moot due to lack of standing. With all due respect to the justices, this seemed unwise and confusing, as it leaves the issues in the

Harris case in a perplexing world of the unknown. Are we to take seriously the thoughtful conclusions of the Ninth Circuit Court? On May 24, 1996, the Third Circuit Court in *American Civil Liberties Union* v. *Black Horse Pike Board of Education* relied heavily upon the Harris decision in declaring student-initiated graduation prayer unconstitutional. In this new case the question of standing could not be an issue because of the ages of the children involved. This decision came too late for analysis in this book but I have included the major findings on the Third Circuit Court of Appeals, meeting *en banc* (all judges for the circuit participating), in Appendix B.

Whatever the final resolution of this dilemma, certain facts in evidence concerning the Harris case suggest all manner of reasons to abandon the student majority policy crafted by the likes of the American Center for Law and Justice (ACLJ) to circumvent the *Weisman* decision. Much of it has to do with the circumstances that faced the Harris family once the suit was filed. For four years the family was abused and threatened by a community in the name of God. That is reason enough to examine with minute care the notion that a student vote on prayer negates the establishment risk. This is not, nor has it ever been, a free speech issue. It is simply a matter of the majority's intent to impose its religious sentiments upon all citizens in the public schools.

The very fact that a challenge to the school's prayer policy at graduation could generate such passion and bitter hatred in the community is proof that the issue is religious to the core. Every sentiment expressed by those who attacked the Harris family reflected the belief that somehow the majority was being denied religious worship by the lawsuit. That in itself is proof of the fact that the graduation prayer is a religious ritual so precious to some that they will threaten mayhem to those who see such public school rituals as government-directed religious services.

Phyllis Harris recalls that her family "suffered an enormous amount of retaliation and torment as a result of filing our lawsuit." On at least two occasions her two sons were "beaten by other boys" who gave the lawsuit as their reason for the attacks. Two pet cats were poisoned and died as the family watched helplessly. Threatening phone calls became a daily experience both at home and at work. "If I were not employed by the federal government I probably would have been fired because of the frequency and threatening nature of the calls," said Ms. Harris.

As the suit continued, the children were afraid to go out alone and the mother was afraid for their safety. When Samuel Harris graduated on June 2, 1995, a group of women surrounded his mother, chanting that she was evil. While a few people in the community were supportive, "after seeing the community's reaction to our lawsuit, I did not feel safe, and to this day, I still don't."

The lead plaintiff in the original suit was Beverly Harris. She initiated the suit when she was a seventeen-year-old senior in the high school. She did so after the school superintendent talked to her government class and told them that he did not expect any protest of their graduation prayer program. She had attended graduation the previous year as a member of the band and was bothered by the prayer. She spoke to her mother and then called the ACLU. Phyllis Harris wrote a letter to the superintendent about the prayer and he told her he didn't anticipate any protest. She informed him she was protesting. By late fall of 1990 the subject was fairly well aired in the community. Finding no movement on the part of the school to change its policy, Beverly and her mother filed a suit in February 1991.

It was then that the personal abuse began. Beverly was ostracized socially. Her friends no longer spoke to her. Students would move their seats to avoid sitting by her. When she walked down the main street of Grangeville, which has a population of 3,500, the majority of whom are Protestant, people crossed the street to avoid her. Of the twenty-odd churches in the town, not one minister gave public support to Beverly and her family. They undoubtedly saw her objection to graduation prayer as robbing them of their private preserve, the public school. Clerks in stores were rude, some refused to wait on her. Beverly received angry notes, some attached to her locker. She was called a Satan worshipper, and she received mostly anonymous hate mail, one-third of which contained death threats. She also received threatening phone calls. All of this has only stopped in the past year.

Beverly's brothers, Samuel and William, were victims of physical abuse. Sports coaches sometimes refused to let Bill play and the other members of the team "roughed him up." In sports this is difficult to prove and is regularly denied. The family believed these things were happening, and if other cases across the country are a guide, they indeed did occur. The older kids picked on Samuel and pushed him around. The joy of high school became a nightmare for the two Harris boys as they became targets of hatred in the name of God.

Of all their acquaintances in the town only a very few publicly supported them. Others, afraid of public reaction against them, told the family privately that they were with them. Business owners were particularly aware of the likely public reaction to them if they were to voice support for the Harris family.

Beverly has moved to another town in Idaho and, except for visits to her mother, tries to stay away from the town where she was reared. "Nothing happens to me anymore, but I stay away because I don't feel at home." To this day Beverly believes that most of the inhabitants, fed on a diet of "Christian America," do not understand the issues involved. "They miss the point and there is no way to have a reasonable discussion about the issues involved in separation of church and state."

Beverly remains committed to the principles she espoused in Grangeville. "It's too important an issue and far too few people are willing to fight for a world in which my children and grandchildren will experience the blessings of liberty."

In the February 3, 1995, *Idaho Statesman* Beverly responded to a letter printed the previous month criticizing her decision to bring suit against the school. Her letter encapsulates reasonableness and dedication to freedom.

Beverly wrote:

Jay Smith of Grangeville contends that graduation prayer is an "issue of free speech." He writes that, in seeking to put an end to having an organized Christian prayer as part of a public high school's graduation ceremony, my family and I would "do away with (students') right of free speech and free exercise of religion." He is quite mistaken on both counts. Whether or not organized prayer ought to be included in an official high school graduation program is an issue of religious freedom. Contrary to Mr. Smith's opinion, in opposing graduation prayer we seek to protect and uphold all citizens' right to freedom of religion.

Grangeville Joint School District 241 and Citizens Preserving America's Heritage argue that the prayers given at Grangeville High School graduations are constitutional because student majorities have voted to have them, and because they are led by students chosen by their peers. The argument goes on that the school district has no part in the prayer, as evidenced by the disclaimer printed at the bottom of the program, in print so small as to be hardly legible.

This all sounds well and good, but it must be understood that the voting process, the practice of having a student (as opposed to a local minister) lead the prayer, and the inclusion of the disclaimer on the program came about only after my family and I filed a lawsuit against the school district.

It is obvious that these measures were enacted as an attempt by district officials to distance themselves from a practice that is clearly unconstitutional. However, as recognized by the Ninth Circuit Court of Appeals, these district officials failed.

According to the Court, there is "no meaningful distinction between school authorities actually organizing the religious activities and officials merely 'permitting' students to direct the exercises." Regardless of who delivers the message, whether it be a school district employee, minister, or student, a prayer offered under the auspices of a public entity violates the establishment clause of the First Amendment.

My involvement in this issue has never been about religion, per se, and I certainly have no wish for people to abandon their religious beliefs. All people have the right to pray anywhere at any time. This is one aspect of religious freedom. The other aspect is that all people have the right not to have any particular religion advanced by a public institution.

Any student may offer a spontaneous prayer at his or her graduation. A public high school may not allow an organized, blanket prayer to be a part of its graduation. When a tax-supported institution encourages and/or endorses religious activity of any sort, it is infringing upon every citizen's right to religious freedom.

When the beliefs of the majority are the only ones presented in a public forum, it appears that the government is endorsing those particular beliefs and rejecting any others that exist among the people of the minority. In 1943, the Supreme Court, in *Board of Education* v. *Barnette,* maintained that "(t)he very purpose of a Bill of Rights was to withdraw certain subjects from the vicissitudes of political controversy, to place them beyond the reach of majorities and officials and to establish them as legal principles to be applied by the courts."

Religious freedom is such a subject, and in order to preserve it, it is imperative that we continue to fight for our individual liberties.[3]

Once again the words of a student ring true and clear. Beverly, like her partners in this struggle in Rhode Island, Mississippi, Oklahoma, Alabama, Utah, and a large number of other states, has articulated in a highly effective manner the issues at stake. These students know the working of our constitutional democracy in a way that is sadly lacking among their peers. The fault usually lies with school systems more intent upon preserving worn out local cultural mores than having the student body perceive the wonder and majesty of our constitutional democracy. As is seen in the next chapter, it was only *after* Rachel Bauchman challenged her Salt Lake City high school that the school administration decided to offer instruction in constitutional principles and democratic process. When the principal of that Henrico County, Virginia, elementary school told me in 1966 that he knew he was breaking the law but he intended to continue, I wondered then what messages in civics were being conveyed to the children. The answer is obvious. If you don't like the law, break it. If you are challenged, claim a godly purpose or tradition as a motivation. And along the way harass and threaten those who call for implementation of constitutional principles.

No one who has brought suit in federal court concerning violations of the First Amendment has become emotionally unstrung even in the face of losing the suit. Note Beverly Harris's comment on the Supreme Court action of 1995: "We were very encouraged in November when the Ninth Circuit decision came down. It felt like all our hard work had been justified. It has been grueling and it is frustrating to come so far and have it dismissed and forgotten about in one fell swoop." Harris found the continued confusion to be the most disheartening of all. "We're left without a resolution here. We're left hanging, and my family has suffered a lot of blood, sweat, and tears to get to this point. It would have been better if they had decided to hear it and rule, and now it's just a muddle. It's now almost worse than even before we started."

Certainly Beverly exhibits frustration and disappointment, but there are no condemnations of the Court, no accusations against those who represented the other side. In spite of losing she believes in the democratic process.*

---

*While the Supreme Court dismissed the case because no more Harris children were in the school, the decision lifts a ban on student-led prayer in Idaho and seven other western states. In that sense Beverly Harris lost.

Having learned little from the struggle, the high school seems poised to resume business as usual; it is as if no one bothered to inquire about the fundamental democratic principles which were discussed in the course of the three-year court battle. Is it just possible that at least one history or civics teacher might undertake an analysis of the arguments in the Ninth Circuit decision? It would seem highly desirable to do so, in light of some student reaction to the Supreme Court decision: "Some of the students really wish we would have been able to have prayer at graduation, and I was one of them," said Jeff McCauley, who graduated from Centennial High this year. "I feel that prayer is a necessary part of the ceremony." McCauley, who describes himself as very religious, considers prayer an important part of his life and doesn't miss a Sunday at church. For him, the loss of a graduation prayer didn't cause a spiritual void, but it was a missed opportunity to give credit where credit was due. "I didn't feel as though I was missing an incredible part of my graduation, but I definitely would have appreciated having a prayer and thanking our God for having the opportunity for graduation."[4]

In these remarks by a sincere student we see the problem Beverly and her family encountered. Cutting through all the legal rhetoric espoused by the American Center for Law and Justice and the school administration about "student-initiated" prayer, Jeff McCauley understands what's going on. For him the prayer was a significant event of religious devotion, a religious ritual of thanksgiving for divine intervention to assure graduation. To return to the argument of the justices in the Ninth Circuit, how can an official activity of the school be given over to religious worship without violating the First Amendment? A sensible history or government teacher could go a long way toward helping McCauley come to terms with the relationship between his own religious sentiments and those of his peers in a democratic society.

Anonymity in the Face of Threats: A Doe Case in Idaho

Following the Supreme Court's action (or inaction) on the Harris case in June 1995, another suit began its way through a District Court of the Ninth Circuit.[5] The unusual character of this potential challenge to religious practices in Idaho schools is the fact that the principles presenting themselves as plaintiffs have chosen anonymity in light of what they perceive to be serious threats to their lives. Only the decision of the district judge to agree to total secrecy regarding their identity has allowed the case go forward. Thus, this chapter could not profit from interviews since no one was willing to be identified. While this book's criterion for recounting the stories of victims has been, in almost all cases, the ability to have personal conversations with the plaintiffs, that rule cannot be applied here.

The attorney for the plaintiffs, Steven Pevar, reviewed the particulars with me via a phone conversation from his office in Denver on December 11, 1995. "The plaintiffs in this lawsuit are three adults and three school children. Their lawsuit seeks to halt two types of school prayers performed by the defendants: prayers offered as an official part of the school commencement program, and prayers offered by coaches with their school athletic teams." The plaintiffs "are convinced that they will suffer retaliation, including the risk of physical violence, if their identities become known. Indeed, they are so scared, that they will dismiss this lawsuit rather than reveal their names."

While infrequent, this procedure is not unusual. It was employed in *Roe* v. *Wade*, the 1973 abortion decision of the Supreme Court. According to court records, Pevar continued, "The common thread running through these cases [those with anonymous complainants] is the presence of some social stigma or the threat of physical harm to the plaintiffs attaching to disclosure of their identities to the public record." Pevar makes the point that this protection is particularly important when some of the plaintiffs are children. Pevar goes on to point out "Not only is there a presence of social stigma, but the threat of physical harm is a real one." Our task in this inquiry is to examine the evidence offered by the plaintiffs. The reader should be aware that while these threats are not the target of the litigation, in a real sense they make all too obvious why the constitutional protections against religious establishment are so critically important. Persons guilty of some of the acts to be described hereafter could be sued in court for such actions irrespective of the constitutional issues raised in the federal suit. We have observed a similar situation in the case of Corine Spurlock, the school cook who beat Joann Bell outside the Little Axe, Oklahoma, school building.

It is reasonable, if not legally actionable, to draw an association between the horrendous acts performed in the name of prayer and the school practice of prayer itself. While it is not a constitutional question, it is a public policy matter when legal challenges to the problematic actions of a school result in insult, threat, and outright violence. That correlation, which we have demonstrated to exist in every example cited herein, should warn all citizens of the sorry state of knowledge concerning our democratic system among much of the citizenry. Further, why would anyone call for accommodation to such religious excess when its proponents are prepared to violate fundamental human rights in order to achieve their goals?

We are dealing with two legally separate issues that are morally bound together. It was that fact which inspired the nation's founders to completely restrict any religious establishment. Madison and his colleagues knew where establishment would lead. In the *Memorial and Remonstrance* Madison wrote,

> [E]xperience witnesseth that ecclesiastical establishments, instead of maintaining the purity and efficacy of Religion, have had a contrary operation. During almost fifteen centuries has the legal establishment of Christianity been on trial. What have been its fruits? More or less in all places, pride and indolence in the Clergy, ignorance and servility in the laity, in both, superstition, bigotry and persecution.[6]

What Madison did not explore was the use of persecution and bigotry as a means of creating an establishment in the name of local cultural and religious mores. We see that in the episodes detailed in this volume.

The public school involved in this anonymous litigation is located in Rexburg, Idaho. The local newspaper, the *Rexburg Standard Journal*, has a feature column entitled "Speak Out!" in which citizens may have letters printed anonymously on public interest subjects. That column has offered numerous unattributed comments on the subject of religion at the Rexburg school directly related to the complaints in the current suit. Examples of references to the plaintiffs included calling them "antichrists" and another writer asked "Why shouldn't we dominate?" It was urged that the plaintiffs leave town. Another writer, aware of the ACLU's part in the suit, claims that that organization is controlled by communists. Yet another writes that the plaintiffs should be "tarred and feathered." The theme of many of the letters is that "a battle is being waged between those who believe in God and infidels."

It is to be noted that the vast majority of citizens in Rexburg are Mormon by persuasion. One writer asserted, "We pay most of the taxes. Why shouldn't we dominate? It is the same in all other areas where the majority religion or culture is [located]." Another commented, "I say if they don't like it here, they have the free agency to move away. There are plenty of places where they can find the godless society they want. They have no right to deny us our right to freedom of religion and of speech." One letter, signed in this case, by Richard Bevan, puts the local situation in stark terms: "When a minority rules, that's dictatorship. Why is their interpretation of the Constitution any better than that of Christians or any other group?" For him and his fellow citizens the Constitution is shaped to fit local majorities and their actions. As another anonymous letter puts it, "We are expected to believe that the Constitution is designed to protect the rights of the minority. These claims are all nonsense."[7]

As Steven Pevar wrote in his plea to the court, "These writers, of course, are entitled to their opinions. However, given their strongly held beliefs, it is no wonder that [the] plaintiffs want to remain anonymous, adult and child alike." No claim is made that all the citizens reflect the feelings of the letter writers. But their number is large, vocal, and threatening.

The letters so affected one Mormon citizen that the following response was written:

We scare me. I have never considered myself a "slumbering saint." I've considered myself a good, temple-working LDS [member of the Church of Jesus Christ of Latter Day Saints], proud of my religion and fellow church members. Now I'm not so sure. . . . On the whole we've bristled about having to change our ways. We can't get it through our heads that minorities even here have basic rights. . . . How would we feel if we went into their schools and heard cruel remarks, or should I say thoughtless, that would make our children uncomfortable? We scare me.

Another Mormon, one of the few to show support for the plaintiffs, wrote, "I admire you for standing up for what you believe. It can't be easy."[8]

In making the case for anonymity Attorney Pevar directed the court's attention to another plaintiff in Rockland, Idaho. The two towns are similar, 150 miles apart, both with an overwhelmingly Mormon population. In Rockland two non-Mormon families objected to prayer in high school activities. Connie Brown, the lead plaintiff, has been a target since the day she filed her suit. Her family has been the object of hatred, contempt, and ridicule, along with threats of violence. Brown's daughter, Joey Lee Long, was persecuted at school and finally transferred to a high school in another town to escape constant harassment. The local newspaper, the *Deseret News,* reported,

> The non-Mormon families who took on the Rockland School District on behalf of their teenage children have been branded "traitors" by many. . . . Brown and her daughter, meanwhile, have become social outcasts. . . . Joey, one of seventeen juniors last year, was given the silent treatment at school. . . . Classmates she counted as friends turned their backs. . . . Seventeen-year-old Jon Howell, basketball and football standout for the Bulldogs, believes Joey betrayed her school.[9]

Returning to Rexburg, the plea for anonymity by the plaintiffs has a definite ring of truth. Recall the words of the young Rhode Island girl as she spoke with the Weismans about her admiration for them and the fear she felt were she to speak up in her school. Fear and intimidation go hand in hand with many who seek prayer in schools. In the name of God proponents of prayer infest their communities with hatred against ideas while insisting that their own ideas, because they are in the majority, must go unchallenged. Such behavior causes permanent damage in the community which pro-prayer people have infected with anger and bitterness.

Notes

1. The account offered here is based upon interviews with Beverly and Phyllis Harris in January 1996, extensive examination of news reports, and the court records.

2. The *Gearon* case (*Gearon* v. *Loudoun County School Board* 844 FSupp 1097 [1993] US Dist) was decided against Loudoun County schools, but the school officials did not appeal it. Therefore, the decision governs all such activities in the Eastern Federal Court District of Virginia.

3. Beverly Harris, "The Prayer at Graduation Was Not Freedom of Religion" (editorial), *Idaho Statesman*, 3 February 1995, p. 6A.

4. David Woolsey, "Ruling Lifts Graduation Ban," *Idaho Statesman*, 27 June 1995, p. 1A.

5. Information concerning this case comes from conversation with the plaintiff's attorney, Steven Pevar; an affidavit from the plaintiffs, David and Diane Roe; various court documents related to the anonymity request.

6. "On Behalf of Religious Liberty: James Madison's *Memorial and Remonstrance*," *This Constitution*, no. 12 (Fall 1986): 30.

7. "Speak Out!" *Rexford Standard Journal*, 25 October 1990.

8. "We Scare Me," published in "Speak Out!" *Rexford Standard Journal*, 21 June 1990.

9. *Deseret News*, 14–15 June 1990, p. 4B.

9

Rachel Bauchman: Variations on a Theme

"I was told not to make waves by my teachers, peers, members of the Jewish community, etc. Basically, it was a feeble attempt to silence me—a hope that I would go away."

"I was told to go back to Israel, called a dirty Jew, Jew bitch, and informed that it was too bad Hitler didn't finish the job."

"I feel that not only as a Jew but as a human being I have a moral obligation to protest against what I perceive to be an injustice."

There are two unique factors in the conflict between Rachel Bauchman and West High School in Salt Lake City.[1] First, the teacher involved in the case behaved in a particularly volatile fashion, making no effort to disguise his use of the classroom to advance his own religious views. Second, Rachel was concerned over a part of the public school year that has received little attention by the courts: celebratory religious music at Christmas. That December season, when observed in public schools through musical performances, is uniquely charged with potential problems.

Through film and popular music, Christmas has been secularized. The U.S. Supreme Court ruled in *Lynch* v. *Donnelly* (1984) that the religious aspect of a creche is diminished when included in a display that

152

involves Santa Claus, Rudolph, elves, decorated trees, and songs such as "White Christmas" and "Jingle Bells." The resulting secularized images make them acceptable on public property, said the Court. But even in that context it is difficult to secularize carols such as "Adeste Fidelis," "Joy to the Word," and "Silent Night." These songs proclaim their message in clear and simple language. Whether sung by Willie Nelson, José Carreras, or Julie Andrews, the Christian faith they proclaim is unmistakable. For many citizens, these traditional Christian hymns provide an unending confession of faith, transforming even the most secular mall display into a semiworship environment. Christians have made these carols so much a part of the season that most assume everyone accepts them. In fact, that is not the case at all.

The focus of the Rachel Bauchman case is a music teacher, Richard Torgerson, a dedicated Mormon. As the story of Rachel Bauchman unfolds, we find Torgerson to be as much a priest as he is a teacher. As of this writing, at the end of June 1996, the federal courts had not resolved the conflict, but the facts regarding Torgerson's actions are, for the most part, undisputed.

If one were to experience an official assembly in a public school organized by a literature teacher who chose to have selected students read exclusively from the Bible, with all citations drawn either from the gospels or Isaiah as interpreted by Christian theologians, one might get a sense of what is involved in the Bauchman case.

Is it not enough that during the Christian holy season of Christmas, every facet of public life is focused on symbols and sounds unique to that faith? Would it be asking too much to implore Christians to recognize that a respite is surely due fellow citizens of other faiths in the schools which they help finance and which their children are required to attend? And before you think it, yes, such citizens can choose to send their children to private schools, but is that thought not the current manifestation of the abominable bumper stickers of the 1970s: "America, Love it or leave it?" Why should the price of freedom be self-exclusion from perhaps the most important institution in our nation, the public school?

As I listened to Rachel tell her story to an audience assembled for a conference held in October 1995 on the *Queen Mary* in Long Beach, California, I recalled the first time I set foot on that magnificent ship. The year was 1955, the place was New York City. Civil rights and southern rebellion were in the air. Public schools were the focus of judicial decisions having to do with equality and freedom and minority rights. At that time black citizens were being told by politicians from Virginia to Mississippi to Arkansas that if they didn't like the time-honored tradition of segregation there would be no school for them. President Franklin Roosevelt could have been speaking of the fifty years succeeding his death when he observed, "The fight for social justice is a long, hard, uphill struggle." So also has it been for the rights of conscience.

In 1955 Ellery Schempp was attending a school in Pennsylvania where he was among the first people to challenge the prevailing customs concerning public school-sponsored religious activity. Rachel Bauchman is the most recent victim of the notion that might makes right. We recall that Ellery Schempp felt he had not experienced too much overt persecution while at the same time noting that his high school principal had sought to undermine his applications to colleges. Rachel, like Ellery, chose to protest. Bright and articulate, she is a worthy successor to those heroic figures who have given voice for half a century to the remarkable heritage that is the First Amendment.

Rachel told her story to a rapt audience in Long Beach:

In October 1994, we received our repertoire for the "Christmas" concerts. I noticed that the repertoire consisted of ten songs, *all* praising Jesus as the Lord, Savior, and King. We're also talking contemporary Christian songs here—not Handel's *Messiah* or Vivaldi's *Gloria* or anything by Brahms, Mozart, or Bach. I didn't feel that as a Jew I could honestly and in good conscience sing these particular pieces. They made me extremely uncomfortable. I wouldn't have felt as uncomfortable singing just one or two of those selections, but the fact of the matter was that all of these pieces were praising a man, Jesus, whom I don't believe is the Messiah. I respect Jesus as a historical figure, but not to the point where I want to worship him. This is a public school supposedly devoted to teaching people of all faiths, including Muslims, Hindus, Buddhists, atheists, agnostics, etc.

I explained my concerns to my parents regarding the repertoire. Also, the performances for November and December were scheduled to be held either in Catholic or Presbyterian churches or on Mormon church-owned property, including the Joseph Smith Memorial Building (Joseph Smith being the founder of the Mormon church) and a church on Temple Square itself! Approximately eight concerts [were scheduled] in all. I asked my father to write a letter to Mr. Torgerson explaining our concerns and asking to meet with him. We had hoped to make Mr. Torgerson aware that using his classroom to further his religious beliefs and attitudes was inappropriate in a public school environment. Let me explain something here. Mr. Torgerson is a devout Mormon and has made it clear on several occasions to the a cappella choir that his religion is the only "true" religion. One example was when he turned off the lights in class and instructed us to visualize Jesus on the cross dying for our sins!

Anyway, Mr. Torgerson's reaction to my father's letter was extremely shocking and very unprofessional, to say the least. Mr. Torgerson gave my father's letter to a parent who is the head of the Friends of the A Cappella Choir, which is a parent support group. That same parent then made 130 copies of my father's letter and sent it along with a nasty cover letter of his own to every single one of the 130 students in the a cappella choir and their parents. The offending parent insulted my father as well as our intentions in his letter, without ever having met my father, or myself, for that matter. This certainly is not the way to create a constructive dialogue between teacher and parent.

Well, as our concerns were so publicly derided and ridiculed, we requested help next from the assistant principal of academics and curriculum, and after running into a dead end there, with the principal. The principal did set up a meeting between Mr. Torgerson and my father, however, Mr. Torgerson never showed up nor did he acknowledge the meeting in any way. The principal of our school then just shrugged the whole matter off. We next contacted the minority rights compliance officer for the board of education, then the superintendent of schools, then the school board itself and finally, the state superintendent. They all just listened, nodded their heads a few times and did nothing. Letter after letter, phone call after phone call, and absolutely nothing. I really shouldn't say absolutely nothing because by this time, the threats, accusations, rumors, religious slurs, and all the other fun stuff was starting to become an everyday occurrence, growing in intensity. Not only was this happening in school and during classes, especially in choir class, but I was also harassed at my home through phone calls. I was told to go back to Israel, called a dirty Jew, Jew bitch, and informed that it was too bad Hitler didn't finish the job. My motives, personality, physical appearance, religious beliefs, citizenship status, my parents, you name it, were discussed, debated, and bandied about on radio talk shows, on television newscasts, and in newspaper articles. I was rarely, if ever, asked my views and reasons about what was happening. I was being ostracized and vilified, a tactic used in Utah quite frequently for those who have the temerity to question anything, especially anything having to do with religion!

Rachel then began a search for legal help. Her efforts met with no success until she reached Lisa Thurau, director of Public Education and Religious Liberty (PEARL). PEARL agreed to represent Rachel. But in the meantime,

Apparently word must have gotten back to Mr. Torgerson to even out the "Christmas" repertoire because we added two new songs. Imagine my disbelief when I learned that those two songs were associated with Judaism and Israel! The two songs were "Bashana haba'ah" which is an Israeli pop-folk song, and "Hanerot Halalu," which is about Hanukah. Apparently, they just didn't get it! My whole objection was that the repertoire was entirely religious in nature. Throwing in two Jewish songs hoping to shut me up was not only embarrassing but insulting as well. I'm uncomfortable having to act as an agent promoting any religion, including my own, in a public school environment. The point is, at the very least the repertoire could have been divided equally between those songs of a religious nature (all types) and those which are secular. Believe it or not, there are more secular a cappella pieces available in music catalogues than religious ones. I know, we checked with the publishers.

I was called into Mr. Torgerson's office one day in early December. Mr. Torgerson told me that he would give me an "A" for the class . . . if I would go sit in the library for the rest of the month, if I was so uncomfortable, and to return to class in January. I guess I really was an outcast! I had felt like one before, now it was a fact. I agreed to sit out the rest of the semester, as by that time I needed the break from being continually browbeaten in a class for an hour and a half every other day! That's not to say that the abuse stopped during the rest of the day. Just during my library time. Well, I somehow got through that awful time in my life and now I am more determined than ever not to give up! No public school student should have to go through what I experienced.

After the holiday Rachel returned to choir class. By that time she had discovered that a few loyal friends intended to support her.

I could never walk into choir class alone. Even accompanied by one of my friends, at least one person would go out of their way to insult me. There were so many occasions when I just wanted to transfer out of the class, but I knew that I wasn't the one who was wrong—they were. You know, when I first told my parents about what was happening in the very beginning of the year, I didn't think that anyone would mind because all I wanted was more diversity in the program. But the funny thing is, I've lived in Texas, Connecticut, and New York without any problems but it took a teacher and his students from Utah to show me what bigotry is all about.

Every year, the choir class takes a spring trip. At the beginning of this year, at the school's open house, Mr. Torgerson announced to the parents in attendance that the choir might not be able to take a trip this year because of complaints about the previous year's trip. Several parents spoke up with remarks like "it's too bad a few kids can spoil a good time" and "what do a few little complaints matter?" Apparently, these "little complaints" were about using the choir class as a Mormon missionary body. The class was promoted as a Mormon choir, performing in Mormon churches and during Mormon religious services, with students of the choir bearing "testimony" that the Mormon church was the only true church. Prayer was led by Mr. Torgerson before performances and several non-Mormon students were asked to read from the Book of Mormon.

Well, March rolled around and it looked like a spring trip was being planned in spite of those "spoilsports from last year." Mr. Torgerson, in an attempt to take a school-independent trip, formed an association, and asked students of the choir to hand out paperwork in class describing a trip being planned by the "association." It indicated that choir members would be performing in churches, singing religious music, and might voluntarily pray. Students were asked to join the Explorer Scouts, a coed branch of the Boy Scouts of America. I and two other non-Mormon students in the choir who were not given any information inquired about the trip. We were told by the choir class president that we could not have applications as we were "not on the list." When I asked Mr. Torgerson personally about the trip he said he knew nothing about it. We later found out his home address was on the application form! The trip failed because the Explorer Scouts learned from scoutmasters in the West

High community that the choir was joining simply to participate in a controversial trip and the Boy Scouts refused to sponsor it. But guess who was blamed for it! The class held immediately after the cancellation was excruciating for me. Mr. Torgerson ranted and raved at me for almost the entire class period, in front of the entire class of 130 students, blaming me for the class being unable to take their spring trip, blaming me for almost everything under the sun. I was in tears and absolutely terrified. One of my friends came and sat beside me and tried to comfort me. I was grateful for the support, but just wish[ed] she and others could have been more vocal about it. The students may not have agreed with my opinions, but I am after all a human being and common decency demanded that they do something! However, the school administration put it all down to "artistic temperament," even Mr. Torgerson's acts of tearing an intercom speaker off the wall, slamming down the lid of the grand piano several times, and hurling a music stand across the room in fits of rage, or should I say, "artistic temperament"?

These tirades continued, varying sometimes more, sometimes less in intensity but always with the same theme. Mr. Torgerson said his religious rights were being violated and denied. He said that I was being intolerant of *his* beliefs!

At about this time the news media got wind of the controversy. According to the *Salt Lake Tribune* of March 24, 1995,

Fred Greer of Midvale pleaded guilty in Third District Court to making harassing telephone calls to Rachel Bauchman, a West High School student who refused to sing Christmas carols because of her Jewish beliefs. Bauchman told police a man called her home and told her "Adolf Hitler should have finished off the Jews." The calls were traced to Greer's residence. He was fined $ 250.[2]

The stage was set for the confrontation that would propel this story to newspapers and television sets all over the nation. In Rachel's words,

In early May Mr. Torgerson presented his selections for the graduation ceremony. Two songs, both undeniably religious, were chosen. Those songs were "The Lord Bless You and Keep You," and "Friends." The first song was undoubtedly chosen for my benefit as, after all, "the words come directly from the Old Testament." The song "Friends" is one that has been on rotation on Christian radio stations since it was written in 1987. Both songs are contemporary. There is no artistic merit to either one, as has been claimed. "Friends" has been represented as being a "traditional" song performed for years by the choir at graduation. In fact, that song only became a "tradition" since Mr. Torgerson started teaching at West some five or so years ago.

I felt that Mr. Torgerson chose those two songs to show me I had no rights at all, which apparently, judging from events so far, I don't. I was also told that attendance at the graduation ceremony was mandatory and that I could not get out of it as I had during December. PEARL and our attorneys asked the school to discuss the matter prior to the graduation ceremony and were told that officials for the school would only be free to discuss the matter the day after graduation. Again, we had done something unheard of at this school or in Utah—we attempted dialogue!

The harassment and intimidation escalated and became very intense at this point. I was elbowed in the hall, had obscenities yelled at me, and vicious rumors and lies were spread about me. Choir class became an absolute nightmare.

The refusal of any responsible official to reply to Rachel's request was clearly tacit admission that they knew she was right. Rachel appealed to the federal district court for an injunction to prevent the singing of the two songs in question. Rachel's own words best describe what happened then:

The threatening phone calls started up again and again, I was discussed in the media. I ran for Junior Class President and had swastikas and other filth scrawled on my posters. Again, no teacher or school administrator did anything to stop this hateful activity.

On May 31st, [Rachel's attorney,] Andrew Hruska, of Sullivan and Cromwell, filed a temporary restraining order with the U.S. District Court to prevent those two religious songs from being sung at graduation, as part of a larger complaint alleging violations of the First Amendment and harassment and intimidation throughout the year. A federal court judge refused to enjoin the singing of the songs, holding that the harm to the graduating seniors who would not hear the songs outweighed the harm to my constitutional rights. Our attorneys proceeded with an emergency appeal to the Tenth U.S. Circuit Court of Appeals. On June 6th, one day before the graduation ceremony, the Tenth Circuit Court of Appeals enjoined the school from singing the two songs "Friends" and "May the Lord Bless You and Keep You" at the graduation ceremony.

I was elated that the Court of Appeals had granted the injunction yet at the same time I really started to panic. The case was all over the media: radio, TV, the newspapers. In addition, our phone was ringing off the hook from every conceivable sort of bigot. I also began to receive many calls of support which really meant a lot to me.

Anyway, I did, unfortunately, have to go to school the next day, the day of graduation, and I was really petrified. By 5 A.M. the morning of graduation, radio shows had started in on the topic of "Rachel Bauchman, Hero or Bitch?" Many students at West were calling in with nasty comments. Also, word was beginning to be circulated that the song "Friends" would be sung anyway in defiance of the Court's injunction! The TV picked that up and camera crews were out interviewing students all over about that possibility. In interviews, students said they would sing the songs to demonstrate their belief that *their* rights were being violated. After all, they claimed, they were the majority here and I was just one little kid trampling all over *them*.

The graduation stage was the site of the closing chapter in that year's long drama. Again, Rachel Bauchman's words best convey the mood of the graduation day:

My father took me to school that morning and I steeled myself to go in. Actually, it wasn't that bad, as no one was even speaking to me except my friends, though it was hard to endure the dirty looks and whispering. School let out early for graduation rehearsal. My mom picked me up and took me to the rehearsal at Abravanel Hall, which is Salt Lake's Symphony Hall, named, by the way, for Maurice Abravanel, a Jew who conducted the symphony for many years. My mother came with me for support. At rehearsal, I was pretty much ignored except for the few shouts of "troublemaker" directed at me. It was hard to have five hundred pairs of eyes staring at me in such hatred, though. There were a few sympathetic friends at the rehearsal, but only a few.

At graduation we sang the two replacement songs, the rest of the choir remained standing and urged the audience members to sing the prohibited song, the lyrics of which were passed out to everyone entering Abravanel Hall that evening, myself included! Up until the very start of "Friends," I really didn't think that people could be so ignorant, hateful, malicious, and spiteful! My mother and I were jeered at and spit at by the audience. We left in shock and disgust. Again, I was an object of ridicule and hate, this time in front of hundreds of people, mostly adults! Why? Because I objected to Christianity being imposed on me in a public school classroom, which after all, is a place for teaching academic and secular subjects. Basically, I'm protesting the teacher's daily proselytizing and being put through hell for doing so.

With the dramatic events of that graduation day Rachel's experience became a national media event. In the following months a lengthy story appeared in *USA Today* and she was featured on ABC's "20/20" and the "Jim Lehrer News Hour." As the fallout continued, it became obvious that the initiating cause of the trouble was Richard Torgerson. And to add to the evidence, Torgerson compounded the problem with the program he distributed for the 1995 Christmas concert.

Convinced that the school administration had failed to act responsibly toward the injunction, Rachel's attorney took that matter to court. In February 1996, the Tenth U.S. Circuit Court of Appeals ruled that West High School administrators did enough to block the school choir from singing a religious song at the 1995 graduation ceremony. The court, located in Denver, Colorado, concurred with U.S. District Judge J. Thomas Greene, who had found the previous November that West High principal Bill Boston had warned choir members they could be sanctioned if they sang "Friends." Greene, of Salt Lake City, also noted that choir director Richard Torgerson had rehearsed substitute songs with the students. In a telephone conversation with the author, Lisa Thurau of PEARL succinctly described her own and Rachel's view of the situation: "To us, the facts before the court were quite clear. The teachers and administrators were aware but chose to make no effort to stop the choir teacher's and students' explicit plans to violate the court order."

While this was a victory for the school, Rachel was determined to get at the primary cause of her particular series of problems, Mr. Torgerson. She filed a federal lawsuit claiming her civil rights were violated by religious undertones in her choir class. While pending in Greene's Salt Lake City court, Judge Greene appeared heavily biased against Rachel's suit, perhaps because he is a part of the Mormon hierarchy and sees this case as a personal challenge to him. Many observers considered his tactics of delay in the case an effort to deny Rachel relief at all costs.

On May 30, 1996, Judge Greene dismissed the suit. Rachel had listed twelve claims demonstrating state endorsement of religion. In his dismissal, the judge evaluated the religious endorsement using the "reasonable observer rule" that is highly controversial. It is also highly suspect considering the evidence we have examined about proselytizing by Torgerson. Rachel and her mother immediately appealed to the Tenth U.S. Circuit Court. An amicus brief on Rachel's behalf has been filed by the Presbyterian Church (USA), the United Church of Christ, the Seventh-Day Adventists, the American Jewish Committee, the Union of American Hebrew Congregations, and the Anti-Defamation League.

In December 1995, Judge Greene did tell Rachel's attorneys that Richard Torgerson's treatment of former students might be admissible in a pending trial, if they can connect it to their case. News sources note, however, that the judge is reluctant to do that. Several former students confirmed that they had had treatment from Torgerson similar to that described by Rachel. Andrew Hruska, Rachel's attorney, has amassed a huge collection of evidence relating to Torgerson's behavior in class with former students.

Meanwhile, another Christmas had rolled around and a program for the annual concert was published by Mr. Torgerson. In a self-serving explanation of the 1995 Christmas Choral Concert at West High, and in order to justify a program of twenty-seven selections, twenty of which were proclamations of the Christian faith, Torgerson explored what he perceived to be the relation between "music and Christmas." In his notes on the program he wrote the following remarks. "Josephus . . . wrote of Jesus Christ in twenty volumes comprising the Jewish Antiquities. . . . The Koran . . . contains portions of both the Old and New Testaments of the Bible. . . . Indeed, historians everywhere have evidenced and documented the events of Jesus' life." In these excerpts Torgerson makes at least four serious errors: (1) Jewish historian Flavius Josephus did not mention Jesus in twenty volumes of his Antiquities, he mentions him but once, when he recorded the stoning of

James, "the brother of Jesus, the so-called Christ";[3] (2) in using the terms Jesus and Christ both together and interchangeably Mr. Torgerson moves from history to faith in his rationale; (3) historians everywhere, whomever they may be, could hardly have documented the events of Jesus' life, since the only source for those events is the Christian Scripture; and (4) Torgerson refers to Hebrew Scripture as the Old Testament. To be sure, that's what Christians call it, but Jewish rabbis and scholars use no such term to apply to the Torah.

All of this is to suggest that dogmatic religious assumptions often color perceptions and actions. In his "rationale" Torgerson has made Rachel's case! Yet, to blame his outrageous behavior and make him the scapegoat is to ignore the unholy silence of the entire school system when it was confronted with what was already known about Torgerson. In a thorough story in the *Salt Lake Tribune*, June 11, 1995, reporter Katherine Kapos presented solid evidence of a long-standing problem with the choir teacher:

> Former students say such practices have gone on for years in Torgerson's classes. A few students say the graduation music was only a small part of the problem. They cite times when Torgerson would call on a student to pray before a concert, selecting an active Mormon. Or the out-of-state trips where the choir would sing almost exclusively at LDS [Latter Day Saints] churches and then stay at the homes of LDS families.[4]

By the fall of 1995 some former students were speaking out. Cameron Alston was a senior choir member in 1992 when the group took a trip to Seattle and the choir performed at the dedication of a new Mormon chapel. Choir members stayed with LDS families.

Alston recalled that Torgerson and several choir members got up at the dedication and bore their testimony, a spontaneous speech that Mormons give detailing what they believe. Alston nearly walked out of the ceremony, and still regrets not having done so. She called her parents from Seattle and told them what had happened, and when she returned home, her mother contacted the school's community council to complain but to no avail.

Alston could have dropped out of the choir at that point, but decided she would rather sing: "At that age it is really hard, even when you are conscientious and know there is a problem, to say something to your teacher that what they did wasn't right."[5]

The extent of these actions by Mr. Torgerson have now come fully to public attention. As a result, Rachel's lawyers made a motion to alter or amend the district court judgment of 1995, based on eight affidavits from former students of Mr. Torgerson, all now graduates of high school. By their testimony the story now extends back to 1977. The list of grievances is so extensive and explicit that the only question that comes to mind is "How did the administration at West High School ignore these events for nearly twenty years?" According to the testimony of the former students, the principal and other officials were fully aware of their complaints. While Torgerson should long ago have found employment where his religious convictions could be expressed as an integral part of his work, the failure of his superiors to stop his egregious behavior is far more disturbing than Torgerson's tirades. What follows are citations from the affidavits that reveal information to which the school officials had access at the time of the abuse and tirades.

Michelle Solvej was a senior and a member of a small choir at South High School where Torgerson taught at the time. "During choir class, Mr. Torgerson made it clear to us that he was a member of the Church of Jesus Christ of Latter Day Saints. I recall feeling it was extremely inappropriate for Mr. Torgerson to bring his religion into the classroom."

In the same year Nanette Barrutia was a junior at South High and a member of the a cappella choir which Torgerson directed. The choir was invited to perform in Hawaii. Students had to raise money and pay their own way. The choir took a bus to San Francisco in order to catch the flight to Hawaii.

> On the morning we were to board a bus for the San Francisco airport, Mr. Torgerson called a meeting of the entire choir. During that meeting, Mr. Torgerson stated to the entire choir that because some students were not behaving, they would not be permitted to proceed to Hawaii. Mr. Torgerson said that he had a list of the people who would not be permitted to proceed on to Hawaii. . . . Members of the choir were crying because they were so upset about Mr. Torgerson's drastic announcement.[6]

The choir director identified Nanette as one who could not go to Hawaii. "I asked Mr. Torgerson what I did to deserve such punishment, and he stated to me that I was not allowed to continue on the trip because I had 'used the Lord's name in vain.' " There were four other students who had also "misbehaved" and could not go on. "Those of us who were being excluded from the trip located our school principal, LaVar Sorenson, at the airport and he told us that we would be going on the trip." While in Hawaii, Torgerson had the choir spend an entire day at the LDS Polynesian Center.

> During the time I was in the choir, . . . [we] performed quite regularly at LDS Church worship services, especially around Christmas time. We performed Christian devotional songs, including LDS hymns, at LDS sacrament meetings, during which we were required to sit through the offerings of prayers and sacraments. I recall being very uncomfortable in the worship services, while the LDS sacrament was passed over me.[7]

Confirming the behavior of Mr. Torgerson offered above, Valerie Davis recalled her teaching career at South High School in 1980, where she taught special education. Sometime that year she remembers seeing a form that was filled out by students interested in joining the a cappella choir.

> At the time Richard Torgerson was director of the South High School a cappella choir. [South High later closed and Torgerson moved to West High School.] The application form . . . inquired as to the applicant's religious affiliation. I inquired of Richard Torgerson as to the reason for asking about students' religious affiliations on the a cappella choir application form. Mr. Torgerson responded that things were much easier if the students in the choir were members of the LDS Church because the choir participated in LDS sacrament meetings. According to Mr. Torgerson that participation included singing and speaking presentations.[8]

Amy Morris graduated from West High in 1994. As a freshman, junior, and senior, she was in choir classes taught by Torgerson. In her freshman year Torgerson assembled the students performing in the musical *Oliver* and offered a prayer, ending with the words, "We say this in the name of Jesus Christ. Amen." Amy said nothing because she didn't want to appear "rude or divisive." Then during her junior year, "the choir performed approximately once each month on Sundays at worship services of the Church of Jesus Christ of Latter Day Saints. Those performances were scheduled and led by Mr. Torgerson." Also as a junior she joined a trip led by Torgerson to Sacramento. During that trip the choir also sang at LDS church services,

> during which prayers were given and the sacrament was passed over me. All of the songs we sang were Christian devotional songs that expressed worship and praise for Jesus and God. No one who was present could have concluded that we were singing the songs for any secular educational purpose; rather, it was obvious that we were singing to convey a religious message at a religious service.

Amy said that while performing at one LDS church "two members of the choir . . . stood up and 'bore their testimonies,' declaring that the LDS Church is the only true church."[9]

Amy recalls that "After the Sacramento trip I informed Mr. Torgerson that I was uncomfortable with the choir performing at religious worship services. However, he did not seem to care, inasmuch as he continued lining up such performances." As a senior Amy stated that "While we were practicing the song 'Lamb of God,' Mr. Torgerson told us to imagine Jesus 'dying for our sins.' "

During her senior year the choir went to Salem, Oregon, to perform at an LDS ward house (the home of an LDS leader) at what was known as a "fireside." At the fireside, "the West High School student body president gave a prayer, as did the bishop of the ward. Also, Mr. Torgerson introduced a member of the choir as 'our seminary president,' whereupon [a student named] Rebecca proceeded to stand up and declare to all present that the Mormon church is the only true church." That whole experience

> was very isolating, alienating, and divisive. By the end of the "fireside" I was crying because of the intense feeling of isolation and frustration at the insensitivity and obliviousness by Mr. Torgerson. . . . Following the "fireside" Mr. Torgerson came up to me and said how pleased he was that I was so moved by the ceremony. His seeming

unawareness of why I had been crying only served to increase my anger and frustration.[10]

After all these experiences, Torgerson had seemingly alienated some twenty or thirty choir members. They signed a petition "informing Mr. Torgerson that we objected to being represented as an LDS choir and performing at religious worship services." The petition closed with these two sentences: "We make music and that is our purpose; not to worship, pray, or represent certain organizations. We believe that when we are forced to host or participate in any religious services, the unity of the choir is lost." Amy and another choir member named Erica took the petition to Mr. Torgerson in his office and, after he read the petition, he yelled at them for thirty to forty-five minutes. Because Erica started crying almost from the beginning, the conversation was mostly between Mr. Torgerson and Amy. Torgerson told the students they had no right to be upset and that they were trying to restrict his religious freedom. Amy recalls that

> Mr. Torgerson launched into an attack on the Supreme Court's decision regarding school graduation prayer and said that if students don't want graduation prayers, they should just plug their ears. I told Mr. Torgerson that we understood that he didn't know we were upset, but that we were only asking him to be sensitive to the fact that people were hurt. Mr. Torgerson responded by accusing me of hating Mormons; I told him that was ridiculous and informed him that half of my family is of the LDS faith. After my meeting with Mr. Torgerson I spoke with our school principal, William Boston, about the petition and what Mr. Torgerson had said to me. Mr. Boston simply said that he would speak with Mr. Torgerson about the matter.[11]

Amy's statement was recorded in New York State (where she was attending school) on September 22, 1995. Erica Brown, the student who accompanied Amy to Torgerson's office, in an affidavit given in Oregon the previous day, confirmed in full the memory of that meeting about the petition and other events involving the choir offered by Amy. An affidavit from another student, Andrea Paluso, fully corroborates Amy's account.[12]

Erica Brown was a classmate and friend of Amy's. She rounded out the petition story by recalling that when she returned home, she phoned a local attorney and discussed the situation with him. The lawyer, Brian Baird, sent a letter to the principal, Mr. Boston, with copies to the superintendent and Mr. Torgerson. That letter closed with the following paragraph: "I request that you investigate this situation, and if in fact, Mr. Torgerson has engaged in such conduct for two (2) years, that you take appropriate action against him. Failure to do so, may result in litigation."[13]

Amy Morris said recently she was glad someone has stepped forward to protect their religious liberty. She commented that while people think this problem just arose and that Rachel is some sort of strange person, that is not the case.

Rachel Bauchman, it now becomes clear, was one of the later victims of Torgerson's persistent behavior. West High School would have the public to believe that Rachel was some kind of malcontent, relating actions by Torgerson unknown to the administration, but they knew about Torgerson before Rachel even moved to Salt Lake City. What Mr. Boston would describe as "artistic temperament" was, in Torgerson's case "religious distemper." Beyond the school, the entire Mormon hierarchy had to know what Torgerson was doing to those public school students. It sounds as if he had visited nearly every Mormon church in the vicinity and beyond.

Torgerson's behavior was so flagrant and so well documented by students over the years that he could not have persisted without official approval. Are we really to believe that he was innocent of contempt of court at the 1995 graduation? It is beyond belief that Principal Boston, now retired, could say, in June 1995, that he found all the allegations to be unsubstantiated.[14]

Comparing the Bauchman story with that of the Herdahls is informative. It demonstrates that in both cases the overwhelming majority in the community was of one religious persuasion, and that in each case the dominance resulted in presumptive capture of the public schools by the majority in the name of faith—Baptist or Mormon. There is not a bit of difference in the fundamental rejection of freedom, justice, and equality by Ecru and Salt Lake City. If you inquire, "Who do these people think they are?" the answer is all too simple. They think they are God's anointed to bring religious dogma through the church and into the state.

Since the unhappy events at the graduation ceremony, West High School has partially responded to what Rachel sought, a dialogue among the students. On September 21, 1995, the *Salt Lake Tribune* reported,

> There stood a West High School choir next to a large sign proclaiming the rights guaranteed by the First Amendment. The snapshot might have been laughable a few months ago under the pressures of a federal lawsuit and a raucous graduation.
>
> But when the West High Chorale opened Wednesday's session of the First Amendment class, it was a happy marriage. It also was an indication that at least one group of students is trying to understand that despite their many differences, they are the same. "A common humanity," is what University of Utah law Professor Edwin B. Firmage calls it. . . . He willingly offered his expertise when it was clear the spirit at West High needed to be reconciled.
>
> "My idea in volunteering to do this was not under any illusion that I could resolve the current conflict . . . but to make a learning event and a healing situation out of a potentially divisive thing," said Firmage.
>
> While the First Amendment class will not fully answer the tough question about religion in the school, it gives students a thorough lesson on their guaranteed freedoms. Since school began three weeks ago, the 30 students enrolled in the course have discussed free speech, clear and present danger, obscenity, and hate speech. Future lessons include nonverbal expression, schools as public forums for free expression, the press and prior restraint and finally, the clauses relating to the establishment of religion.
>
> "After graduation, I wanted to find out what was right and wrong," says student Eryn Caamano, "But sometimes it is undeterminable. We need to accept both points of view." . . . For the students who have enrolled, as well as the handful of parents and community members who attend, discussions are informative and lively.[15]

All of this is well and good as an aftershock response, but it cannot hide the hideous behavior of an entire community when faced with a clear moral and legal choice. Is religion so demanding of the faithful that it condones outright cruelty by large portions of an entire city toward a sixteen-year-old high school student? In the name of reason, what kind of teachers persecute their students? Even worse, what kind of teachers remain silent in the face of such outrages? Salt Lake City, sadly, is not the exception but rather the most recent illustration of an all too common pattern, as we have observed in the previous chapters.

Rachel Bauchman's experiences on this subject are not yet over. She continues to experience harassment, although not as severe as last year. Her case, on appeal, now has a focus upon the horrendous behavior of Richard Torgerson, but the entire school system is implicated in the suit. It puts one in mind of the song so popular in the 1960s, "Blowin' in the Wind," which poses the question, "How many times can a man turn his head and pretend that he just doesn't see?" Rachel encountered this same theme in reading the moving words of Pastor Martin Niemoller, a leader of the German Lutheran Confessing Church in the 1930s and 1940s. Niemoller opposed Hitler, but in his mind, not soon enough. She tells us that his words have shaped her life ever since she first read them:

> In Germany they came first for the Communists, and I didn't speak up because I wasn't a Communist. They came for the Jews, and I didn't speak up because I wasn't a Jew. Then they came for the trade unionists and I didn't speak up because I wasn't a trade unionist. Then they came for the Catholics and I didn't speak up because I was a Protestant. Then they came for me and by that time no one was left to speak up.

In the fall of 1995, as Rachel reflected on her experiences, she concluded,

> My brothers and I have been raised to think and to question those in authority with whom we disagree, and not to remain silent for fear of retribution. To stand up to wrongdoing, whether or not it directly affects one is not only right; it is a responsibility which we all must take. I feel that not only as a Jew but as a human being I have a moral obligation to protest against what I perceive to be an injustice. As I said before, I think the world would be a much better place if we all could truly show a basic degree of respect and tolerance when we interact with one another.
>
> All I've ever wanted is for the diverse population of Utah to be truly acknowledged and appreciated. I would only hope that the people who are claiming that they want diversity and tolerance would

understand that we don't live in a democracy where majority rules about the inalienable protections set forth in the Bill of Rights.[16]

Of course Rachel is correct. As noted earlier, Thomas Jefferson warned his successors that if any legislature were to abandon the religious freedom protected by his bill[17] it would infringe upon natural rights. Democracy can never completely escape its own fundamental weakness lurking in the potential irresponsible behavior of a majority that could restrict civil and human rights. It is, as we have seen, generally true that in the more complex governing bodies individual rights are better protected. Madison noted this in his October 17, 1788, letter to Jefferson: "I am sure that the rights of Conscience in particular, if submitted to public definition, would be narrowed much more than they are likely ever to be by an assumed power."[18] Convinced of this potential for local mischief, Madison proposed to the first Congress in 1789 an unsuccessful amendment that would have read, "No State shall infringe the equal rights of conscience, nor the freedom of speech, or of the press, nor of the right to trial by jury in criminal cases." He considered it "to be the most valuable amendment on the whole list."[19]

The senate demurred, in large measure because in 1789 several states still had established religions. Eventually, of course, through the Fourteenth Amendment, the Bill of Rights was applied to state actions. That in turn led to the Supreme Court's now fifty-five-year series of precedents respecting the religion clauses. And the record we have amassed from Utah, Mississippi, Rhode Island, Oklahoma, Virginia, New York, Pennsylvania, Maryland, and Texas is testimony to the wisdom of Madison. State administrators have demonstrated a serious reluctance to challenge local mores and habits, particularly respecting public schools.

Rachel Bauchman reminded both her friends and detractors that she planned to stay the course on the issues she raised. "I was told not to make waves by my teachers, peers, members of the Jewish community, etc. Basically, it was a feeble attempt to silence me—a hope that I would go away. The problem is that I will not go away. I am in for the long haul. Whether I'm forty-five or one hundred and five, I'll still be here." That tenacity, combined with a calm spirit and quiet reasonableness, is typical of the persons we have met in this study.

One other item catches the eye as we leave Salt Lake City. In June 1996, another high school in the city, East High School, was embroiled in a confrontation with a group of gay students who wished to form a club. On February 23, the Utah Senate passed a bill aimed at preventing public-school employees from promoting homosexual acts and other illegal conduct. This ban was clearly heavily influenced by the religious sentiments of Mormons, who condemn homosexuality. Fearing a federal lawsuit based on the Federal Equal Access Act, the school board voted to ban all extracurricular clubs in the high schools. The Equal Access Act was initially passed to protect the rights of religious groups to use the same type of school facilities as those assigned to other groups. It received strong support from a wide range of religious groups.

A news report in the *Salt Lake Tribune* informed its readers that

West High students rallied outside their school and later marched on the state Capitol, while their counterparts at East amassed on each side of busy 1300 East [Street]. One side appeared to support the point of view of gays and lesbians and their backers, and the other seemed angry about the cancellation of clubs with interests ranging from chess to Frisbees.[20]

There was a certain irony in all this. The majority in the community is Mormon, and here was that majority seeking to impose its moral code on the schools. But this time it had an unexpected effect: it trod upon the majority of students eager to have their clubs. Then came Senator Orrin Hatch to his home state. Hatch had been a strong advocate of the Equal Access Act at the time of its passage. Obviously, he saw it as a protection of the rights of minorities, including his own Mormon faith, against discrimination. But Mormons are the majority in Utah. So how did the senator suggest dealing with the act? He said, "the Equal Access Act is written in such a way as to allow school boards to make decisions concerning what is in the best interests of the student." However, he said the school board need not have banned all clubs. "I don't see a problem with just banning the sexually oriented clubs—both homosexual and heterosexual." Then, as if he felt he had not made his point, he digressed to a totally different subject. He argued that students do not have the same rights as adults do, citing as examples drug testing of student athletes, locker searches without warrants, and the ability to censor school publications.[21] Senator Hatch is surely aware that the Equal Access Act requires all groups acting within the law be given equal treatment. However, how issues like drug tests and locker searches relate to equal access is clear only to him.

Rachel has not been idle in this most recent series of events. She participated in the protest with her classmates. She has been asked to speak to two local groups about the relationship between her case and this new crisis. And in June 1996 she was selected as a Young Woman of Courage by the National Organization of Women.

It would be interesting to know whether any of the students protesting the ban saw a connection with Rachel Bauchman's lone stand for her rights.

Notes

1. Resources for this chapter include a taped interview with Rachel Bauchman which took place in October, 1995; several conversations with Lisa Thurau of PEARL, the organization which is representing Rachel, in the winter and spring of 1995–1996; an address to a church/state workshop in Long Beach, California, in October, 1995; a ceremony in which the author made an award to Rachel in the name of the James Madison Memorial Foundation; and numerous news accounts and television programs.

2. "Bad Calls," *Salt Lake Tribune*, 24 March 1995, p. B2.

3. See Howard Kee, ed., *Understanding the New Testament* (Englewood Cliffs, N.J.: Prentice Hall, 1965), p. 54. See also Josephus, *Antiquities*, XX, 9.1.

4. Katherine Kapos, "Expert Calls Students' Singing Act of Civil Disobedience," *Salt Lake Tribune*, 11 June 1995, p. A1.

5. Cited in Kapos, "Expert Calls."

6. Nanette Barrutia, sworn affidavit signed September 22, 1995, United States District Court for Utah. *Bauchman* v. *West High School*.

7. Ibid.

8. Valerie Davis, sworn affidavit signed September 20, 1995, United States District Court for Utah. *Bauchman* v. *West High School*.

9. Amy Morris, sworn affidavit signed September 22, 1995, United States District Court for Utah. *Bauchman* v. *West High School*.

10. Ibid.

11. Ibid.

Using

12. Andrea Paluso, sworn affidavit signed September 20, 1995, United States District Court for Utah. *Bauchman* v. *West High School*.

13. Letter from Brian Barnard to William Boston, dated April 4, 1994. Filed as an exhibit attached to Erica Brown's affidavit.

14. Kapos, "Expert Calls."

15. Katherine Kapos, "Law Professor Enlightens West Students on Rights," *Salt Lake Tribune*, 21 September 1995, p. D2.

16. Interview with Rachel Bauchman, November 4, 1995, Long Beach, California.

17. See Thomas Jefferson, *Virginia Statute on Religious Freedom*.

18. *JMPapers,* vol. 11, p. 297.

19. *JMPapers,* vol. 12, p. 344.

20. Samuel Autman, Jennifer Skordas, and Robert Bryson, "SL Students Rally," *Salt Lake Tribune*, 24 February 1996, p. A1.

21. Ibid.

10

The Herdahls:
Challenge to a Closed Society

"I want to know where in the Constitution does it guarantee anybody the right not to be offended."

"Go find a school you like. But don't dictate to everybody else in
your community based on your particular prejudices."

"How can Christians have such evil ways?"

Ecru is a small town in northeastern Mississippi. A ninety-minute
drive from Memphis, Tennessee, the town is only thirty minutes from
Oxford and Tupelo. Pontotoc County, in which Ecru is located, has
two public schools, each containing grades K-12. Ecru children are
enrolled in the North Pontotoc facility. While the immediate environs
of the county are rural, the University of Mississippi is only a few minutes away. In that county a drama with national implications far
beyond the local controversy is being played out. In 1995 the conflict
drew the attention of numerous major newspapers and their reporters
as well as a segment on the program "60 Minutes."[1]

So what is going on there? In an effort to understand the dynam-
ics of a story now over two years old, I went to Ecru in December
1995, to interview Lisa Herdahl, the center of the storm, and to discuss the conflict between her family and the community, centered on

the public school. Lisa and Darel Herdahl, with their six children—
Elizabeth, age four; Christine, age six; Jason, age nine; Richard, age
ten; David, age twelve; and Kevin, age sixteen—lived in a modest
home on State Route 15, about a mile from the North Pontotoc
school. Arriving in late afternoon, I was greeted by Kevin and Elizabeth. Two other children, Jason and Christine, joined the gathering,
all curious as to why I was in their driveway. A menagerie of cats, dogs,
and an overweight pet pig moved contentedly among the children. It
was a delight to listen and observe the genuineness of these young tots
and teens. It was difficult to imagine how this happy family had
enraged the citizens and the authorities in the county.

Lisa Herdahl is both articulate and gracious. As we began our conversation in her living room, she had just returned home from a long
shift as manager of a local convenience store. There were signs of
exhaustion, yet she patiently explored ground she had surely discussed
with inquisitive visitors from out of state almost daily for over a year.
We were frequently joined by the two youngest children, Christine
and Elizabeth. While we discussed a book I had brought with me,
Elizabeth brought a volume from a set of classics, Milton's *Paradise
Lost*, and quietly showed me the title. The girls proudly turned on the
lights on their twelve-foot Christmas tree and called for me to look. As
Lisa and I talked, I met, by name, most of the gentle animals that
moved freely through the home. The phone rang. It was the local
ACLU attorney, Danny Lampley. Lisa called Kevin to speak with their
lawyer. All of the children were delightful, inquisitive, and clearly
loved. The home was awash with family values. So what had raised the
ire of local residents?

Lisa recounted the events of October 1993, which resulted in a
confrontation between school officials and her family, beginning with
the decision to move to Ecru. The Herdahls had lived in Wisconsin for
several years when they decided to move south, away from the cold and
nearer to Darel's parents. Before the move Lisa traveled to Ecru and
visited with her mother- and father-in-law. "They mentioned that the
school had prayer and Bible. We never went into anything about it. I
thought maybe occasionally they had it." The Herdahls moved to Ecru
in October 1993. Because she had been forewarned of possible religious practices in the school, "when I went to enroll the four children
in the school I asked if they had prayer and Bible in the school and

they started bragging on that point. They said, 'Yes we do every morning. We have Bible for them every day.' "

Suddenly Lisa Herdahl was faced with a major decision. She spoke with her family that evening and "instructed the children not to attend" the Bible class. As for the prayer, the children "couldn't do much about that because it was over the loudspeaker throughout the whole school." And the school made no effort to make changes. "They really didn't do anything about it. When it came time for them to go to Bible class they either were sent out in the hall or stuck in another classroom that was just available. Basically they were kind of shuffled around."

Clearly the school administration had not faced the problem previously and there "wasn't any certain class that was set aside for students who weren't going to Bible. They tried to adjust because they knew they were not doing what they should do."

By keeping their children out of Bible class, the Herdahls "set the children apart." The effort to accommodate this new situation "created a problem for my children with other students. Because they didn't attend the class they were called devil worshippers, atheists, you name it they were called that. The children in the school just assumed that because my children didn't go to Bible class they weren't Christian." The situation deteriorated quickly, and by the second day "they were already being looked [upon] as strange and were called names."

Remember, these four children had just arrived in a strange town and entered a school where they knew no one. Word of this situation moved quickly through the community, and making friends became difficult.

> I don't recall them ever coming home and saying any student actually said that they agreed with them, but they did have a few friends that would hang around with them. It has gotten a little bit better, but they did go through a time for quite a while there when almost nobody would have anything to do with them. And the other kids were threatened. If their parents saw them with my kids [the other children] would be beaten up [by their parents].
>
> Actually a kid in David's class wrote him a note and told him that if he was caught talking to David or playing with him his parents would beat him up. We have that piece of evidence.

Kevin was in high school, the other three in elementary school. Christine, who was in kindergarten, never complained. "She would let me know that 'we prayed before we ate in school or we sang Sunday School songs.' But other than that the kids didn't seem to pick on her. They were too young to do that unless pressed by teachers or parents."

The first months were hard, and many cruel comments were made to the three older children. Misidentified as non-Christians and attacked by local clergy, the Herdahls sought a place of Christian worship. Darel is Lutheran, and the children had been baptized in that faith, but Lisa was born and raised a Christian Scientist. Neither of those options were open, however, and Lisa looked for a church. She chose the Pentecostal Church,

> because it was the only church that at the time accepted us for a family, who we were, and didn't bring the school issue into it and how we were different from everybody else. The kids really enjoyed going there. I figured at least they would have that Sunday school background. Sunday school is not all the same from church to church, but they are getting the basics.

While they were attending that church, "one Baptist minister came up in the yard early in the year and asked me if I'd go to his church and I said 'No, the kids are going to the Pentecostal Church.' He told me I was going to burn in hell." Sadly, by February 1996, Lisa told an *Atlanta Constitution* reporter,

> The kids did go to a Pentecostal church for a while. It was the only church in the area that seemed to accept us for who we were, and I really feel that the kids needed some kind of religious background. But one person in that church was telling the Sunday school kids that I was going to go to Hell. I pulled them out of there, figuring if they were talking behind their back when the kids weren't there, I didn't know what they were doing when they were there.[2]

Meanwhile, Lisa tried to explain her concerns to the school officials.

> I went through trying to talk to the principal and the vice-principal. It was back and forth and back and forth. I talked to Mr. Horton, the superintendent, and I finally went to the school board. I'd come

home so upset because it was like hitting my head against a brick wall. I kept telling them from the beginning that if they didn't do something I would go further. I didn't know what I was going to do because I couldn't get anybody around here to back me up. Their constant response was, "we've always done this here and we're going to continue." At that point I decided something had to be done. I didn't know it was going into a lawsuit. But that is the only thing they understood. A friend of mine told me about the ACLU and I got in touch with them. I wrote them a letter and it seemed like forever before I heard from them. And then I got a response from them. Then it seemed like forever again before I talked to the first attorney. Things after that went pretty quickly. People for the American Way came in later and talked to the ACLU. They wanted to help. I didn't really talk to the ACLU until a month before we filed the suit, just before Christmas break a year ago [1994].

The public school which the children attended had two practices that troubled Lisa Herdahl. First, she learned that prayer was broadcast over the school intercom into each classroom. Second, there was a class, which was expected (by the school) to be taken by elementary school children, that was unmistakably an introduction to Christianity from the perspective of the dominant Baptist culture. The former practice had been common in large numbers of Southern schools prior to 1962. And even after the *Engel* decision of that year and the *Schempp* decision a year later, which together declared unconstitutional any school-sanctioned prayer or Bible reading, the Court was frequently ignored in communities where one Christian tradition was overwhelmingly in the majority. But it is important to note here that there is no single "Baptist position" on school prayer.

Indeed, the very core of the developing tradition of church/state separation received overwhelming support from eighteenth-century Baptists in Virginia. James Madison depended upon the strong Baptist voice in 1785 to defeat efforts to fund Christian education with public monies. You will recall from chapter 1 that in 1801 President Thomas Jefferson received a letter from a group of Baptists in Connecticut which prompted the now familiar phrase "a wall of separation between church and state" from the pen of the sage of Monticello.

A month after the Herdahl's lawsuit was filed Stephanie Saul of *Newsday* reported "red-white-and-blue signs" everywhere in the rural community. "This normally quiet, almost exclusively conservative Christian area," she wrote, "is embroiled in a controversy over the right to maintain a decades-old tradition here: prayers and Bible classes in public schools."[3] The school in Ecru had inaugurated a class in "Middle Eastern History" which, according to the ACLU, was "a way to get around the Constitution and have Bible study in schools." Referring to the classes, one clergyman who requested anonymity, stated, "I knew they were precarious. But there was a 99 percent chance that no one would object, unless someone came in from outside."[4] Local churches pay for the instructors and appoint a committee to review the curriculum. The classes are taught as electives in the high school. The reporter noted that the Mississippi Department of Education was pressuring the school to make the classes "more of a world religion course." Olen White, a furniture factory worker and chair of the church oversight committee observed that the instructors were trying to do that. As an example, he explained that, when the instructor mentions Judaism, the students are taught that 'the Jews are still looking for Christ to come the first time.' "[5] Mr. White seems oblivious to the inherent bias against Jewish interpretations of the Hebrew scriptures. At best such a statement is paternalistic.

Outraged by the Herdahl lawsuit, Doug Jones, a local Baptist minister, organized a rally that drew perhaps 1,500 people. Speaking to the crowd, newly elected U.S. Congressman Roger Wicker (R-Miss.), said, "Now I want to say this to the plaintiffs in this lawsuit: You could not have inflicted a deeper wound upon the souls, upon the very core of this community, than to do what you have done." He concluded, "I want to know where in the Constitution does it guarantee anybody the right not to be offended."[6]

Lisa Herdahl sees herself as an outcast in the community, the victim of "women whispering about her in grocery stores and rumors of a boycott against the convenience store she manages." Perhaps the most pathetic observation in the *Newsday* article was the following: "'One hundred percent of the community is not one hundred percent in favor of school prayer,' said one local clergyman who objects to the practices, but who asks not to be named."[7]

Reports in February 1995 confirmed that not a single person in Ecru had publicly supported the Herdahls. The *Dallas Morning News* reported, "motorists drive by her house and yell insults. Her children come home each day with the latest rumors from school—that Mrs. Herdahl and her husband, Darel, are getting a divorce, that she's doing this for money."[8]

The American Civil Liberties Union entered the case in late 1994 and made the court challenge to the school routines a few weeks thereafter. When we sat in Lisa Herdahl's living room and talked in December 1995, it had been a year since the lawsuit was filed. The court date of March 4, 1996, was still three months off. I wondered how Lisa felt about the impact on the children.

> It has helped the older children quite a bit. It taught them that saying no and being different is all right. There's nothing wrong with being different, nothing wrong with saying no. The younger ones are doing well with it. They have a little harder time [though] because I think the kids are more cruel at that age. In the long run I think they are going to look back and remember. I wouldn't do it different. I think it has been a valuable lesson for all of them. I was wise to do it. I thought about that a lot. What are the kids going to go through? But I wouldn't change any of it. As hard as it's been I still wouldn't change any of it.

As the 1995 Christmas season approached, the mood of the community was calmer, but Lisa expected the turmoil to erupt once more in March, with the opening of the court case. Even so, the Herdahls knew they did not stand alone:

> I've had supportive letters from out-of-state religious leaders. Nobody locally would come forward. At work people will come in, see that nobody is around, and come up and basically whisper to me. "We know who you are. We back you, but we can't say anything." One business owner said he was actually told that if he did not put "Religious Freedom" signs in front of his store, (with the orange and blue ribbons representing North Pontotoc School) his business would be burned or boycotted. There is a fear running through the town. I think there are [a] lot more people that agree with us than the community wants to realize, but they are scared to death. I can fully understand why.
>
> It's sad and scary that no one will speak up. No one has enough nerve or enough guts to stand up. Sooner or later they are going to

182
Without a Prayer

want that same Constitution to stand up for them. If they can't stand up for it now, what are they going to do later? There is a misconception that we are isolated. Ecru is a town of maybe three hundred or four hundred people. There are maybe 22,000 people in the county and the whole county is in on this.

Lisa's emotions had been intense in the two-year struggle.

My first reaction . . . was anger that nobody would listen. The anger then turned into being terrified for our life. At one point I seriously thought of not filing the lawsuit because there were threats to our [lives]. And I think now it's gone to basically a sad feeling for the people. It's gone from angry to scared to death to sad and it's starting to get to that scared point again because, as it gets near the court date, I have a feeling we are going to go through a lot of the same threats and stuff we did before. It's going to be difficult if we win . . . they will appeal. They are going to take it as far as they have to.

She was on the mark in most of her expectations. By mid-January 1996, Lisa had given up her job because of threats against her children: she had to be home to protect them. After she left, a sign reading "Under new management" was placed at the convenience store where she had been manager. Threats against the children were frequent as some members of the community orchestrated an effort to drive the Herdahls out of Ecru. Meanwhile, the county had raised over $150,000 for legal costs.

As I prepared to leave the Herdahl home, a warm, friendly place with delightful children, I was both alarmed and heartened by the visit. I was alarmed at the cruelty, not of the local children, but of the adults in the community, particularly the school officials and the clergy. But I was heartened by the conviction and stamina of this remarkable woman and her devoted family.* On stepping outside I stopped to speak to Kevin, the oldest son. People for the American Way attorney Elliot Mincberg informs me that Kevin was one of the best witnesses he has had the pleasure to hear. My conversation with him confirmed that fact.

---

*I did not have the opportunity to meet Darel Herdahl. He is an auto mechanic who has made no public statements. He is supportive of Lisa's efforts but, as she says, he listens and learns about community attitudes as he goes about his daily work.

Kevin said the students in his school

have adjusted, but they would not have adjusted if I had not told them our side of the story. They were hearing the stuff from parents that wasn't true about our family and that's the reason they were mean to me. But once I started talking to them most of them . . . understand what it's about. They have learned that what their parents have been telling them about us was not true. . . . Things are getting better. It was hard at first. I never thought it was going to be so bad. We got bomb threats and people following my mom's car. Now it is better.

It was obvious from our conversation that Kevin had mastered the intricacies of the legal jargon and the constitutional questions:

In the beginning I understood, but . . . [not] very well. I understood what the concept of it was and because I was taught about separation of church and state I knew what was happening in school was wrong. I knew about that but I didn't know all the details. Then I started learning all the details and all the laws. I read different cases. I feel good about what we did. I am sure that once we go back to court it will start up again and I'll get questions. And of course, some don't like me because of the lawsuit. Most teachers treat me fine. From a few you get the feeling that they don't think you belong, but most are pretty good. Some teachers stopped speaking to me in the hall. They haven't been mean. I think I got the grades I earned. I am active in the athletic program and I play football. The coaches treat me well. I think we are going to win the case.

Kevin Herdahl is bright, reasonable, and kind. For over two years most adults in Pontotoc County have simply ignored that truth. Death threats, meanness, and ostracism have not made Kevin bitter. Although his detractors don't realize it, Kevin is a citizen any community should cherish.

There is, of course, another side to this story. While we have focused upon a family in distress over what appear to be egregious violations of their First Amendment rights, the Pontotoc community's stand for public school religion has drawn strong praise from Mississippi political figures, including Congressman Roger Wicker, as mentioned previously. During the summer of 1995 Lisa was engaged in a public exchange with House Speaker Newt Gingrich. The House speaker said he believes it is "nonsense to say that one person can dictate to 3,000." He continued, "My attitude is that we'll give you a voucher for the value of your child's education. Go find a school you like. But don't dictate to everybody else in your community based on your particular prejudices." Gingrich, clearly devoid of information on the Herdahl case, nevertheless commented at length, calling the federal lawsuit an example of "antireligious bias." Gingrich told a town meeting in Roswell, Georgia, that such a lawsuit favors people with minority views at the expense of the majority.[9] Lisa described his remarks as "goofy."

By the close of 1995 the Herdahl case had become a rallying point for political action on the part of vocal advocates of biblical literalism and exclusivistic fundamentalism. Ed McAteer, leader of the Religious Roundtable* and a Southern Baptist who had much to do with the organization of the Moral Majority, announced a "National Affairs Briefing" to be held in Memphis, January 20, 1996, which he coordinated. McAteer predicted an attendance of ten thousand. In Pontotoc County citizens were being recruited to attend in order to show support for school prayer. "We're going to do something special on the effort that's going on down in Pontotoc and it will be one of the main issues addressed," said McAteer.[10]

And special it was, according to published reports in the *Memphis Commercial Appeal*. "We're here to support school prayer," said Pontotoc resident Rebecca Grant, mother of two children in the public school. "Without God, we don't have anything." The newspaper reported that a caravan from Pontotoc consisted of some 1,300 persons

---

*The Religious Roundtable was founded by Ed McAteer in 1980. He has been a lifelong advocate of rigid government control over private lives of citizens in the name of a special brand of Christian fundamentalism. The first major action of the group was to sponsor a gathering of 10,000 Christian ministers in Dallas in August 1980 to endorse the election of Ronald Reagan, featured speaker at the gathering.

The Roundtable originally had fifty-six members, a number equal to the signers of the Declaration of Independence, because, says McAteer, "our theme is patriotic." The number included Jerry Falwell and Pat Robertson along with virtually every right-wing political leader. Through the years McAteer has been a prominent spokesperson for the extreme right social agenda—a school prayer amendment, creationism in public schools, and an antiabortion amendment.

who "waited in the cold until Phil Gramm stopped talking, then took their seats to a roar of applause." According to the reporter they "appeared to almost double the crowd already present."[11]

Ecru, with perhaps four hundred residents, is a part of Pontotoc County. It is, like most such American villages, largely congregated on one main street, which, in the case of Ecru, measures little more than a mile. A few stores, gas stations, and a railroad track join a collection of houses, a few expensive, most modest. One building, the Ecru Baptist Church, is a prominent landmark.

The first national attention directed toward the conflict in Ecru resulted from a widely read column in the *San Diego Union Tribune* by James Yardley. He caught the flavor of the situation effectively when he wrote: "Lisa Herdahl fears Sundays. She dreads prayer meetings and the fervor they induce. She knows the preachers shout her name and ask God to forgive her. She worries that the people in the pews will not be so merciful. She doesn't sleep easily anymore. Death threats will do that."[12]

As I drove down the Ecru mile, a main street so common in the rural South, it was evident that adults had not forgotten the conflict nor flagged in their ardor to maintain their way of life. I counted more than twenty red, white, and blue signs with the words "Religious Freedom" boldly displayed in front of homes and businesses and the Baptist Church. I had seen the first such sign in the Herdahl yard. "After all," Lisa said, "we believe in religious freedom. That's what this is all about." But the signs were intended to condemn the Herdahls, accusing Lisa and her family of denying *their* religious free exercise. The signs have been in place for nearly a year, a silent reminder of the bitterness that greeted the Herdahls and their attempts to protect First Amendment rights. Ecru Baptist Church felt the need to display two signs, both of which are prominently situated on the large lawn in front of the sanctuary. Certainly to the people of Ecru, where prayer has been in school as long as anyone can remember, Lisa Herdahl's lawsuit is an attack against their way of life. Nevertheless, the question posed by Barbara Reynolds, writing in *USA Today,* February 10, 1995, still haunts the Herdahls, and the families who have fought to ensure the liberties that can only come with complete separation of church and state: "How can Christians have such evil ways?"[13]

Angry voices screamed from cars whizzing by on the highway outside the Herdahls' house. Women in the grocery store turned their backs. The children came home from school every day with the latest nasty rumor. There have been threats to firebomb the house and to kill Lisa. Such are the "Christian" ways of Pontotoc County.

After the lawsuit was filed by the ACLU and People for the American Way (PAW), the federal judge issued a restraining order respecting the loudspeaker prayers and Bible reading, as well as classroom blessings before lunch. That order remained in force until a trial set for March 4, 1996. How were the Herdahls' attorneys preparing for that date? They responded to the school's questionable "adherence" to the court order (to be detailed shortly) in their request for summary judgment* prior to the date set for the trial. (That appeal was denied and the case went to trial as scheduled.)

In their request for the summary judgment the attorneys for Lisa Herdahl made several salient points about alternatives devised by the school to replace the intercom prayer.

The attorneys directed attention to the district court injunction of April 18, 1995:

> While enjoining [preventing] the defendant's school prayer practice, the Court advised the defendants that they could create "a *neutral* activity period, prior to classes, . . . during which students in grades 7 through 12 are free to participate in *any* club of their choice *or in no club at all. . . .*" The Court further advised that, with the consent of their parents, children in grades K–6 could also attend the "pre-school activities." [Emphasis in original.][14]

In response to the court order, the school created an activity period in the gym before classes.

The Herdahls' lawyers noted that a videotape of the devotional period shows "the elementary grade children being led into the gym and seated by their teachers and then led out at the conclusion of the service. The teachers remain for the service." One of the tapes "shows teachers standing against the wall bowing their heads during the prayers."

The attorneys conclude this section of their argument with the following observation:

> Regardless of parental permission slips, a five-year-old child who is led with her classmates from her classroom by her teacher to a prayer ser-

vice in the school and then led back again cannot distinguish between impermissible school sponsorship and endorsement of the religious event and school "supervision" for purposes of student safety.

Quoting from the *Bell* v. *Little Axe* circuit court decision of 1985, Lisa's attorneys noted,

> Elementary school-children are vastly more impressionable than high school or university students and cannot be expected to discern nuances which indicate whether there is true neutrality toward religion on the part of a school administration. A child, for example, is unlikely to distinguish any difference between school sponsorship and mere faculty supervision.

Concurrent with the developing drama in Ecru, the elections of 1994 brought new political winds to Washington and the control of the Congress passed to the Republicans. As noted earlier, one of the first promises made by Speaker Newt Gingrich, when he addressed the House of Representatives in January 1995, was to pass a school prayer amendment by July 4 of that year. While that promise went unfulfilled, both the Senate and the House committees concerned with the judiciary focused on school prayer in separate hearings in the summer of 1995.

Lisa Herdahl was invited to testify before the two Congressional committees. Her testimony in September before the Senate Committee, chaired by Senator Orrin Hatch (R-Utah), contains a recounting of events in a formal presentation that, while repeating some of the materials covered above, adds the dynamic of a public forum. For that reason her testimony is offered here.

Testimony of Lisa Herdahl Before the Senate Judiciary Committee, September 12, 1995

My name is Lisa Herdahl and I have come to Washington today at the request of the committee to speak to you firsthand about the religious harassment that families like mine, who live in communities where they are in the religious minority, suffer when the separation of church and state is breached. For two years, my family has been harassed and stigmatized because we live in a community in which our religious beliefs and practices differ from those of the majority of people in our community and because of what happens in our public school.

In October 1993 my husband, my six children, and I moved from Wisconsin to the small community of Ecru, Mississippi, of less than 500 people so that my husband could find work and my children could be near their grandparents. I enrolled my five oldest children in the North Pontotoc Attendance Center, a public school that serves grades kindergarten through twelve, and the only public school in our community. At the time that I enrolled my children in this school, I learned that vocal prayers were broadcast over the school intercom and recited in classrooms during the school day, and that students at the school attended religious Bible instruction as part of the school curriculum. In fact, I heard the prayer myself over the intercom when I registered my children in school. I stated that I did not want my children to attend the Bible classes or to participate in the prayers.

I am a Christian and I am raising my children as Christians. I believe that it is my job as a parent, and not the job of the public schools, to teach my children about religion and prayer. Religion is something that my children learn at home and in church, and I did not and do not want the public schools telling them when and how to pray. Because prayers were being broadcast over the school intercom as classes were beginning in the morning, however, my children could not avoid them. I was particularly concerned because the intercom prayers were in the name of Jesus. That is directly contrary to my family's religious beliefs, because I teach my children to pray directly to God. My ability as a parent to teach my children to pray and our religious freedom was being undermined.[*]

Because I requested that my children not participate in the religious instruction at the school, my children have been ridiculed and harassed by teachers and classmates, and falsely called "devil worshippers" and "atheists." For example, as my son David was leaving his elementary classroom before one Bible class one of his classmates also asked to leave the classroom. His teacher said words to the effect that: "David doesn't believe in God. People who believe in God go to Bible class—those who don't, don't go to Bible class." David was later harassed by other children who falsely accused him of not believing in God.

---

*This statement caused Brother Doug Jones, on Oprah Winfrey's television show in May 1996, to assert that Herdahl is not a Christian.

Another time, when my son Jason was seven years old and in the second grade, his teacher placed headphones on his head during the period that the prayers were being broadcast over the intercom. After the teacher put the headphones on Jason's head, his classmates responded by calling him "football head" and "baseball head." Jason, who is now eight, has continued to be called names by his classmates and to be thumped on the head and grabbed by the ears. It is no wonder that he sometimes does not want to go to school in the morning.

There are many other examples as well. When the religious Bible classes take place my elementary school children leave the room and sit in another class, sometimes with older or younger children, or go into the hall for a full class period, and are teased and ostracized as well. One of my sons told me that a friend of his said that he couldn't play with him anymore, because if he did, my son's friend would get beaten up. Once, one of my children asked me if the people at the school and in town who were making things so hard for us were Christians. I said that they were. He replied that in that case, he didn't want to be Christian because he didn't want to be like them. I did my best to explain, but as a parent and a Christian, that disturbed me very much.

I had many conversations with school officials to request that the school stop the Bible classes and prayers. I went to the assistant principal. I went to the principal. I went to the superintendent of schools. I was told that this was just the way things were done in Pontotoc. I even went to the Pontotoc School Board last September. They said that they would "look into" my concerns, but I never received a response from them.

In order to protect my children, I had no choice but to file a lawsuit in federal court to stop the school's unconstitutional practices. As a result, the harassment of my family got even worse. Signs appeared all over town in support of the school's practices. I have been called an atheist and worse names. I personally have received a death threat in the mail and my family has received bomb threats. For several months, I was afraid even to start my car in the morning, and my husband did our shopping so that I wouldn't have to go into the stores.

Fortunately, the First Amendment protected us in court. In response to a request for a preliminary injunction from my attorneys from People for the American Way and the ACLU of Mississippi, the federal court in Mississippi issued a decision finding that the prayers over the intercom and in the classrooms were unconstitutional. The judge said that even if the prayers could be considered, as the school called them, "student-initiated," they were still unconstitutional because they had the school district's seal of approval and because they constituted government sponsorship of religion and students were captive audiences during the prayers. The judge ordered the school to stop allowing the intercom and classroom prayers. This was done. A trial was set for the following March on the remaining issues, including the Bible classes.

My family's experience demonstrates clearly that the public schools are certainly not hostile to religious practices, as some people suggest. I have heard from families all over the country, many of whom have faced similar violations of their religious freedom. The pressure these families face to accept religious oppression is, in my opinion, far greater than the pressure against those who push for government-sponsored prayer. Many of these families are afraid to come forward. I know their fear. People warned me not to complain about organized prayer in the Pontotoc schools. They warned me of the danger and the ridicule we would face. I stood up for what I believe is right; but many families live in fear of coming forward. Even in Pontotoc County, I have heard from people who agree with me privately, but are afraid to say so publicly.

My family believes deeply in God, and our religious faith is important to us. But because our religious beliefs are different from those of others in our community, and because of the organized religious practices in our public school, we have been harassed and stigmatized. It has been difficult for my family, but we have drawn even closer together and my children are learning an important lesson about standing up for what they believe in and about real religious liberty. I hope our experience will help other families who are concerned about religious liberty as well. Thank you very much.[15]

Lisa Herdahl was one of five persons to appear before the Senate Judiciary Committee on September 12. While Chairman Hatch and Senator Joseph Biden both decried what had happened to her and her family, neither asked her a single question. In sharp contrast, an extended dialogue took place between Hatch and Colleen Pinyan, Coordinator of the Office of Public Affairs of the Rutherford Institute.*

---

*A Virginia-based legal aid organization, the Rutherford Institute provides volunteer attorneys to litigate church-state separation cases on a *pro bono* basis. The institute denies an association with the Religious Right, but an examination of its current and past caseload indicates otherwise.

Pinyan argued in favor of a constitutional amendment to protect student-initiated graduation prayers and the First Amendment rights of teachers. She also advocated applying the free exercise clause as a means of countering the establishment clause. She cited instances where student rights had been denied by school officials. And while admitting that such violations were clearly forbidden by the Supreme Court, she feels the need for an amendment to aid the courts.

In response it is proper to examine the record. The Herdahl children were harassed by almost the entire community for their protest of existing conditions in the Pontotoc school. Lisa had to go to court to stop violations of her children's rights. The policies in Ecru were not the result of an overzealous administrator afraid he might violate a court order. In nearly every case cited by the Rutherford Institute where rights were denied, no court test was required. All it took was a phone call by an attorney, clarification of the law, and the problem was solved. When Lisa Herdahl cited the law, the entire community rose up against her and her family. The ACLU would have joined with the Rutherford Institute of in most of the cases cited by Pinyan. It is a far cry from an overzealous individual administrator or teacher erring in judgment on the one hand and an entire community blatantly violating the rights of children on the other. Pinyan makes no mention of instances in which a child was abused and ridiculed. In Ecru it was the Baptist Church that set the standard of vicious attacks on the Herdahls. The anecdotal evidence supplied by the Rutherford Institute nowhere cites community harassment and angry denunciations of students who prayed over lunch or carried a Bible to school. In sum, the Herdahl case involves organized hate and anger, consciously defying the law. The Rutherford cases supply us with a collection of individual officials who, while trying to enforce what they understood as the law, violated rights. By failing to question the witness on those fundamental differences, the members of the Judiciary Committee simply ignored their responsibility.

To understand this case properly it helps to examine the religion courses being taught in the Pontotoc schools. Inherent in the very organization of the curriculum is a clearly defined plan of intimidation and coercion leading to a specified point of view on the Bible. Since the arrival of the Herdahls, there have been two teachers of the religion classes in North Pontotoc, Larry Dean Patterson and Mike

Thompson. Patterson, who is now a Christian minister in Colorado, provided a clear picture of the nature of the Pontotoc situation in a revealing deposition in 1995.

The school district in Pontotoc does not employ teachers for the Bible class. There is a church committee, consisting of preachers and lay people, that employs and pays the teachers. The State of Mississippi does issue teaching certificates specifically for Bible. Patterson had one. Interviewing and hiring are the work of the committee, which then sends its choice to see the school principal, who approves that choice.

Patterson graduated from the local high school in 1970 and recalls, "It was the best class I had in high school." Asked if he were actually saved in that class, Patterson replied, "Sure, it happened as a result of exposure to the Bible." It was further established that he believed one is "only saved through Jesus Christ." In 1982 Patterson got his state teaching certificate in Bible. He hoped to have the same influence on students that his teacher had had on him. In 1984 Patterson was hired by the church committee. His deposition revealed that as the teacher he told the students what he believed and he taught the Bible as literally true. In no sense was the course "an historical and literary perspective" on the Bible, as the school administrators claimed. It was taught, unapologetically, from an evangelical Protestant viewpoint. The Bible, the only text, was presented as without error. This was not a course *about* the Bible, it was instruction in an interpretation *of* the Bible. Its purpose was to advance religion. Without doubt the class was religious indoctrination. Patterson was refreshingly candid. The defense would later find his affidavit an embarrassment in the court trial on March 4, 1996.

In one of the classes the teacher did use one book besides the Bible, the *Kids-Life Bible Story Book,* which described itself as a means to help "kids learn the truths of God's Word." The children were met with words such as, "In the beginning was our wonderful God. Our world was empty. Everything was dark and gloomy. So God decided to make our world a happy place for us to live in."[16] Unfortunately, no thought was given to making the public school classroom a happy place in which to learn for all children, irrespective of their beliefs.

In the upper grades Mr. Thompson currently teaches the pre-existence of Jesus (the Christian doctrine that Jesus, as Son of God, was with God before he was "made flesh and dwelt among us"), the miracles of Jesus, and the resurrection. All of these are Christian interpretations of the text, not historically verifiable events. The arrogant presumption that in a public school classroom such beliefs may be appropriately thrust upon young citizens, no matter what their own persuasions, is the heart of the issue. In the face of the Patterson and Thompson testimony, the attorneys for Pontotoc obstinately contend that the "Biblical History of the Middle East" course is taught "from a historical and literary perspective, and a nonsectarian, nonproselytizing matter [although they probably meant 'manner']." The school district claims it is teaching "about" the Bible as a part of a secular program of education. That is an astounding claim considering the fact that the only text is the Bible, which is presumed to be self-authenticating by the administrators and teachers. No one conversant with history and science, however, would be so foolish as to presume that the Bible is historical and scientific truth without error.

The Pontotoc attorneys finally came to grips with the Herdahl concern, perhaps without knowing it.

> It should be noted that many of the complaints raised by the Plaintiff are stated in terms that the teaching of the class is unconstitutional because Jewish beliefs concerning certain Biblical subjects are not presented as equally as Christian beliefs concerning those same Biblical subjects. Of course, again it should be kept in mind that this is a *Biblical* history of the Middle East course. The fact that people of the Jewish faith do not believe much of the content of the Bible, at least as compared to Christians, really is a moot point with regard to the purpose of the class, which is to teach students about the content of the Bible in an historical and literary fashion.[17]

The observation about "Jewish faith" clearly misstates fact. The Hebrew Scripture, usually tagged the "Old Testament" by confessing Christians, is the Bible for persons of Jewish faith. It could, in fact, be more easily noted that Christians "do not believe much of the content of the Bible, at least as compared with Jews" since Jews and Christians have in common only the Hebrew scriptures, which are by far the larger segment of the Bible. What some Christians believe about Isaiah or Genesis is completely affected by New Testament interpretations of these writings, and of course Jews do not consider the New Testament sacred. It is impossible to teach the Bible as Pontotoc has sought to do without inculcating Christian dogma. The sad part is, the school knew this. The only reason the course is taught is to teach a specific dogma, and the Christian churches of the community pay for the instruction. The class is an outreach of the Christian faith and is as unconstitutional as the programs forbidden in the McCollum case of 1948 (see chapter 4). The attorneys reveal their reverential perspective on the Bible when they regularly capitalize the adjective "biblical."

From the testimony offered it is clear that the Pontotoc teachers believe and teach that the Hebrew scriptures predict the birth of Jesus and his mission as the Christ. Mr. Thompson admits he teaches the pre-existence of Jesus. That is a matter of faith, not fact. How did the Bible come to us? The teachers assert that it was through revelation and inspiration. Again, faith, not fact. It is claimed, with a straight face, that there are no contradictions between the creation accounts in Genesis 1 and 2.* That is faith contradicting fact. And it is asserted that Moses wrote the first five books of the Bible. It is interesting how Moses might have written about his own death, which is detailed in Deuteronomy 34:5–12. The Pontotoc schools protest too much. If, in fact, these courses are truly nonsectarian, why does a committee of local clergy fund the project? Every shred of evidence points to the fact that the issue is not the Bible as history, but the God of faith. That is why the motorcade from Pontotoc to Memphis was labeled the "School Prayer Caravan." If this were only an academic debate about Middle Eastern culture it would hardly stir 1,300 residents to travel ninety miles to Memphis to protest Lisa Herdahl's actions. It would be nice if the proponents of "Christian America" could take a cue from Jesus, their chosen leader, and tell the truth about their motives. Are they ashamed of proclaiming Christ in the classroom? No, rather they are fully aware that they are breaking the law, violating consciences and abusing children.

✛   ✛   ✛

*This is clearly not the case. For example, Genesis 1:26–27, states that man was created on the sixth day of creation. In 2:7, man was created first. Genesis 1:27 has God creating male and female together, 2:22 has God creating woman as an afterthought following efforts to have man's companion be a beast or bird.

With the mood in the town of Ecru charged by the Memphis rally in January, lawyers prepared for the legal confrontation in the courtroom in Oxford, Mississippi, some thirty miles to the west of Pontotoc County. As I sat with attorneys Elliot Mincberg and Judith Schaeffer in the offices of People for the American Way, situated in the heart of Washington, D.C., the events in Ecru took on an eerie unreality. Even though we were surrounded by thousands of pages of evidence, depositions, and interviews, it hardly seemed possible that within weeks a federal court in a little university town would be assessing the constitutionality of mental harassment by a mob in the name of religion against a single family in rural Mississippi.

As the deadline for this book approached, it became obvious both to the publisher and me that we could not omit the drama unfolding in the Mississippi federal district court beginning March 4, 1996. District Judge Neal Biggers had granted a temporary injunction forbidding the morning devotionals at Pontotoc. Beyond the consideration of making the injunction permanent, the court was to hear Lisa Herdahl's complaint against the biblical history course.

It was a rainy Tuesday when I drove from Memphis to Oxford on March 5 to spend three days in the courtroom, observing during the day, writing in the evening. As I entered the courtroom the Herdahls' lawyers* were concluding the calling of witnesses. The attorneys included Robert McDuff, Elliot Mincberg, Judith Shaeffer, and Danny Lampley. Monday morning Robert McDuff, representing Lisa Herdahl on behalf of the ACLU, had opened by directing attention to the two basic issues, the devotional prayer broadcasts over the school intercom and the Bible classes. As noted, a year earlier Judge Biggers had issued a preliminary injunction suspending the devotionals over the public address system. That resulted in the school creating a devotional period in the gym sponsored by the Alethia Club, whose members had recited the morning prayers and Bible verses over the intercom. This was deemed unsatisfactory by the Herdahls. Part of this conflict was resolved when "attorneys for both sides agreed in court to allow high school students to continue having voluntary devotional services before school in the gymnasium."[18] The agreement was contingent upon eliminating all stigmas associated with nonattendance, such as

---

*Also referred to as "the plaintiffs" in this discussion.

having students who arrived at school early stand outside until the devotions were completed. A similar devotional exercise for elementary and middle school children was not agreed to by the plaintiffs and became one of the issues to be addressed by the court.

Turning his attention to the Bible course, McDuff contended that Pontotoc County schools don't hire the Bible teachers through normal channels. Later he elicited from George Owen White, chairman of the Pontotoc County Bible Committee, that area churches give money to the committee and the committee pays the teachers. In describing a typical job interview, White stated that the candidate would give details of his or her "salvation experience." When William Sims, pastor of the Pontotoc First Baptist Church, took the stand, he said he would not want to pay a teacher who would teach that the Bible could contain errors. His church gives $9,200 a year to the Bible teacher fund.

David Herdahl was the first member of the family to be called as a witness. A seventh grader, he testified that he did not attend the Bible class and, as we noted earlier, his teacher, Mr. Thompson, said to him that by leaving he was saying he didn't believe in God. Kevin Herdahl testified at length on Monday afternoon, describing the experiences recounted above. One sharp point of contention came from Kevin's description of a history class taught by Frank Cayson. Kevin said that Cayson repeatedly related to his class his "salvation experience." This was denied by Cayson the next afternoon. Kevin also testified about an animated cartoon shown in class depicting Jesus on the cross. Cayson admitted his use of the cartoon but insisted it was not religious, only informational.

The teenage Kevin recounted for Judge Biggers that his instructor once pulled out a Bible and began telling the class how his life had been changed through a personal communion with Jesus Christ. Kevin also told the judge about the hostility and isolation he and his siblings suffered after their mother began complaining about prayers being broadcast over the school intercom and about Bible instruction winding up in classes devoted to other subjects. "I get picked on because I'm different than anybody else. . . . Everybody in school is talking about my mom, that we didn't believe in God, and that we're trying to take prayer out of school and that we were devil worshippers." In front of the federal building that same day some 150 persons held a rally against the Herdahls. Another group of about twenty-five supporters carried signs on their behalf. Don McCutchen, a Baptist preacher, was quoted as saying, "People say pray at home, not at school. But our students spend seven to eight hours a day in school. . . . We hope to keep everything. We're not giving up hope, and we're not giving up anything." He went on to claim that prayer in Mississippi schools should be a fact of life that Herdahl and others should get used to. "She is offended by that. I know that her children are not accustomed to that, but we are. This is the Bible Belt. We believe in it, and we're not giving up on it. We're offended by her, but are we suing? We're here because they put us here."[19] Perhaps McCutchen is confused, since he also stated that the school system will appeal all the way to the Supreme Court, if necessary. That is a threat to "sue" Lisa Herdahl. Another minister, Anthony Collier of Cherry Creek Missionary Baptist Church in Ecru, asserted that "Lisa Herdahl has been used by the devil to divide the Ecru community."[20]

Tuesday morning the former Bible course instructor, Larry Dean Patterson, was called as a witness. As one would expect from reading his deposition, noted above, Patterson quite honestly stated, "I don't believe they [the Bible Committee] would hire a person with non-Christian belief. That's not the perspective of the people of Pontotoc County. The people of Pontotoc County understand the Bible is the word of God." This forthright testimony would sharply contrast with statements later made by other teachers, school officials, and a Baptist seminary president. However, Patterson's remarks conformed completely with the testimony and statements made by numerous Pontotoc preachers outside the courtroom. It is interesting to note that had Patterson not appeared in court, the plaintiffs' lawyers would have been confined to using Patterson's affidavit as proof that the course was overwhelmingly filled with expressions of commitment to faith. That option appeared to frighten the defense because the affidavit contradicted their case. Hoping to avoid having the plaintiffs use the written word, they flew Patterson from Colorado to Oxford, Mississippi, at their expense, in order to blunt the use of the pretrial statement. As we have indicated, Elliot Mincberg spent much of Tuesday morning exploring with Patterson his unapologetic presentation of his faith to the students as part of the course. The defense might have been better served to go with the affidavit because on the stand Patterson made it clear that the defense was not forthcoming in its account of hiring policies.

Each side chose to present a single expert witness on the teaching of religion in post-secondary education. Herdahl's attorneys called Thomas Lewis, an ordained Methodist minister and, for thirty-seven years, Professor of Religious Studies at Millsaps College in Jackson, Mississippi. It was a master stroke since Lewis had been teaching at the small Methodist college his entire career and is highly respected in the state of Mississippi. He affirmed that after reviewing the Bible class at Pontotoc, newly named "Religious History of the Middle East," he was convinced that the class was a religious proclamation using the Bible as a religious document. He also stated that a text used for kindergartners through third graders was religious, "written for the purpose of persuading them [the children] to that belief and moving them to a position of faith."

In the afternoon the defendants opened their case with a string of eleven witnesses. Most were students who were asked identical questions. The defense lawyers were intent upon proving that the public address (PA) system, when used by the Alethia Club, previously called the Christ and Us Club, was no different than any other club using it. The point was to show that the morning devotions consisted of announcements exactly like the other clubs. The school's lawyers sought to accomplish this by proving that the PA system was open to all student groups. No one had ever denied that. But as student after student testified, it became painfully obvious that each of them knew that the Alethia Club was holding its meeting on the PA system with prayer and Bible reading, while the other clubs merely announced that anyone who was eligible could voluntarily come to a meeting of the math or science club.

Judge Biggers saw through the defense strategy and interrupted: "The Alethia Club doesn't announce its meeting, it has the meeting. It would appear all of the students are having to attend the meeting. They are required to be in the classroom when the message is broadcast."[21] For what it was worth, the defense appears to have established as well that there was no written policy on the use of the PA system. One supposes that, in the mind of the defense, not having a policy means not being at fault.

One of the defense witnesses had helped get the devotions on the PA back in 1978. Lisa Gooch said she and a friend got permission from the principal to use the PA. Written policy or not, the administration chose to allow the Alethia students to broadcast devotions daily. And, as proof that everyone knew this was different from announcements, the devotions always came at the close of the public PA period, like a benediction. Plaintiffs' attorney Judith Shaeffer got one of the defense witnesses to admit that the religion club announcements on the PA were not pertinent to school activities in the same way other clubs were.

A sad demonstration of the influence so easily transferred from adults to children highlighted the testimony of a seventeen-year-old senior. Having just stated to the court that, contrary to Kevin Herdahl's claim, she never saw him ridiculed or embarrassed by other students, she was reminded by Elliot Mincberg of a letter she had written to the local newspaper. She admitted writing, "We do need prayer and devotion in [all] our public schools. I hope Lisa Herdahl knows what she's done. She'll pay for it in the long run." During the further cross examination the defense attorney got the young lady to say she believed she was correct and remained convinced of the truth of everything she wrote. The attorney saw the letter as a case of free expression and seemed to gloat at her steadfastness. He did not seem to understand that the young lady admitted having done to Kevin Herdahl what she said no student had ever done to him.

As the afternoon wore on the defense called to the stand Frank Cayson, a history teacher who was also one of the school's athletic coaches. Kevin Herdahl had accused Cayson of preaching in his classroom. "Not so," said an aggressive Cayson. He protested that he was just giving the facts of American history. He had a textbook to prove it. He insisted he never taught anything not in the text. Cayson immediately contradicted himself when the defense asked him about videotapes he showed in class. He showed the video *The King Is Born* at Christmas which, in his words, is about the "birth of Jesus Christ." *He Is Risen* was shown at Easter to tell about the arrest, death, and resurrection of Jesus Christ.[22] Obviously, neither of these videos would contain information found in an American history textbook, but Cayson vigorously denied that he was proselytizing. Anyway, he said, "I let students who might be offended go to the library. Students who are Moslem or Jewish might have discomfort." Surely he should have known that the Herdahls' attorney would nail him on that. And attorney Danny Lampley did just that, asking Cayson why they might be offended. Didn't that prove the videos were religion-driven? Cayson failed to see the point of that question. Asked how the video *He Is Risen* related to the text in American history, Cayson said that like the text, the video dealt with Judas and his betrayal of Jesus. It was a dramatic moment when Lampley pointed out that the video never mentions Judas.

But it was Cayson's choice of a third tape that would appear to call into question his ability to teach an American history course. He showed the tape *America's Godly Heritage*, narrated by David Barton, a well known Religious Right leader, claiming it to be a historically accurate presentation about the founders of the United States.[23] (The very title, with its use of the adjective "Godly" is a faith statement.) In truth, Barton's take on history includes his contention that SAT scores declined immediately following the *Engel* decision of 1962. The previous day Kevin Herdahl had made the point that, according to Cayson, when prayer went out of the schools SAT scores went down and teenage pregnancy rates went up. Clearly, Cayson had endorsed the Barton tape. Barton functions in a historical vacuum to promote the "true faith." He is the source of much of Pat Robertson's fictionalized version of the nation's founding and the early years of the Republic (see chapter 3). Judge Biggers suggested that perhaps Lampley's questioning of the witness on the Barton tape was unnecessary because surely the school officials would be willing to insist that Cayson no longer use it in class. But no, the school lawyers, citing the sanctity of the teacher's academic freedom, said they would not stop him from using the tape. In a response to the attorneys' remarks, the judge implied that he would likely remove the tape himself.

With the defense out of witnesses for the day, Judge Biggers adjourned the court until Wednesday morning when the school would call its biblical expert, Albert Mohler, president of Southern Baptist Theological Seminary. Mohler has presided over the dismissal of several faculty in his brief tenure. The firings resulted from theological differences between Mohler and some faculty over women in the clergy, which Mohler opposes.[24]

Mohler was led through testimony that in some ways pitted the Religious Right agenda against American jurisprudence and the federal courts in particular. He testified that he believes we are living in a secularized culture where a crumbling Christianity is being replaced by secularism and atheism. It is, he asserts, the "new dark ages where a brooding hostility to religion is evident everywhere." He believes that this hostility is evident in the *Engel* decision, and if the school district were to lose the Herdahl case, Judge Biggers would become a part of that hostility to religion.

Mohler went on to insist that there is a secularist agenda in the courts, and the nation needs an amendment to the Constitution to correct the problem. This points to an interesting flaw in the Religious Right arguments as they are currently being presented. Mohler surely knows that the single issue in the *Engel* case was school-sponsored prayer, but he willingly states that religious activities in public schools should not include sponsored prayer in the classroom.

One of the sillier moments took place when the defense attorney, Michael Whitehead, tried to draw an analogy between the death of John F. Kennedy and that of Jesus. The point being developed was that an eyewitness is an eyewitness no matter what millennium or document. Presumably this made the point that the biblical record of Jesus' death was somewhat comparable to the Zapruder film, the famous cinematic record of Kennedy being shot.

When Elliot Mincberg opened his cross examination he challenged the claim that Mohler was an expert on the subject under discussion, the teaching of religion to children in public schools. It was established through Mohler's own words that apart from Sunday school, he had just that year taught his first class, a course in Baptist theology. Further, he had never constructed a curriculum, a subject on which he pontificated at length in response to questions from the school lawyer. Moreover, he had never taught the Bible and never constructed or taught an objective, secular Bible course. The "credentials" that brought him from Louisville, Kentucky, seemed to be that he was a friend and Baptist colleague of defense attorney Whitehead.

Under Mincberg's questioning Mohler admitted his belief that no religious test should be required by a public employer, but he was vague about whether the procedure followed by Pontotoc for hiring Bible teachers through a church committee might be an exception. After Mohler endorsed the curriculum used in the Bible classes in 1994–1995, Mincberg pointed out that on December 5, 1995, the Mississippi State Committee for Appraisal of Curriculum had concluded that the one used at Pontotoc could not be continued because (1) it is not objective and does not have a balanced viewpoint; (2) it does not emphasize the history of the area outside of biblical material;

(3) the terminology employed suggests topics for preaching; (4) additional resources were infrequently used.

When asked if he were aware that the Bible for Jews did not include the New Testament and that the Bible for Roman Catholics included the Apocrypha,* Mohler stated that he had indeed known that. He was then asked if the term "Bible," when used to include the Hebrew Scriptures and the New Testament, but to exclude the Apocrypha, was a sectarian or faith term. "Yes it is," Mohler replied.

In conclusion, Mincberg asked Mohler about his view of the current federal judiciary. He responded, in keeping with his previous deposition, that the courts "reveal a secularist agenda." Did that indictment include Judge Biggers's Court? Mohler responded that, depending upon its decision, this district court could either continue that "overall pattern" or help the Pontotoc schools.

When the current Bible teacher from North Pontotoc took the witness stand after a lunch break the real core of the case was directly addressed. Michael Thompson is certified by the State of Mississippi to teach Bible and social studies in grades nine through twelve. In fact, he is teaching a Bible class to students in kindergarten though grade six as well as at the high school level. The defense attorney asked how he taught the course. Thompson responded that it was a chronological approach. After creation, Thompson begins with the life of Abraham and goes through the Book of Esther. He said he dealt with the conflicts in the Palestine area and used *The Middle East: Cradle of Conflict?* a film, he told the court, narrated by Barry Kasdam, a Jewish convert to Christianity who states on the film that the conflict will be resolved when everybody accepts the Messiah. He also showed *The Evidence for Creation*, which, he said, introduced people who believe in creationism not out of faith but through scientific evidence. By using the words "believe in creationism" Thompson confirmed what most scholars know: there is *no* evidence for creationism outside the Bible. Further, the video is introduced by a Mr. Oakland, who gives his Christian testimony. Thompson said he did not show that part, as if that would neutralize a proselytizing film.

---

*The Apocrypha is a collection of writings dating from 200 B.C.E. to 100 C.E. These fourteen books or parts of books are not accepted as canonical by Protestant Christians, but are included in the Bible by the Roman Catholic Church. The canon of Hebrew scriptures (90 C.E.) does not include these books.

It was also revealed that Thompson taught identical courses each year in grades K–3, resulting in the children having four exposures to the exact same material over a four-year span. In conclusion, Thompson said that in light of the rejection of the curriculum he had been using it would be necessary to make some adjustments.

Judith Schaeffer then began to question Thompson for the plaintiff. She demonstrated that beyond any reasonable doubt Thompson was using the class to promote his own confessional position.

Schaeffer first confirmed from Thompson that his education was obtained at Columbia Bible College, an institution that made belief in the inerrancy of the Bible a condition of graduation. It was established that he believes that the "Bible is a record of what occurred in the past." He posed questions to kindergarten through third grade children that included, "God made our world. What day was the moon created?"

In teaching the Christian scripture he divided his long attention to the life of Jesus into pre-existence, preparation, ministry, and closing events. In the first section he dealt with the length and purpose of Jesus' life as presented by the Gospel of Luke. In the Jesus section he used the video *Jesus* produced by the fundamentalist group, Campus Crusade for Christ, organized, as Thompson admitted, to convert persons to Christianity.

The next incident was surreal. Thompson, an inerrantist, who teaches the life of Jesus for several months each year, entered into a discussion with Schaeffer. Thompson had previously insisted that he used as a text only the New Testament Book of Luke. Attorney Schaeffer asked if he were aware that the final scene in the video depicted Jesus ascending into the sky while saying, "Go ye therefore and teach all nations, baptizing them in the name of the Father, and of the Son, and of the Holy Ghost: Teaching them to observe all things whatsoever I have commanded you: and, lo, I am with you always, even unto the end of the world. Amen" (Matt. 28:19–20). This quotation, attributed to Jesus, is commonly called the "Great Commission" by Christians. "Isn't that passage from Matthew, not Luke?" Schaeffer asked. Thompson faltered and appeared confused. He accepted Schaeffer's offer to lend him a Bible. She did so while informing him that it was the King James Version. Thompson read it aloud and said it was the gist of what the film presented. Here was a self-confessed inerrantist unable to identify the location of one of the three or four most frequently quoted statements attributed to Jesus.

Schaeffer turned to the film *Jesus* again pointing out that omitting the introductory confession of faith by Oakland did not remove the interpretations remaining in the film, including concepts such as free will, Satan enticing Eve, and the Fall of Man. She asked if these were terms acceptable to Jews. Thompson, who teaches the Old Testament, the main component of Jewish scripture, said, "I don't know what Jews believe."

Returning to *America's Godly Heritage* by David Barton, noted earlier in Frank Cayson's testimony, Attorney Schaeffer pointed out that this video was distributed by the American Family Association in Tupelo, Mississippi, and supplied by them to the Alethia Club. That association is directed by Donald Wildmon, a fundamentalist Methodist preacher. One can safely assume that a highly fundamentalist organization such as the American Family Association would be unlikely to promote and distribute a separatist, secularly oriented film.

Finally, Schaeffer focused on *The Middle East: Cradle of Conflict?* The message in that film is delivered by a Jew who converted to Christianity. That person, Barry Kasdam, states that the conflict in the Middle East will only be resolved when everyone accepts the Messiah.

As the cross-examination concluded, one more surprise lay in wait. In his course Thompson distributed a paper naming the theme and purpose of the Bible. As a part of the class testing, Thompson asked, "What plan did Yahweh have for Jesus in the Old Testament?" For Thompson, the answer was to be found in chapter 42 of the Prophet Isaiah. Schaeffer asked if Jesus were mentioned in the Hebrew scriptures. Thompson said, "I don't know, I'm not sure." Of course there is no mention of Jesus in any of the books Thompson called the Old Testament, a term that in itself is theological and is employed only by Christians. The testimony made it clear that Thompson was interpreting Hebrew scripture to fit certain Christian interpretations.

On redirect* defense attorney Edwards asked if Thompson taught his own views in class. He said no.

The final witness for the defense was Pontotoc School Superintendent Jerry Horton. He was prepared to defend the devotionals over the

---

*After cross examination by opposing counsel, the attorney originally calling a witness may ask further questions to clarify points arising in cross examination. This is called redirect examination.

PA system and the Bible class because both were supported by the community. He did not indicate whether he thought those who didn't offer support were excluded from the community. He agreed he would obey the court order whatever it might be.

Plaintiffs' attorney Elliot Mincberg asked several questions of Horton, but the most telling was his final query regarding a letter Horton wrote to the *Pontotoc Progress,* the local newspaper. Horton believed the case was bound for the Supreme Court. "It'll be difficult in Oxford because of the history" in this federal district. He asserted both in the letter and on the witness stand that the district was biased against the Pontotoc position, "but it may get corrected at the Supreme Court."

Late Wednesday afternoon the court was adjourned by Judge Biggers and the crowd in the courtroom slowly departed. It showed a cross section of Pontotoc citizens, men and women, and many students. As I chatted with one young teenager, Jamie Graham, a classmate of Kevin Herdahl, there did not appear to be any of the anger so evident among the religious, school, and political leaders in the community. Jamie said he is a friend of Kevin; he likes him. He has had numerous conversations about the controversy with Kevin (which Kevin confirmed to be the case), but he supports the Bible classes and devotions over the PA. He had come to the trial out of curiosity and in support of the school policy. Jamie had been impressed with the defense attorneys, something that should give them considerable pause. This pleasant, bright young man should have been reason enough for the defense to be honest, to themselves and everyone else, about what they were doing at Pontotoc. Instead, they betrayed the students at Pontotoc when they entered the court, a place of law, and seemingly, in what they perceived as a righteous cause and with no apology, misstated what they knew: namely that they had been violating the Supreme Court's *McCollum* decision since 1948. Jamie Graham deserved better.

As I departed Oxford, Lisa Herdahl assured me that the behavior of the community was not going to run her out of town. She would not give them the satisfaction because she believes in the principles underlying her protest. The failure of her neighbors to understand her deep convictions has led to horrendous mistreatment that was once more on the rise in early 1996. Ultimately this is a battle she will not win alone. Of course it will require legal assistance to prevail, but beyond that it must include an awakening of millions of American citizens to the threat posed to our democratic freedoms in communities like Ecru, where the spirit of seventeenth-century Salem, Massachusetts, and its witch hunts is all too frequently in uncontested evidence among the populace.

As for Kevin, he was optimistic about the outcome of the trial as well as about his future at Pontotoc School. He does have friends there who want to understand his point of view and it was clear to me as I listened to him that he is fully capable of explaining the nature of religious freedom to his peers. Kevin and Lisa, along with Elliot Mincberg, appeared on "Oprah" in May 1996, along with two Pontotoc residents, Brother Doug Jones and school board member Pat Mounce and their attorney, Michael Whitehead. As Kevin detailed his experience with the anger that had been directed toward him, he exhibited a mature grasp of the events storming around him. Coupled with that were the tears of a child abused by unfair and cruel treatment on the part of his neighbors. He could tell the audience why he believed as he did, but he was at a loss to explain why peopled hated him for it. It was a moment never to be forgotten. "They can pray," Kevin said, "anytime they want . . . I have my right to bow my head and pray. But when they get on the loudspeaker and pray their prayer and tell me the way I should believe . . . I think I should go to church and learn in my home and not be forced or harassed."

Brother Jones denied that he had said Lisa was not a Christian and then proceeded to tell her that unless she believed as he did she wasn't one. All three supporters of the Pontotoc school position decried threats of violence, one stating that her friends just wouldn't do that. "This did not come from anyone we are associated with," said Pat Mounce. "How do you know?" asked Lisa.

On June 3, 1996, Judge Biggers rendered his decision in the case. (Excerpts from that decision are to be found in Appendix A.) There were five issues to be resolved: (1) Judge Biggers found that use of the intercom by the Alethia Club was unconstitutional. The defendant cannot "sanitize an endorsement of religion forbidden under the Establishment Clause by also sponsoring nonreligious speech in the coercive context of public schools." A permanent injunction was issued forbidding such use of the intercom. (2) Since the preliminary injunction was issued in 1995, the Alethia Club conducted morning prayers before the school day began. The Judge ruled that that practice could continue, but noted that "in this present practice teachers are not permitted to participate in the religious meetings." (3) As to prayers in the classroom directed by teachers, the judge stated, "This conduct clearly violates the dictates of the Establishment Clause." He further noted, "The defendants' practice in directing teachers to pause before the class leaves for lunch, to specifically announce and provide an opportunity for vocal group prayer . . . is patently contrary to the separation of church and state." (4) Concerning the Bible class, Judge Biggers wrote, "Thus, all three prongs of Lemon are violated and the Bible class fails constitutional muster." He further noted concerning an endorsement test that the school was "clearly favoring religion over irreligion and preferring fundamentalist Christianity to the exclusion of all others." Finally, the Bible classes were found to be coercive. The judge accepted the right of a school to teach about the Bible and religion. But if such courses were to be taught, he instructed the school officials to "monitor the course closely and require any teacher to comply with the ruling herein, and that District shall satisfy itself that teachers it accepts have not been selected on the basis of a religious belief test and do not have an agenda to proselytize." He specifically enjoined the defendants "and anyone acting in concert with them . . . from teaching . . . concerning the Bible or religion in any manner that is not consistent with this court's decision and the United States Constitution." (5) Concerning religious instruction in all other classrooms, "These practices obviously violate the neutrality that a public teacher is required to maintain toward religion, and constitute impermissible religious instruction and endorsement of religion by a public official which crosses the wall the constitution erected between the scepter and the cross, and the defendants are directed to not allow any such activities by its teachers and to take swift and strong action if the District's policies are violated."

This is a sweeping victory for Lisa Herdahl and her children. The school district called two citizen meetings in June, but decided not to appeal the decision to the Court of Appeals. Judge Biggers's ruling therefore applies directly only to those counties in the Northern District of Mississippi. But it is another beacon from the federal judiciary that sets forth the guarantees of the Bill of Rights and is a reminder, as Judge Biggers wrote, that "The Bill of Rights was created to protect the minority from tyranny by the majority."[25]

Despite the resounding victory for Lisa and her family, the unregenerate Board members actually claimed victory on the ground that the judge did not overturn the *Schempp* decision. The claim was made that since the county can still teach "Bible classes," albeit to be monitored by Mississippi officials to guarantee that any such courses are strictly secular, "we are thankful that the school district can continue to graduate students who are literate in the Bible."[26] That is sheer nonsense. The evidence makes clear that for those fifty years the children were systematically denied an opportunity to be literate in the book. If they become so under the judge's ruling it will be because the instruction has left every shred of biblical inerrancy and literalism behind. But the arrogant response from officials does not bode well for the future.

The report of this response led Lisa Herdahl to comment to me on July 5 that she is relieved but believes "it is not over. We will likely be back in court in a few months because I am skeptical that the Board members have learned anything."

Notes

1. Information for this chapter is taken from taped interviews with Lisa and Kevin Herdahl in Ecru during December 1995. In addition, the author has spent considerable time discussing the case with Lisa's attorneys David Ingebretsen of the ACLU and Judith Schaeffer and Elliot Mincberg of People for the American Way. A huge number of newspaper articles have been examined. Finally, the author was present for three days of the district court trial in Oxford, Mississippi, during the first week of March 1996.

2. Doug Cumming, *Atlanta Constitution*, 10 February 1996.

3. Stephanie Saul, "A Lonely Battle in Bible Belt," *Newsday*, 13 March 1995, p. A8.

4. Ibid.

5. Ibid.

6. Ibid.

7. Ibid.

8. Jim Yardley, "Suit Challenges Mississippi Town's Fervent Support for School Prayers," *Dallas Morning News*, 18 February 1995, p. 12A.

9. "School-Prayer Foe Dismisses Gingrich Criticism," *Memphis Commercial Appeal*, 20 June 1995, p. 2B.

10. "Ride for Religious Freedom," *Pontotoc County Progress*, 30 November 1995, p. 2.

11. Bartholomew Sullivan, "Mississippi Caravan Takes Prayer Issue Up Front," *Memphis Commercial Appeal,* 21 January 1996, p. 1A.

12. Jim Yardley, "Foe of School Prayers Has Bible Belt Boiling," *San Diego Union Tribune,* 17 February 1995. ˙

13. Barbara Reynolds, "Closed Minds, Cold Hearts Make School Prayer a Mockery," *USA Today,* 10 February 1995, p. 11A.

14. "Memorandum of Points and Authorities in Support of Plaintiff's Motion for Summary Judgment," filed by Lisa Herdahl's attorneys December 12, 1995.

15. Lisa Herdahl's testimony before the U.S. Senate Judiciary Committee, September 12, 1995 (not yet published).

16. Mary Hollinsworth, *Kids-Life Bible Story Book* (Elgin, Ill.: Chariot Books, 1994).

17. Defendant's Memorandum Brief, filed by the school district's attorneys January 12, 1996, p. 28.

18. Neal McCready, "Plaintiffs' Witnesses Testify as Trial Begins," *Oxford (Mississippi) Eagle,* 4 March 1996, p. 1.

19. Steve Mullin, "School Prayer Trial Underway." *Oxford (Mississippi) Eagle,* 4 March 1996, p. 1.

20. Ibid.

21. McCready, "Plaintiffs' Witnesses Testify."

22. Both of these videotapes are referenced in the decision of Judge Biggers released on June 3, 1996, *Herdahl* v. *Pontotoc County School District,* US Dist Lexis 7671, 55.

23. *America's Godly Heritage,* produced by Wallbuilders, Inc., Aledo, Texas, 1994. The tape is narrated by David Barton, head of Wallbuilders. In the past few years this video has been released several times in new editions.

24. See in particular the dismissals of professors Paul Simmons and Molly Marshall from Southern Baptist Theological Seminary, which are discussed in George H. Shriver, ed., *Dictionary of Heresy Trials in American Christianity* (Westport, Conn.: Greenwood Publishing, forthcoming).

25. *Herdahl* v. *Pontotoc County School District.*

26. Bartholomew Sullivan, "No Appeal But Still Prayers at School," *Memphis Commercial Appeal,* 4 July 1996, p. 1B.

11

And Bear in Mind

In the planning of this volume, space considerations and publisher deadlines prevented the exploration of the hundreds of other cases that could otherwise have received attention. In order to remove any suspicion that the experiences detailed above are anecdotal exceptions, it seems advisable to offer a brief look at five other similar cases that have been active in the past ten years. In researching the following stories I am particularly indebted to several state directors of the American Civil Liberties Union for their time and energy in making files and contacts available to me. Not all the examples below are about confrontation and insensitivity. Some communities have discovered ways to communicate across cultural and religious boundaries within the democracy common to all.

Mistaken Identity

> "It was insinuated that parents with concerns like mine could create problems for a child in school."

In the fall of 1994 the Louisiana ACLU director, Joe Cook, notified the East Baton Rouge Parish School Board that it should stop the promotion of prayers by Zachary High School. This action followed a request by the mother of one of the students in the school that the ACLU examine the practices of the physical education department.

The complaint came from the mother of a girl named Jane, who was a member of the school dance team. Although the team was supposedly an extracurricular activity, the girls received grades and high school credit in physical education for being on the team. The mother's concern was aroused after an incident involving another girl in the class.

> At the end of the practice the girls would join together in a circle and pray. . . . My daughter's friend informed me that she had been called in to discuss her so-called bad attitude. In this meeting, the child was informed that one of her infractions was that she had "walked out before the prayer" at the end of practice.[1]

Jane was upset at the treatment her friend received.

Jane's mother had assumed that the prayer at the end of practice was voluntary, but when the friend was called in to discuss her "bad" attitude she began to inquire about the school policy. Jane's friend received a "penalty point" for her action, something that could affect her grade.

Knowing all this, Jane's mother contacted a representative of the school board, who explained that they were "just trying to instill morals in our children" and in any event, "dance teams did not come under the rules about forced prayer in school." When the mother made her dissatisfaction clear, she was directed to see the school principal, Jerry Boudreaux. She met with him and two of the team sponsors, both teachers, and was informed that the dance team was strictly voluntary. The school representatives "insinuated that parents with concerns like mine could create problems for a child in school, which as you can imagine, did not sit well with me."

One of the sponsors told the mother that not all the rules for the team were written and that one of the unwritten rules was that participation in the circle is mandatory because sometimes announcements are made during this time and it gives the girls a time to discuss their own concerns.

Jane's mother wrote to the ACLU asking for help. The ACLU sent a letter to the school board in the fall of 1994, requesting the cessation of the practice of prayer in the dance class. In their letter the ACLU pointed out that the principal had suggested that Jane's friend quit the team if she didn't like the way it operated. The school board replied in November that the charges made by the ACLU were false and that the prayers were student-initiated and "student-given." In that single response the school officials admitted violating the fundamental principles set forth in the ruling Supreme Court cases of *Engel*, *Schempp*, and *Weisman*: time in a class, taken for credit in the public school, was being employed for the purpose of prayer.

It was at this juncture that a most astounding action by Boudreaux occurred. He publicly claimed that Jane's friend "complained about the prayers because she wasn't chosen as captain of the team this year."[2] Can one imagine a more outrageous thing for a principal to say to a teenager he has chosen to help learn? Is it appropriate for an educator to give a public pop psychological analysis of any student who raises question about school rules and procedures? But that is not the worst of it. The principal assumed, incorrectly, that the complaint to the ACLU had been made by Jane's friend, which was not the case. Thus, the principal publicly attacked one of his own students for standing up for her convictions and in the process named the wrong child.

The school board responded by refusing to alter its policy about student-initiated prayer in a class for school credit. In reply to the school board, the ACLU pointedly noted that the principal had "fingered the wrong student as being the person who lodged the complaint." The principal attempted to guess who the complaining student was, but erred and ultimately embarrassed a young girl who had absolutely nothing to do with the protest.

When it became evident that the community was heaping criticism on a young girl who was in no way involved in the complaint, Jane's parents decided not to press the matter with a suit.

The Spirit of Christmas

"I believe non-Christians will go to hell when the Judgment Day comes."

In Lee's Summit, Missouri, the R-7 School District held an annual Christmas candle-lighting ceremony. "The ceremony—a tradition at the high school for more than thirty years—centers around the Christian theme of the coming of the Messiah—Jesus Christ." After receiving a protest in 1986 from a Jewish family, the ACLU challenged the ceremony on constitutional grounds, leading to the editorial remark, "To protect the rights of a few, the rights of the many are trampled."[3] The editorial writer went from that expression of opinion directly to a fictional account of eighteenth-century events: "Most of the drafters of this country's Declaration of Independence and Constitution were deeply religious men who believed that religion and government went hand-in-hand."[4] Unfortunately for the editor, it was, as we know, the author of the Declaration of Independence, Thomas Jefferson, who created the phrase "a wall of separation between church and state."

By November, the school board was prepared to convene to determine further action, if any. The vice-chairman of the board, Bob Bruce, was quoted as saying "People are just old-fashioned enough they don't like outsiders coming in and telling them what to do."[5] Other board members were more prepared to examine the merits of the ACLU case. After consultation with their legal counsel, they were informed that the Christmas program as it was planned was unconstitutional.

Acting on that advice, the board voted five to one to drop the Christmas ceremony. The vice-chairman, later engaging in a dialogue with a Jewish parent, stated, "I believe non-Christians will go to hell when the Judgment Day comes. . . . Anyone who has not accepted Jesus Christ as his savior [is doomed]." He was earlier reported as saying that it didn't matter whether non-Christians felt ostracized by the ceremony "because they're going to be ostracized anyway when they go to hell."[6]

It is heartening to report that the reasonableness of the board and the superintendent made possible a solution which led the ACLU director for the state to call the members "a courageous bunch of people." Clearly the community preferred to retain the ceremony, but it became clear to the leadership that defying the mandate of the Supreme Court was folly, and more than that, irresponsible stewardship.

Why Should a Kid Be Put Through This?

"Christmas is the same as any other day to him."

In an especially thoughtful report in a Michigan newspaper, Gerald Frawley wrote about separating church and state. He began his essay with these words:

> The boy, seven years old, maybe eight, sat down and looked at the paper before him. *A Christmas Carol* by Charles Dickens—[it was] an essay test on values and the feelings evoked by the classic piece of literature.
>
> The teacher had assigned the book to the class to read, think about, and be prepared to answer questions. No grade, no hassles, just an exercise in values in the spirit of Christmas.
>
> First question: What do you do at this time of year to promote the Christmas spirit? Second question: Is it better to give gifts for Christmas or receive them? Third question: What should you do for a charitable organization during this time of year? And so on.
>
> The little boy couldn't answer any of the questions—his family was Jewish and didn't celebrate Christmas.
>
> This is a true story, according to Jewish Community Council spokesman Howard Wallach. Several years ago, it happened in Mt. Pleasant in central Michigan, he said, and fortunately, the child was intelligent enough to know what the correct answers were—if he had not, and had answered the truth—that Christmas is the same as any other day to him—he would have been scorned as a "Scrooge" by the test's grading scale and held up for ridicule in front of his classmates.
>
> "Why should a kid be put through this?" Wallach asked.
>
> "I know that the teacher never meant to ostracize anyone, but that's what happened," he said, adding that most teachers cannot teach topics related to religion without instilling some sort of bias and that can insult without meaning to or actually cause a religious minority grief.[7]

The image of that seven-year-old child left by Frawley's comments is an emotional one. And it is one that can possibly assist in breaking through that all-too-frequent blindness toward other people's feelings that is manifest when religion becomes an issue in the public arena.

Win One for the Savior

"We heard about you in Sunday School the other day and you're not a Christian."

In 1986, Douglas Jager's father filed a suit on his son's behalf against the Douglas County Board of Education in Douglasville, Georgia.[8] At issue were the prayers before the home football games of Douglas County High School. Jager felt such prayers were a violation of his constitutional rights. At the time of the filing William Jager made the following comment: "The prayers are being controlled by Southern Protestants, and have been since the beginning. How could you have freedom of religion when there's only one group doing it? It's a joke."[9] In February 1987, a federal district court ruled against the school, holding that the practice of having ministers give pregame prayers appeared to endorse Protestant Christianity and violated the Constitution. The judge found that the prayer "has no secular purpose." He did allow an "equal access" plan in which a lottery would be held to pick a person to pray at each game. This "compromise" was offered by the school system, but on January 3, 1989, the Eleventh U.S. Circuit Court of Appeals upheld the original lower court finding and ruled that the equal access plan also violated the Constitution. The circuit court found,

> Therefore, the likely result of the equal access plan will be the continuation of Protestant Christian invocations, which have been delivered since 1947. Moreover, the equal access plan places those attending football games in the position of participating in a group prayer. Consequently, the plan violates the primary effect prong of the *Lemon* test.[10]

Pregame prayers had to stop. In May 1989, the Supreme Court refused to review the circuit court decision. Douglas Jager, by then twenty-one years of age and a sophomore at Georgia Tech, had prevailed. Reflecting on his experience, Jager had two pointed observations. He said he would do it again, "but, if circumstances had been different, the suit would never have been filed." He expounded on these remarks:

> Initially, if I had been treated with some respect and there was no hostility or anything, there would probably still be a prayer before the local high school football games. I was more than perfectly willing to just be quiet and show respect for their religious beliefs and them doing the same for me.[11]

In 1986 Doug Jager played the saxophone in the marching band. A local reporter, Lucy Warren, wrote, "This serious kid with braces, who said he was agnostic, had had enough of a practice he saw as blatantly unconstitutional."[12]

In his freshman year in high school, at his first football game, Doug stood during the prayer without bowing his head. Fellow students noticed him and called his action disrespectful. They began to harass him. Doug makes an important distinction here: "The harassment was never kidding. The friends that I hung around with all love to tease, cut people down and everything. But it was never associated with this. This was always harsh every time it ever would come up." Soon the "Jager" affair was a matter of community discussion. He was talked about in local Sunday schools: "We heard about you in Sunday School the other day and you're not a Christian."

Doug reflected from a distance of three years on his puzzlement over what was going on. "At first I . . . kind of . . . just let it be. There's not that much wrong with just having prayer. I can sit there and be quiet through this however long it is." But he soon noticed that these people had no concept of separation of church and state, "because prayer was so ingrained and so routine they didn't think about it." In a nice turn of a phrase Doug continued, "When I wouldn't pray, it was kind of like, 'whoa, someone who doesn't believe in God.' "[13] That led to regular efforts by some students to debate him about religion. In response, the bright young student began to read about civil disobedience in the works of Thoreau, Gandhi, and Emerson. "I always knew the prayer was unconstitutional but I figured somebody needed to say something to somebody." That somebody was John Stone, the principal at the time. Stone referred him to the band director, who told him there was nothing he could do about it, and then proceeded to give him a religious lecture.

Even as Doug imagined how he might make a public response to the minister's prayer, he really wanted to resolve it without upset. Troubled by the events, he discussed the matter with his father, who suggested he call the ACLU. Doug and his father then met with the superintendent. They were distressed to find ministers from the local ministerial association at the meeting. Doug, obviously having researched *Lemon* v. *Kurtzman* by that time, saw this as "entanglement" with religion. The ministers said they were willing to make it a nondenominational, but still Christian, prayer. A short time later one of the local ministers informed a church member about the Jager complaint and the story reached the local newspaper.

With the lack of a resolution, the Jagers filed suit in September 1986. The judge granted a temporary restraining order that ended the prayers. As the *Los Angeles Times* reported it,

> At the first home football game after the judge's decision, many in + the crowd wore T-shirts and carried banners with slogans such as "Pray today" and "I feel a need for prayer." One man broke into a recital of "The Lord's Prayer" and was joined by part of the crowd of 3,000. David Hill, principal of Douglas County High, which has a student enrollment of 1,400, said that the tradition of praying before home football games goes back at least to the 1920s. "We don't think that this is an issue that involves religion and government," he said. "People go to the football games voluntarily, and no particular religion or religious viewpoint is being pushed in the prayers." He said also that, up to the time of the temporary ban on the prayers, the Tigers had a 7–0 record, but, afterward, the team lost the remaining three games. But he hastened to add: "I certainly wouldn't want to say there was any connection."[14]

Inevitably, the heightened controversy led to greater pressure on Doug. "I knew I was going to get a lot of flak over this," said Jager, who was born in Denver and moved to Douglasville with his family in 1976. "I've been living with these people for the last ten years." Bryan Barnett, one of Jager's friends, says Jager has shown tremendous courage. "I have the same views as him, but I don't think I would have the guts to go through what he has," he told a reporter after Judge Tidwell imposed the temporary restraining order.[15] Frequent insulting remarks coupled with students throwing things at him made life at school difficult. But he did have a good group of friends who stuck with him and were supportive.

By this time other serious harassment had begun. Typical of the hundreds of calls they received was this one: "I'm a Christian and I think you're going to hell. You ought to go to Russia." Doug was bemused by the fact that people identified themselves as Christians and then cursed him. Indeed, Doug feels that it was the Christian community in his town that showed him how important church/state separation is.

In February 1996, William Jager, Doug's father, spoke with me about the case and the types of pressure exerted over the three-year period. He confirmed that his son had initiated his complaint without consulting with the family; in fact, he is very proud of his son's mature handling of the situation. Regarding harassment, the phone was the weapon of choice by anonymous detractors. Threats to the family's life and property became so constant that William Jager kept the answering machine on all the time and screened incoming calls. As a result, he has a record of all the insulting and threatening remarks. In 1988 he played a couple of them when he was on "Donahue."

William notes that after the suit became public the "media went wild and Georgia went crazy." The calls continued with upswings in number corresponding to court dates and newspaper coverage. Hate mail was heavy. Two of the Jagers' cars had the tires slashed while parked in the garage. The house and mailbox were egged. The local papers were not sympathetic, nor were the local politicians, who used the case to parade their own "piety" to the public. Unlike many of the media, the *Atlanta Constitution,* the main offices of which are located about thirty miles east of Douglasville, was editorially sympathetic.

The local clergy, so intimately associated with the football prayer issue, found no compassion for their agnostic neighbor. Rather they sought to justify what was being done even in the face of court rejection. The Rev. Jamie Jenkins, a Baptist minister in the town, made this point: "There is a subculture that surrounds football—it's almost a cult unto itself. When you mix that with the religious history of the Deep South, you have an exercise that is very important to the community."[16] After the Supreme Court, without comment, upheld the circuit court decision, reaction spread across the South. Whatever the application of the Eleventh Circuit decision in the other forty-seven states, it was now law in Florida, Georgia, and Alabama, the states included in the Eleventh Circuit.

Douglasville is a town of nine thousand people and forty churches. That proportion is more the rule than the exception in the region. And the resentment in Douglasville spread quickly. In Montgomery, Alabama, "Mayor Emory Fulmer and County Commissioner William Joseph marched to the 50-yard line in Crampton Bowl and led a prayer before the first game of the year."[17] Before the prayer Fulmer announced to the crowd, "Prayer is a tradition here in Montgomery, in Alabama, and in these United States." In Cedartown, Georgia, the football coach observed, "This is the South, the Bible Belt—religion is a part of our life. I don't know if this will become as emotional as abortion, but it has the potential. I hope it does. I hope we get this overturned."[18]

A pastor of a Baptist church in Columbiana, Alabama, was proud to assert, "I'm a law-abiding person, but if it comes to a choice between obeying the Lord and following the Constitution, the Bible is more important to me than the Constitution."[19] In Pensacola, Florida, preachers with bullhorns led spectators in impromptu prayers at a game.

Doug has now graduated from Georgia Tech and holds a Master's degree from that institution. He prefers now not to discuss the days of the 1980s when he served an entire nation in the cause of freedom. What he accomplished with his suit is a permanent reminder of what a single, dedicated teenager can achieve. Beyond that, it is a remarkable example of an emotional issue transforming city and town residents into unruly mobs challenging the Supreme Court because "this is the South."

To close this particular drama it is useful for the reader to consider some of the words from the federal judges who ruled for the Eleventh Circuit. Judge Frank Johnson wrote,

> When a religious invocation is given via a sound system controlled by school principals and the religious invocation occurs at a school-sponsored event at a school-owned facility, the conclusion is inescapable that the religious invocation conveys a message that the school endorses the religious invocation.[20]

He went on to note that the school system's rejection of a proposal to allow secular inspirational speeches proves its officials improperly "wanted to have invocations that publicly express support for Protestant Christianity."

It was noted by the court that the

> Jagers offered to accept a pre-game invocation consisting of a secular inspirational speech. Since the school district rejected this compromise even though it would have fulfilled the three secular purposes of pregame invocations, it is clear that the school district was most interested in the fourth purpose served by the invocations. That is, the school district wanted to have invocations that publicly express support for Protestant Christianity.[21]

The Primrose Path

> "Minority rule is the sort of thing that was promulgated by the likes
> of Hitler and Mussolini. . . ."

In Barrington, Rhode Island, Primrose Hill School became the center
of a major controversy in December 1994. As Christmas approached,
a new music teacher, not native to the community, was planning the
annual holiday concert. She was working with third graders who were
required to take the class. She chose as one of the songs to be included
in the program, a carol written in 1992 which contained the line "For
Jesus Christ was born today." A Jewish boy in the class didn't want to
sing it. His mother went to the principal, who told her the song was
all right. She appealed to the school superintendent, who told her
there could be songs in the program that were religious but not songs
that embarrass a child. He chose to rely on the first part of the rule,
ignoring the embarrassment question.

The mother, convinced that the song was a celebratory endorsement of Christianity, appealed to Roni Phipps, one of the school committee members. Phipps, in turn, called other members of the committee, expressing her view that the mother was right in objecting.
When the committee met they discussed the matter with the chair of
the music program, the principal, and the superintendent. It was suggested that if the child didn't like the song, he could sit down. That
was no solution in the minds of those present and it was clear the boy
felt that if he sang the words then he was confirming belief in them.
The superintendent suggested dropping the word "Christ" from the
song. A rabbi was consulted and he explained that there was no problem in the child saying Jesus was born, but "Christ" is the label
assigned to Jesus by believers in his messiahship as the son of God. In
other words, it is a Christian term. Based upon this discussion the
word was removed and the children sang the song. The superintendent
issued a statement in which he pointed out, "Whether the majority of
the students are Christian or not, this statement of religious belief is
not appropriate in the public schools."[22]

Unfortunately, the meeting where the decision took place was held
thirty minutes prior to an open session of the school committee to
which citizens had come to express their views on the subject. Upon

discovering that the decision had been reached before citizens were heard, many in attendance were angered, producing many letters in the local paper, the *Barrington Times*.[23] There was considerable criticism of the committee for deciding in secret before a scheduled hearing.

At the request of the family the boy's identity remained unknown. Consequently, there was no direct effect on the child, but the letters and the general public reaction became an issue for the boy's father. The tone and spirit of the response by his neighbors sickened him and he informed me that he was not sure he could remain a resident of Barrington. He expressed deep disappointment in his community's reactions.

And just how did the neighbors react? A local headline dated December 14, 1994, proclaimed "Christmas Carols Cause School Uproar." Numerous letters followed. One such letter read:

> It is a person with no tolerance or acceptance of others who caused the uproar by complaining. . . . Instead of the superintendent of schools changing policy for a handful of malcontents, maybe we Christians, as the majority in town, should vote to exclude all non-Christians from attending holiday activities so they won't be offended.[24]

By the week after Christmas the "Letters" section of the paper had expanded. "This wonderful democracy of ours is firmly founded on the premise of majority rule. . . . Minority rule is the sort of thing that was promulgated by the likes of Hitler and Mussolini. . . ." Another wrote, "I am a Christian, and I am sick and tired of all this censorship. . . . It's about time the majority speaks up and stops the minority from taking away what is rightfully ours." An angry letter attacked "a courageous (but, alas, anonymous) whiner" and went on to mock the "embarrassment of the town's sophisticated and culturally sensitive third-graders. . . ." Early in January one correspondent wrote, "The anonymous complainer has sent his/her child the message that if you disagree with what someone else is doing, it's appropriate to force him to stop, laws to the contrary notwithstanding." Forgetting the child altogether, one writer noted, "Someone should have just suggested to this individual that if they did not like the song selections do not attend the concert!" During the same week these letters appeared, the newspaper editor weighed in against the school decision.[25]

There were, of course, personal letters as well. One addressed to the school committee began, "I am absolutely livid and outraged at the decision to eliminate the word *Christ* from a *Christmas* song at a recent school holiday concert. I do not believe a public school has the right to tell a Christian what words go into their Christian song."

One of the most interesting letters came from Rabbi Leslie Gutterman, the target of the Weismans' complaint that led to the Supreme Court's 1992 decision in *Lee* v. *Weisman* outlawing school-sponsored graduation prayer. A resident of Providence, some sixty miles north, the rabbi commented on the Primrose case: "I think that it is ironic that at a season of good will to others, when the message of peace on Earth and good will toward humankind is the clarion call, that such incidents tend to be divisive. It trivializes the essential religious meaning of Christmas to apply theological tests to songs."[26] The good rabbi had not understood the Weismans' concerns respecting their daughter Deborah and he clearly missed the point again in 1994. It was precisely because the song had "Christ" in the lyrics that it had religious meaning and was theological.

As best one could ascertain, only two citizens wrote in support of the school decision. Meanwhile, in a Catholic Church in Bristol, where the superintendent's eighty-five-year-old parents are communicants, the resident priest denounced the school's decision and the superintendent in particular. When this incident was reported in religious circles it drew hate mail against the superintendent from as far away as Seattle, despite the fact that he had acted in good conscience to seek a solution that would be satisfactory to both sides.

The school committee met in January and members were blasted by residents for operating in secret. At the meeting, the chairman apologized to the residents. "We were in the wrong." Following this the committee revisited the issue and devised a policy stating that the school may recognize either all religions or none. "All," however, meant only Buddhism, Christianity, Hinduism, Islam, and Judaism. In June 1995 the school committee met to face further criticism for their revised policy, particularly the fact that they had submitted their proposed policy to the Barrington clergy for approval. After that meeting, sensing a possible embarrassment that would attend a second round of debate, the committee agreed to meet again in a week to discuss their new policy. At that meeting a committee was assigned the task of writing a new policy regarding religious holidays. Meeting for the first time since June, on August 31, 1995, the school committee reported the revision at an open meeting. The policy was adopted. The Christmas season of 1995 passed without incident on this front.

By then Barrington residents were in an uproar on another church/state front—plowing church parking lots at public expense following snow storms.[27] It was a serious issue, but lost somewhere in the public uproar and the attacks on the school committee's inept confusion over simple procedure is a little boy who felt very isolated by his school when it urged his participation in a Christian faith statement. The story is presented here because the battering administered by local residents against a caring parent was not only insensitive, it was hypocritical since most people who wrote pointed out their own great tolerance.

Notes

1. Letter from Jane's mother to the Louisiana ACLU (made available by that organization to the author of this book).

2. Fred Kalmbach, "ACLU Wants Zachary Prayer Nixed," *The (Baton Rouge) Advocate*, 26 October 1994, p. B1.

3. "Our Opinion," *Lee's Summit Journal*, 5 October 1988, Several other newspaper accounts of this case were used in writing this section.

4. "Protecting Anonymity at the Majority's Expense," *Lee's Summit Journal*, 5 October 1988.

5. Bob Bruce, quoted in *Lee's Summit Journal*, 9 November 1988, p. 1.

6. Ibid.

7. This section is based on Gerald Frawley, "Separating Church and State" (Union Lake, Michigan) *Spinal Column*, 28 December 1988. It is an effective presentation of the dilemma facing minorities every day in public schools.

8. I am indebted to William Jager for an interview he granted by phone in February 1996. Also used in telling this story were numerous newspaper reports.

9. *Los Angeles Times* Newswire, 25 September 1986, Pt. 3, p. 1.

10. *Jager* v. *Douglas County School District* 862 F2d 824 (1989).

11. Lucy Warren, "Fighting School Prayer," *Douglas County Sentinel*, 18 May 1989.

12. Ibid.

13. Ibid.

14. David Treadwell, "Dixie May Face End of Ritual Pigskin Prayer," *Los Angeles Times*, 14 November 1986, Pt. 1, p. 1.

15. Ibid.

16. Jerry Schwartz, "Student Gains in Fight to Bar Pregame Prayer," *New York Times*, 8 January 1989, Sect. 1, p. 16.

17. Peter Applebone, "Football Prayer Ban Stirring Anger in South," *New York Times*, 2 September 1989, Sect. 1, p. 1.

18. Ibid.

19. Ibid.

20. *Jager* v. *Douglas County School District.*

21. Ibid.

22. "Christmas Carols Cause School Uproar," *Barrington Times,* 14 December 1994, p. 1.

23. In addition to the newspapers, I am indebted to school committee member Roni Phipps and to the father who lodged the complaint on behalf of his child for granting taped interviews during 1995. I am also grateful to my nephew and niece, Bob and Zoe Alley, along with their two wonderful children, Cassie and Max, residents of Barrington, for keeping me informed about this story and introducing me to the participants.

24. "Letters," *Barrington Times,* 14 December 1994, p. 6.

25. "Letters," *Barrington Times,* 4 January 1995, p. 6.

26. Jerry O'Brien, "School Edits 'Christ' Out of Grade 3's Holiday Time," *Providence Journal-Bulletin,* 16 December 1994, p. 1A.

27. Jerry O'Brien, "The Forum on the Constitutionality of the Town's Plowing Snow for Houses of Worship," *Providence Journal-Bulletin,* 29 March 1996, p. 1.

12

Conclusion

The personal experiences examined in this book, gleaned from fifty years of history, should send at least three significant messages to concerned citizens of the United States.

First, the Supreme Court case law on First Amendment religion issues has been consistent, interpreting the establishment clause as erecting a wall of separation between church and state. The Court message has varied over those years from a strict interpretation to a degree of accommodationism. But the key cases—*Barnette, McCollum, Everson, Engel, Schempp, Jaffree, Edwards,* * *Berger, Kyrias Joel,*† and *Weisman*— have been effective beacons setting forth precedents which have settled hundreds of conflicts at the appellate level. The Supreme Court, as it is presently constituted, appears inclined to maintain that direction. Future appointments could easily alter the situation, but for over fifty years the First Amendment has consistently secured the rights of minorities and has remained a bulwark against religious establishment. Listening to the children and teenagers who endured abuse and harassment is a lesson in true character.

Edwards v. *Aguillard* 107 US 2573 (1987) ruled against inclusion of creationism in Louisiana public schools.

†*Kyrias Joel* v. *Grumet* (1994) forbade the state of New York from creating a school district solely for persons of one religious belief.

Second, the tradition of religious establishments is still very much alive in the United States, particularly in smaller cities, towns, and counties. Majoritarianism, a type of populist oligarchy, grips the political leadership in smaller jurisdictions across the nation. There is no mystery here. Strongly held opinions easily devolve into imposed dogma when there is no counterforce strong enough to check that trend. Since so much of popular sentiment concerning democracy is fixated on majority rule, minority rights are frequently ignored or even denied. That this is not a new phenomenon is clear from examining nineteenth-century history.

The founders, armed with the memories of the population at large still fresh from religious persecution, crafted a Constitution and Bill of Rights that assumed free conscience to be a natural right requiring government guarantees of freedom. Nevertheless, there was ample evidence of persecution in the name of religion in the nineteenth century. This was true even after the last state, Massachusetts, abandoned its religious establishment in 1833. Justice Joseph Story (1811–1845) was no less vigorous in support of the United States as a Christian nation than large numbers of Protestant clergy. In a fairly homogeneous environment, a degree of tolerance among denominations allowed for the creation of a popular theology which presumed the unquestioned authority of the Bible and the attachment of this nation to the Christian cause. This of course did not prevent a century of persecution of Roman Catholics who, in turn, challenged and then toppled the Protestant era in American history.

In the past fifty years such dramatic changes have occurred in our national character that the old traditions have passed away into mild memory. New directions of thought and culture, combined with massive technological and communication revolutions, have frightened many Americans. The old fabric of social order is passing and blame is frequently more effective as an explanation than is reasoned analysis of the multitude of causes. Since one of those phenomena is the fading, but still active, myth of a homogeneous religion of the nation, it is natural to hear voices of doom in the land decrying the loss of a spiritual center, a moral compass, or a faith in a specific deity.

Blame quickly falls on institutions which espouse policies that seem somehow to fly in the face of moral rectitude. Thus, when the Supreme Court carefully assessed the intentions of the founders and the content of the First Amendment, thereby stating a national policy preventing officially sponsored prayer and Bible reading in the public schools, it became a natural target for local political majorities in the process of losing their grip.

Third, the notion of majoritarianism, still functional in smaller political jurisdictions, challenged by a national trend of a different type, has spawned bitter recriminations over the school prayer issue. On occasion this has taken the form of accusations against intruders from outside, such as Lisa Herdahl and Rachel Bauchman. In other circumstances, where the disruption of majoritarianism comes from natives of the area, attacks are made on those disloyal to their heritage, traitors to the culture they once supported.

History One Last Time

We know that until 1940 public school students were subjected to sanctioned prayer and religion courses with no avenue of defense save through state constitutions and courts.

In the nineteenth century public schools were considered to be de facto Protestant enclaves. Most historians argue that by the year 1850 free public primary and secondary schools were available to most children. Generally the earliest schools reflected the religious hegemony of Protestantism in the United States, a condition that was soon to be challenged by thousands of immigrants from Ireland and southern Europe, the majority of whom were Roman Catholic. In 1844, riding on anti-immigrant sentiment in Philadelphia, persons with an anti-Catholic bias organized to fight a concession by public schools to Roman Catholic requests that children of their faith be allowed to use the Douay Bible, the accepted Catholic translation. One child was killed and two Catholic churches were burned down. This anti-Catholic sentiment was a direct result of a confrontation about the proper use of the Bible in the public schools. The Bible became the catalyst for destruction and killing. The "Word of God" became a weapon in a war among Christians that was evident across the northeast.

By the 1930s the rhetoric had cooled and the reality of a powerful Catholic minority had a certain conditioning impact upon Protestant claims. Discrimination against Jewish citizens became more subtle but no less real. As a boy growing up in Richmond, Virginia, in the 1930s

I recall my experiences in a middle-class neighborhood quite vividly. The relatively few Jewish families in the city at that time tended to congregate in blocks along certain streets. That was equally true of Roman Catholic families. However, this did not create segregated neighborhoods in the way in which race clearly did in those days. Most of my Jewish friends went to the local public school and tolerated the Protestant cultural control of the classrooms. My Catholic friends were, for the most part, enrolled in a parochial school nearby.

A large majority of Protestant ministers assumed they possessed the right to impose their religious perceptions on the public school curriculum because it was really "their" country first. The Virginia Council for Religious Education, all Protestant, never doubted its right to create religion classes for the schools, taught by devout church members. This was not fundamentalism as it is now defined, but it presumed no less certainly that this was a Protestant nation. The elementary school religion classes did not seek to convert, merely to confirm the faith of the overwhelming majority of the local population. Insensitive and arrogant, Protestant leadership encouraged genteel anti-Semitism. In those days, for most citizens, the notion of other religions and nonreligion having perceptible presence in the community was close to nonexistent.

White political and religious leaders created and maintained a totally segregated society along racial lines. Staffed by dedicated and gifted teachers, those schools created for black citizens were underfunded and ignored by the power structure. While, for many communities, Protestant and Catholic enclaves of power have disappeared, nevertheless, memories of that past, real or imagined, still grip much of the nation's population. Those "good old days" are all too often romanticized and become an antidote to an unknown future. We have examined in this book some of the more egregious examples of the impact of that nostalgic way of thought, a pattern of thinking that threatens the very future that rightfully belongs to our children. The persons we have met who speak glibly of the power of the majority seem terribly frightened of the present and abnormally fearful for the future. Religious extremism has fueled that fear while generating a longing for what never was—a Christian nation.

Over and over again prayer and other forms of religious ritual have become, since 1980, the excuse for outrageous behavior in the name of

God. Every time one of the horror stories described in this book is recounted to a broader public many who adhere to the Christian Coalition publicly deplore such malice. They always end, however, by noting that this is the exception, not the rule. And they quickly return to advocating local actions that defy the Supreme Court. Based on my research, I am convinced that the level of local harassment of persons who appeal to the religion clauses for protection is on the rise. Charged with the notion that Washington is the seat of evil and godlessness and statism, defiance of the Supreme Court is a natural result. And that translates into "siege mentality."

Lisa Herdahl has won her suit and, if necessary, her family will be protected by U.S. Marshals from threatened bodily harm and violations of the children's rights in the school. But the persecution will not abate. Sadly, those hundreds who crowded Oxford, Mississippi, streets on March 4, 1996, will not likely cease in the face of reason and law. The level of their anger will likely rise higher and defiance will spread to other communities facing similar challenges.

Lillian Gobitis recently stated, "It has been more than fifty years since I took a stand on the flag salute, but I would do it again in a second. . . . They persecuted me, and they will persecute you also."[1]

The common thread in the case histories we have examined in the previous chapters is an abuse of students who differ in religion and/or culture from the prevailing majority. Proclaiming the glory of their deity and the justness of their cause, the majority of self-righteous persons have employed prayer and the Bible as weapons against fellow citizens who take exception to the majority opinion.

Late in the eighteenth century an enlightened group of gifted statesmen set forth a "more perfect union" which removed from the purview of the government all the doctrinal preachments which had so torn the fabric of European society in previous decades and centuries. But the Protestant majority in the several states held firmly to many of those prejudices which, of course, were exacerbated by an equally doctrinaire Roman Catholic system. Now, in the United States, two centuries later, the Catholic-Protestant conflict is largely memory. American political leaders are active in the amelioration of religious conflicts in Northern Ireland and Bosnia. But, sadly, as a more and more religiously diverse population emerges here at home, we see signs of new tensions respecting Muslim, Hindu, and Buddhist citizens. If we look to our constitutional heritage, the answers exist to avoid repetition of the meanness and anger so vividly exhibited in Salem, Massachusetts; Danbury, Connecticut; Culpeper, Virginia; Philadelphia, Pennsylvania; Little Axe, Oklahoma; and Ecru, Mississippi. History makes it clear that the only genuine answer to religious discrimination is the removal of religion from the "cognizance" of the civil government. If, in fact, the United States is learning that lesson, it is sinking in ever so slowly.

Following World War II there was no serious religious fracture in the nation which pitted Christian against Christian, and there is little real evidence that politicians were hunted down and destroyed by action groups using religious dogma as a litmus test. Even as late as the 1962 *Engel* decision, which certainly caused an enormous uproar against the Supreme Court, a strong voice of reason from the mainline Protestant churches and the Jewish communities, coupled with able support from leading Roman Catholic public figures, seemed finally to be turning the corner on the old patterns of religious divisiveness.

But that was not to be. In 1981 a "search and destroy" mission was launched by the Moral Majority against members of Congress who failed the test of real Americanism. Remember "America, love it or leave it?" The slogan was given religious content as politics became for the Moral Majority a series of loyalty tests. And how did the Religious Right know they were correct? We are told by its leaders that God acted in the historical continuum to manifest his allegiance to the burgeoning Christian Coalition.

Our founders provided us with a remarkable gift in a Constitution which excluded religion from its domain. Operating on that principle religious institutions succeeded in making this nation the most religiously diverse populations on the globe. For over two hundred years that "wall of separation" has served well in maintaining the integrity of our democracy.

The framers of the Constitution did not exclude God from the language of the document.[2] They excluded religious doctrine, dogma, and exclusivism from its cognizance. They intended to place agnostics, deists, theists, and atheists on equal footing and assumed that the document they drafted was a result of political sagacity, not divine guidance. Any citizen can believe otherwise, protected in full by the guarantee of free exercise, reason notwithstanding. But skewed theories concerning the religion clauses, based on some notion of a holy nation, simply will not stand in the face of rational analysis by the Supreme Court and historical scholarship. The Constitution does not allow it. Ralph Reed, the executive director of the Christian Coalition, knows this. That is precisely why he and his group want to alter the seminal document known as the First Amendment. It is because they *know* it rejects their position.

From the case of Gobitis to that of Herdahl is a road littered with angry and vicious attacks on citizens who had the courage of their convictions. Too often those horrendous experiences in the formative years of childhood have been lost in history lessons and constitutional arguments. And while those horrors could never have been remedied without history and the Constitution, we ignore this human side of the struggle to implement the First Amendment at our peril. I am confident that James Madison would be alarmed at current experiments on the liberties of courageous citizens who have been at the vanguard in protecting our freedom. By the same token he would surely be pleased by this courageous group of teenagers and their siblings who, by taking alarm and acting on their convictions, made a phenomenal difference both locally and nationally.

To reiterate, the details of the cases just reviewed tell a consistent story of harassment and intimidation carried out in the name of prayer and religious rectitude. The Bible and prayer have been employed to threaten and cajole citizens seeking redress from grievances having to do with state-sponsored religion. The query by *USA Today* reporter Barbara Reynolds rings sadly in our ears: "How can Christians have such evil ways?" A devout Mormon in Idaho absorbed the horrors of Rexburg (in which the anonymous litigants were viciously attacked in the local newspaper) and commented, "We scare me." Much of the solution to our problem lies in persuading those dedicated believers belonging to the Religious Right to come to terms with their own history, particularly the Baptists, whose forebears insisted that righteousness gives no one the right to impose upon others one's own definitions. One of my kindest friends is as religiously conservative as any dedicated fundamentalist, but Baptist minister Henry Lankford has always defended anyone's right to explore ultimate questions with a totally unfettered conscience. He believes with Roger Williams that any effort by the government to prescribe faith should be rejected by persons of faith. He knows that prayer in public schools is not only unconstitutional, it is a sham perpetrated by people who value appearance over substance.

It is obvious from what we have learned about prayer as a rallying cry for violence that it is a national disease. From the horrors faced by Jehovah's Witnesses in 1940 to the threats aimed at the "Doe" family in Rexburg, Idaho, in 1996, we have a panorama of egregious behavior in the name of God.

Our founders knew well the sickness inherent in European religious wars and terrorism of the sixteenth and seventeenth centuries, which is to say this is not a new phenomenon. We've been there and done that until we should be sated with it. Yet it continues. Religion in the service of violence and bigotry stained our nation in the nineteenth century with claims of God-given superiority of white citizens. And who promoted that theme most effectively? It was the clergy who used the Bible to "prove" racial inferiority.[3]

It is incumbent upon citizens to insist that political discourse not be reduced to exchanges of religious credentials, as some commentators would wish. The creation of genuine dialogue concerning religion and government is a daunting task. As an example, the Tennessee Senate, in February 1996, by a vote of 27 to 1, endorsed the Ten Commandments and urged all citizens to observe them and post them in schools and churches. Senator Roscoe Dixon, a Memphis Democrat, voted with the majority even as he remarked, "This is a political issue. I wish we could debate this on its merits and not have to think about what's going to be in the paper tomorrow. . . . But I don't have time to explain to 150,000 constituents about how this is America and this was about choice. I'm not going to get into a fight with those right-wingers."[4] So he compromised his convictions for lack of time to convince his constituents otherwise. We have to find that time and create that debate.

The Christian Coalition has every right and responsibility to enter the political arena, but its self-righteous denunciation of those who differ with them on moral issues does not automatically translate into "We are right and they are wrong." Saying one is religious, parading one's faith in the limelight, is proof neither of correctness nor of sincerity. And it is past understanding why self-styled biblical literalists wish to force our children into public prayer in the face of the words attributed to Jesus: "But thou, when thou prayest, enter into thy closet, and when thou hast shut thy door, pray to thy Father which is in secret" (Matt. 6:6a). Interestingly, in the context of that statement Jesus presents a model of what to pray in secret: "The Lord's Prayer."

Is it possible to effect a rational discourse on the subjects addressed above? The answer is assuredly yes. But it will require full disclosure of the mischief and persecution that have been nationwide phenomena since 1940. For every case we have examined, there are hundreds of other communities that have experienced similar conflict surrounding efforts to establish religion in public schools. It is past time to observe that even if we did not have a First Amendment, the damage generated by majority tyranny in matters of conscience is sufficient alone to say emphatically, desist! But we do have the religion clauses, so we may combine constitutional principles, history, and current experience as we call for genuine implementation of "total separation of the Church from the State."[5] In his remarks before the Virginia Constitution Ratification Convention in 1788, James Madison gave us a blueprint: "There is not a shadow of right in the general government to intermeddle with religion. Its least interference with it would be a most flagrant usurpation." But this issue is not only about government "intermeddling." Madison also remarked, "Strongly guarded as is the separation of Religion & Govt in the Constitution of the United States, the danger of encroachment by Ecclesiastical Bodies may be illustrated by precedents already furnished in their short history."[6]

Armed with information and reasonableness it *is* possible to "explain to 150,000 constituents about how this is America." In so doing we would need to consider a method of explanation consistent with John Marshall's description of James Madison as a person not so much concerned with persuading his opponents, but with convincing them. With the goal of convincing, citizens should take a discussion to the public square supporting the separation of religious institutions from the state as the most effective and secure way to preserve the richness, diversity, freedom, and integrity of each and all.

Notes

1. Lillian Gobitis, "Here Comes Jehovah," in Peter Irons, *The Courage of Their Convictions,* p. 35.

2. See Isaac Framnick and R. Laurence Moore, *The Godless Constitution* (New York: W. W. Norton, 1996).

3. See H. Shelton Smith, *In His Image, But . . .* (Durham: Duke University Press, 1972).

4. In the Supreme Court decision in *Stone* v. *Graham* 449 US 39 (1980) a Kentucky statute requiring the posting of a copy of the Ten Commandments, purchased with private contributions, on the wall of each public classroom in the state was declared unconstitutional. In spite of that fact, and defying the Tennessee attorney general's opinion, the State Senate on February 21, 1996, "passed a resolution urging all Tennesseans to observe the Ten Commandments, teach them to their children, and post them at home, at work, in schools and places of worship. The Senate rejected an amendment that would have exempted from the measure non-Christian and non-Jewish temples and mosques. . . . The vote was 27-1." See "Laugh's on Us," *Memphis Commercial Appeal*, 23 February 1996, pp. 8A and 1B.

5. James Madison letter to Robert Walsh, March 2, 1819, included in Gaillard Hunt, ed., *The Writings of James Madison,* vol. 9 (New York: Putnam, 1910), pp. 1–13.

6. James Madison, "Detached Memoranda," Elizabeth Fleet, ed., *William & Mary Quarterly* 3 (October 1946): 534–67.

Appendix A

Decided: *Herdahl v. Pontotoc County School District*

LISA HERDAHL, on behalf of herself and her minor, school-age children, Plaintiff v. PONTOTOC COUNTY SCHOOL DISTRICT; PONTOTOC COUNTY BOARD OF EDUCATION
UNITED STATES DISTRICT COURT FOR THE NORTHERN DISTRICT OF MISSISSIPPI, WESTERN DIVISION
1996 U.S. Dist. LEXIS 7671
June 3, 1996, Decided

OPINION BY: NEAL B. BIGGERS, JR.

. . . A bench trial was held on March 4–6, 1996. The claims that remain for review by the court are: (1) the school-wide intercom prayer and devotionals; (2) the new pre-school activities of the Aletheia [*sic*] Club as to grades K-6; (3) classroom prayer prior to lunch in grades K-6; (4) the current teaching method of the Bible class; and (5) the alleged injection of religious materials in American History class. Upon due consideration of the issues presented, the evidence produced at both hearings, the exhibits and arguments submitted by the parties, the court is prepared to rule.

Discussion

The court is once again confronted with a conflict between the goals of two divergent but well-meaning groups. At issue is the meaning each wants to ascribe to the Establishment Clause. "Neither a state nor the Federal Government can, openly or secretly, participate in the affairs of any religious organizations or groups and vice versa. In the words of Jefferson, the clause against establishment of religion by law was intended to erect 'a wall of separation between Church and State.' " The founding fathers believed that this clause would guard against the abuses of government and the abuses that might be committed by the community itself.

The District's witnesses testified that the school prayers should continue because a majority of the students and parents are in favor of the practice and Mrs. Herdahl is the only person who opposes the practice; however, the Bill of Rights was created to protect the minority from tyranny by the majority. Indeed, without the benefit of such a document, women in this country have been burned because the majority of their townspeople believed their religious practices were contrary to the tenets of fundamentalist Christianity.[*] To say that the majority should prevail simply because of its numbers is to forget the purpose of the Bill of Rights. It is not insignificant that the opening line of our enumeration of individual rights reads "Congress shall make no law respecting an establishment of religion . . ." Of course, that amendment has been interpreted by the Supreme Court to prohibit not only Congress but also the states and their subdivisions, such as counties and school districts, from inserting themselves into religious practices. The court is now called upon to give effect to the words of the Constitution as they relate to the practices of a public school in Pontotoc County, Mississippi, in accordance with the opinions previously issued by the United States Court of Appeals for the Fifth Circuit and the Supreme Court of this land.

---

*Judge Biggers is here referring to the burning of witches in colonial Salem, Massachusetts.

I. Intercom Prayer

. . . At the preliminary injunction hearing, this court held that the plaintiff established that there was a substantial likelihood of prevailing on the merits of this issue, and a violation of the Establishment Clause was clearly evident. The District did not appeal the ruling at the preliminary injunction stage; however, it is still the District's position that it has created a "limited open forum" as described in the Equal Access Act ("Act"). The Act prohibits public secondary schools that receive federal financial assistance and that maintain a "limited open forum" from denying equal access to "students who wish to conduct a meeting within that limited open forum." By permitting student clubs or organizations the right to request and use the public address system for a brief moment for announcements or such other appropriate use following the official morning announcements, the District contends that it cannot now discriminate against the Aletheia [*sic*] Club on the religious content of the club's message. This argument was analyzed by this court in its April 18, 1995 opinion and found to be unpersuasive. At trial, the court permitted the defendants to present evidence of their forum theory. Accordingly, the defendants have introduced evidence that other student clubs and organizations frequently utilize the intercom system for making announcements, such as fund raisers, pep rallies, yearbook sales, and election results. Furthermore, they have attempted to introduce evidence of student use of the intercom as a vehicle for their free expressions beyond mere announcements; however, the evidence nevertheless shows that, excluding the Aletheia [*sic*] Club, the intercom was used only for announcements of club activities, including announcements to encourage students to participate in activities, and not for the actual conduct of substantive club activities themselves. For example, the yearbook staff has made announcements over the intercom that it will meet at designated times and places, but it has not conducted the substance of its meeting over the intercom. The Aletheia [*sic*] Club, however, has not only announced the times and places of its meetings over the intercom, it also has said the prayers and read the devotionals that it gives in its meetings. That is a significant distinction that the defendants have refused to recognize, or at least admit.

The defendants' arguments notwithstanding, it is evident to the court that the Equal Access Act is not applicable to the practices of the District and the Aletheia [*sic*] Club. First, the Act applies only to secondary schools, while it is undisputed that the intercom prayers were broadcast into all the classrooms at the Center, a K–12 school. Moreover, the Act applies by its terms only to voluntary meetings of secondary school clubs.

. . . The court therefore concludes that the broadcast of religious messages over the public address system is not a "meeting" under the definition provided in the Act or as contemplated in the legislative history. It is not the type of activity in which student clubs at the Center are already permitted to engage in. Other student clubs are not permitted to conduct their club business during the morning announcements and in fact are only permitted to meet during the activity period set aside during the school day or after school. Only announcements of school or student activities are permitted with the sole exception of the Aletheia [*sic*] Club's practices. This special accommodation of the Aletheia [*sic*] Club for its admittedly religious messages is clearly prohibited by the Establishment Clause, and not authorized by the Equal Access Act.

Although the student members of the Aletheia [*sic*] Club expressed their views voluntarily, the students to whom these views were broadcast did not voluntarily choose to be there; rather, they were there under the mandate of law. Prior to the injunction previously issued herein, the Aletheia [*sic*] Club apparently considered all the school classrooms its meeting place. Such practices over a school intercom broadcast to captive audiences of students are clearly not meetings and are not "voluntary in the truest sense of the word." Indeed, Superintendent Horton conceded during his trial testimony that the activities of the Aletheia [*sic*] Club were not meetings, and it is obvious that those practices go beyond mere announcements of the club's activities. Activities which are voluntary both for those who initiate them and those who participate in them are the activities which Congress envisioned protecting under the Act. Thus, the District's reliance on the Act as a defense to these intercom prayers is misplaced.

Additionally, the following stipulation was accepted by the court in the pretrial order: "During the morning announcement period, students sometimes made announcements over the school intercom of school and student activities, such as when senior yearbook sales would begin or when a particular club would be meeting next. . . . There is no evidence of student use of the school intercom during the morning announcement period other than for announcements of school and student activities as set forth above and the broadcast of prayers and morning devotionals."

Clearly then, the District's reliance on its policy of providing a brief moment for wide-open discussion of any free speech comments by the student body is belied by this stipulation. . . . In fact, the only club that has been provided the opportunity to actually espouse its beliefs over the intercom is the Aletheia [*sic*] Club. Thus, while the District may have a valid argument that it has created a forum to permit announcements of school and student activities, the evidence clearly shows and indeed the District stipulates that it is not maintaining a soapbox for the religious, social, or political expressions of members of the student body who want to preach, teach, or politicize over the intercom system.

The case law in this country has consistently recognized that the conduct of such morning devotionals broadcast by students over a school intercom system is an unconstitutional practice. As a matter of law, even if the defendants established a limited open forum for student speech over the intercom, devotionals and sectarian prayer broadcast over the public school loudspeaker would still violate the First Amendment. As the Supreme Court noted in *Schempp,* it is the act of turning over the "machinery of the State" to the students in the religious majority to broadcast their religion which violates the Constitution, and that act cannot be justified as accommodating the First Amendment rights of the students who wish to do so. The defendants cannot "sanitize an endorsement of religion forbidden under the Establishment Clause by also sponsoring nonreligious speech" in the "coercive context of public schools." The preliminary injunction opinion will therefore be adopted in all relevant respects and a permanent injunction will issue.

II. Pre-School Activities

Since the court's injunction, the Aletheia [*sic*] Club has been conducting its morning prayers and devotionals starting at 7:50 A.M. in the high school gymnasium. The students in grades 7–12 who wish to participate in the morning prayer and scripture reading go to the gym. At 7:58 A.M. a bell signifies the impending commencement of the school day. Students then have three minutes before the final bell rings at 8:01 A.M. to arrive in their homeroom class. The plaintiff does not object to this practice as it relates to grades 7-12. The students in grades K–6 are also allowed to participate in the Aletheia [*sic*] Club's morning activities on the condition that they furnish written parental requests for them to do so. . . . Because of the large turnout for these activities, the Center allowed students in grades K–3 to go to a separate activity room where members of the Aletheia [*sic*] Club would administer the same devotional that was given in the gym. Students in grades 4–6 were permitted to attend the activities with grades 7–12 in the main gym. The plaintiff objects to the participation of grades K–6 in any morning religious activity period on the basis of the age and impressionability of the children. (See *Bell* v. *Little Axe Indep. Sch. Dist.,* . . . holding that requirement of teacher supervision at religious meetings in elementary school would create impression of state sponsorship).

It had been generally held that mere teacher supervision necessarily leads to interference with or advocacy of religious activities and thus ran afoul of the Establishment Clause. . . .

The court is of the opinion that this delicate situation is resolved in favor of the current practice based on the informed written consent of the individual child's parents. Without question, parents possess the inherent right to control the religious upbringing of their children. The Court explained "that the parental right to guide one's child intellectually and religiously is a most substantial part of the liberty and freedom of the parent." Having the authority to act in the stead of the child, a parent's maturity and ability to discern the difference between faculty supervision and implicit endorsement of the religious ideals expressed at the meeting is imputed to the child. Through parental consent, the elementary children are on equal footing with secondary school students, who the Supreme Court has held are mature enough to differentiate between sponsorship and mere custodial oversight. Furthermore, the court finds that no imprimatur of state involvement is exhibited in this practice as it relates to the non-participating students. The risk of the appearance of improper state involvement is significantly diminished in an opt-in type of situation as exists here, as opposed to an opt-out situation in the classroom prayer practices. Students who wish to participate in the pre-school devotionals actively seek out involvement in the religious activity without burdening those who do not. Moreover, the compulsory attendance laws that have driven many courts to find subtle coercive pressures do not operate prior to the commencement of the school day. Therefore, students who are present before the school day begins are not compelled to be there and do so of their own free will. Without such a determination, there would be a per se rule against the participation of elementary students in any organized religious activities based solely on the required custodial oversight of the children.

Accordingly, the court finds that the current practices of the Aletheia [*sic*] Club for all grades prior to school should be permitted to continue. The court therefore modifies the preliminary injunction opinion . . . to reflect the current changes. Additionally, the court notes that in this present practice teachers are not permitted to participate in the religious meetings.

III. Classroom Prayer

The issue of organized classroom prayer in elementary classrooms at the Center prior to lunch was also dealt with in the preliminary injunction. As Superintendent Horton testified, subject to the discretion of individual teachers and classes, such prayer was authorized to be led by students prior to the preliminary injunction. Until this court's order, such prayer was facilitated directly by elementary teachers. For example, kindergarten teacher Suzanne Montgomery testified that she designated one child each day as a "blessing sayer-helper" to lead the pre-lunch prayer. In January 1995, Principal Flowers instructed teachers concerning the "Blessing for Lunch," directing them specifically to tell students that they could conduct "the lunch blessing" in the classroom before the class left for lunch and the teachers were to separate out non-participating students by having them "step out in the hallway with [the teacher]."

This conduct clearly violates the dictates of the Establishment Clause. Organized prayer in the classroom, where students have no choice but to participate or to conspicuously "step out in the hallway," is unconstitutional whether led by students or teachers. . . . By informing students of the appropriate time to conduct a lunch blessing, the state is facilitating this prayer. The courts have clearly ruled that inviting or encouraging students to pray violates the First Amendment. . . . The defendants' practice in directing teachers to pause before the class leaves for lunch, to specifically announce and provide an opportunity for vocal group prayer, and to separate out in the hallways those who do not wish to pray is patently contrary to the separation of church and state. Nothing herein interferes in any way in each student's right to individually pray at the lunch table in the cafeteria, or to individually pray silently at any other time.

IV. Bible Class

For the past fifty years, a committee in Pontotoc County comprised of members from some of the local Protestant churches and commonly referred to as "the Bible Committee" has sponsored classes in which the Bible has been taught in the local public schools. Under this program, the Bible Committee hires teachers who are allowed by the District to conduct classes on school property during normal school hours. The Bible teachers have no employment contracts with the District, and are the only teachers working in the school district who are not paid by the District. The District maintains that it has supervisory authority over the teachers. The District provides classroom space at the Center for the Bible class in all grades in which it is taught, as well as related materials such as bookshelves. In addition, the District provides public funds to the Bible teachers to be used for the purchase of books, supplies, and other materials to be used in the course, and such funds have been expended for such purpose.

Previous to the 1993–1994 school year, a course simply known as "Bible" was offered to the students at the Center. Prior to the plaintiff's enrollment of her children in the local public school, the Mississippi State Department of Education ("MSDE") rejected the "Bible" class as an approved accredited curriculum at the Center. In an effort to "preserve the integrity and essence of what they had been teaching already," the Bible Committee developed a new curriculum entitled "A Biblical History of the Middle East." The Committee submitted a three-year pilot program for approval by the MSDE, which was granted. The Center began offering the approved curriculum for the 1993–1994 school year. This same curriculum is the basis for teaching the participating grades at the Center, with the obvious exception that the teaching methods are adjusted to the level of the age group being taught.

In the elementary grades at the Center (K–6), the course is taught as a "rotational class," alternating once every four days with music, library, and physical education. The Bible teachers come into the students' regular classrooms and replace the regular teachers, who generally leave the rooms. Although the other rotational classes are required classes, the District has made an exception for the Bible class. Students who do not wish to participate are excused and may get up in front of their classmates and leave the classroom. During this period, the only alternative instruction for them is to be sent to another rotational class for their grade, which merely duplicates a rotational class they have already taken or will take, so that the children end up taking the same class twice. The plaintiff's children who are subject to the District's rotational class program are now excused from participating in the Bible class and are escorted to and from another rotational class by the teacher or assistant. The plaintiff claims that being singled out in this manner has exposed and continues to expose her children to harassment and ridicule, and they have been accused of being atheists and devil worshippers.

The Bible class taught in the high school grades (9–12) is open to any student as a one-hour elective. Kevin Engle[*] is the plaintiff's only child old enough and therefore eligible to attend the high school Bible class. Engle has not attended this class and indicated that he has no plans to do so in the future.

The issue currently before the court is not whether it is appropriate for public schools to teach the Bible, rather, it is the method of that instruction that is in question. Both parties agree that the study of the Bible in public schools is not per se unconstitutional. . . . [See] *Schempp,* 374 U.S. at 225 (1963).

The District does not contend that its practice of allowing private organizations to operate and fund a course involving the teaching of the Bible serves to free the District from the constraints placed upon it by the Constitution. Indeed, such a position could not be supported. . . . Instead, the defendants argue that the course is taught from a "his-

---

*"Engle" is Lisa Herdahl's maiden name. Kevin was given that name when Lisa divorced her first husband.

torical and literary perspective, in a non-sectarian, non-proselytizing manner, for the primary purpose of educating students with regard to important historical figures, historical events, and literary contributions, during this time period in world history, and the relationship of such events, persons, literary contributions to future civilizations." Thus, the court is faced with the constitutional question of not that the Bible is taught, but the selectivity, emphasis, objectivity, and interpretive manner, or lack thereof, with which the Bible is taught. . . .

A. The Lemon Test

. . . Under Lemon, a government practice is constitutional if (1) it has a secular purpose, (2) its primary effect neither advances nor inhibits religion, and (3) it does not excessively entangle government with religion. The court finds that the Bible class in its current form not only fails one prong—enough to render it unconstitutional—it fails all three prongs of the test. Each prong is examined below.

1. Secular Purpose Prong

The Bible class clearly lacks a secular purpose. From its inception by the local Protestant churches, the aim of the instruction has been overtly religious in nature. The District's profession of educational instruction in this relevant time period of world history is belied by the evidence presented to the court at trial. First, the fact that the District contracted out the teaching of this class indicates an attempt at avoiding the constitutional ramifications of this instruction. If the class were truly secular, there should be no necessity of disassociating itself (and thus the state) with such a practice. The District cannot accomplish through others what it is forbidden to establish itself. Second, the selection procedures for the Bible teachers indicate a religious agenda unquestioned by the District. As the acknowledged "sponsor" of the Bible classes, the Bible Committee seeks out prospective Bible teachers for the public schools, interviews and then selects them, using religious criteria that have resulted in a teaching staff of Christian teachers who teach the Bible, and are expected to teach the Bible, from a fundamentalist religious perspective as the inerrant word of God.

When a Bible teaching vacancy occurs, it is the Bible Committee, not the school district, that initiates the hiring process, and it does so not by an open job search or through advertisements, but by personally soliciting names of potential teachers from the present and former Bible teachers. The District is well aware of this religious testing, and has to date not turned away any selected Bible teacher. Prospective Bible teachers are interviewed by the Bible Committee, and their religious beliefs and "salvation experience" of the candidates and their "personal spiritual background [and] beliefs about the Bible" are routine topics during job interviews. The chairman of the Bible Committee, Mr. Olen White, stated at trial that he personally believed that it was important for the prospective teacher to consider the Bible as literally true. It is also his understanding that the teachers who are currently teaching the Bible class at the Center are teaching their classes from the perspective that the Bible is literally true and without error. . . . Reverend William Sims, a pastor of a local church and member of the Bible Committee, testified that he expects that a teacher of a Bible course would teach the Bible as the inerrant word of God. He further stated that if it came to his attention that one of the Bible teachers was teaching the Bible as if it were capable of error or that one of the teachers was not of the Christian faith he would not want the Committee to continue to fund that person's salary. This religious testing, plainly imposed on prospective Bible teachers, alone makes the practice an unlawful intrusion into the school curriculum.

For over ten years the high school Bible class was taught by Pastor Larry Dean Patterson, including the first year of the pilot program. . . .

It is Patterson's belief that the Committee would not consider hiring a Jew or a Muslim for the teaching position because they would not be teaching the Bible from the "perspective that the people in Pontotoc understand the Bible." That perspective, and the perspective that the Committee expected to be taught was the fundamentalist Christian perspective. This, according to Patterson, was the reason for having the Bible class in the first place. Indeed, according to Patterson, without this interpretation one can "miss the whole purpose of the Bible." The court does not have to analyze the testimony in great depth to conclude that the predominant purpose of Patterson's instruction was to espouse to his students the tenets of Christian fundamentalist views.

According to Pastor Patterson, the Bible classes were taught using the Bible as "a historical text," meaning he taught it "as events that actually happened," e.g., teaching Genesis as "actual literal history." Furthermore, Patterson testified that he believes the Bible to be the inerrant, revealed and inspired word of God. He tells his students of his personal belief and, most significantly, he testified that he taught the Bible in accordance with this belief. Significantly, the Bible is the only text used in his course and only tests that are given are based solely on the content thereof. The primary version used is the King James version, commonly accepted as a Protestant translation of the Bible. Neither the Catholic Bible nor the Jewish Bible have been used.

Other indicia of the religious purpose of the course is evidenced by the reasons for continuing the course for the 1993–1994 school year. When the MSDE dropped the accreditation for the Bible class, the teachers and the Committee were concerned that the number of students who would wish to participate in the class would significantly decrease because they would not receive credit for it. The response was to establish a pilot program so that, in the words of Pastor Patterson, they could "preserve the integrity and essence of what they had been teaching already." Despite its new name, there is no indication that the "Biblical History of the Middle East" class was any different than the course that was previously dropped. In fact, Patterson explained that there were virtually no changes from the methods or subjects taught in the new pilot course. The fact that the teachers were teaching the same course that was disapproved by the MSDE indicates a motive by the sponsors of the program to continue to impart religious doctrine to the students at the Center, and raises the question of how many years the MSDE would allow a District to continue teaching an obviously illegal course by merely changing the name and proposed teaching method but not the substance or actual teaching of the course.

This "business as usual" practice by the Bible teachers in the District did later meet with criticism but no action when the MSDE sent a social studies expert to observe the classes. Joann Prewitt observed several classes taught at other area schools by Patterson and [Mike] Thompson during the first two years of the pilot program. . . . Prewitt testified in deposition that what she observed being taught was religious Bible instruction presented from a Christian perspective, not the objective teaching of a secular social studies course. She explained that Pastor Patterson's class was "taught as a Bible class, not history," and similarly when she observed Thompson's class the next school year she noted that "from Mr. Thompson's class, tests and materials" that "he was teaching a religious class," not "a history class." According to Prewitt, the tests, lesson plans and student activities that she reviewed and observed "represented a Christian Biblical viewpoint and did not bring in to play . . . any other viewpoints from a different perspective." . . .

. . . The court is firmly persuaded by this and other evidence that the predominant purpose of the Bible class is not secular, rather, it is a part of a concerted effort by the religious sponsors of the class, fully condoned by the District, to inculcate students at North Pontotoc into the beliefs and moral code of fundamentalist Christianity—an admirable goal perhaps for some private citizens or for a private religious school, but a forbidden one for the government.

2. The Primary Effect Prong

As can be expected of a practice that is religious in nature and purpose, it is by no means accidental, and certainly not incidental, that the primary effect is that of advancing religion, and moreover, a particular sect of religion. The same evidence validates the conclusion that not only does the course have a religious purpose, that is also its primary effect. It therefore violates the second prong of Lemon. The testimony of the Bible teachers themselves, the lesson plans, exams and Bible class materials, as well as other evidence adduced at trial, all confirm that the Bible classes offered at the Center advance religion in general and, specifically, fundamentalist Christianity. It is not "presented objectively as part of a secular program of education." Mike Thompson, the current Bible teacher in the elementary and high school grades at the Center, uses *The Kids-Life Bible Storybook* to teach in grades K–2. . . .

After reading the Bible stories aloud, Thompson asks the children what he calls the "fact" questions at the end of each story, in addition to some of his own. These "fact" questions frequently concern the religious beliefs and theological lessons of the stories. For example, some of the questions have been: "Which day did God make the sun and the moon?" and "How did Jesus want us to treat our enemies?" Thompson also has the young children act out the Bible stories contained in the book. This practice cannot legitimately be contended to be of secular education. The stories and their titles are and contain proclamations of religious doctrine and plainly reveal the book's religious perspective. Indeed, the cover of the book proclaims that it will teach children "the truths of God's Word" and how to relate it "to everyday experiences." . . .

In grades 3–6, Thompson uses the King James Bible as the basis for the class. In direct contrast to regular secular subjects like math, there is no homework, testing, or grades given. In these classes, Thompson continues the tasks begun in kindergarten of repeatedly teaching the students the same events depicted in the Bible. Moreover, he adds other lesson plans that deal with the application of the Bible to daily life—a pastoral or religious task in itself. Similar to his method of instruction in grades K–2, Thompson's lesson plans for grades 3–6 are all identical for each grade and from the previous year's lessons. This repetition of the same course for four more consecutive years illustrates an intent to indoctrinate a specific philosophy or belief system into the students which is obviously fundamentalist Christianity.

Thompson further testified that he teaches the Bible not as a work of fiction, but as a historic record, i.e., as a record of what actually occurred in the past. When asked how he deals with the virgin birth and Jesus' miracles and the resurrection as historically viable events, Thompson stated, "We just study it as the Bible explains it: This event happened, this event happened, this event. We're teaching the historical account, so I want my students to understand the details of those events." This is inherently religious instruction, rather than objective, secular education, since much of the Bible is not capable of historic verification (such as divine creation, the "pre-existence" of Jesus, Jesus' miracles, and the resurrection), and can only be accepted as a matter of faith and religious belief. . . . To simply read the Bible without selectivity is to read a religious book and to teach the Bible literally without interpretation is to convey a religious message or teach a religious lesson.

The District's argument that the course can be saved (no pun intended) by prefacing each discussion of a biblical event with "The Bible says . . ." or noting that not everyone believes the Bible, is without persuasion. Even the defendant's experts agree that, insofar as the young elementary grades are concerned, that distinction is meaningless. . . . Furthermore, the daily teaching of the content of a book of religious proclamation does not become secular instruction merely by informing students that the content is only what the Bible says; indeed, for many students, that may well heighten the religious effect of the course.

Other evidence of the course's purpose and effect can be seen in the films shown by Thompson during 1994–1995. The film *The Evidence for Creation* is a clearly sectarian product designed to persuade the audience to accept the creationist's view. It consists in large measure of Bible verses and preaching. The defendants have not explained the relevance of creationism in a course that is supposedly a historical survey of the Middle East from 2000 [B.C.E.] to 100 [C.E.], nor can the court conceive of any reason why it would be relevant.

Likewise, *America's Godly Heritage* has no place in a history class focusing on the ancient Middle East. The significance of what the past 200 years of America's heritage has to do with 2,000-year-old cultures in the Middle East is lost on the court. The film teaches that "the United States was founded as a Christian nation" and that the current "moral and social crisis of America" are "due largely to the elimination of Christianity from the public sphere." While some or all of this film may be very true, the only implication the court can draw from the showing of this and other religious films to a class of students supposedly studying Middle East history is that the teachers are attempting to indoctrinate the students in their religious beliefs by claiming to teach Middle East history. This practice cannot be condoned in the context of a public school system. It is best left to the family and the church. . . .

3. The Entanglement Prong

The third and final prong of *Lemon* is also well represented in the case *sub judice*. Although a separate and distinct element of the test, many of the factors considered by the court above are applicable to the entanglement analysis. Suffice it to say that "if an evidently religious study course is taught on school grounds during regular school hours, the school is excessively entangled in it regardless of who teaches the class." Furthermore, the court cannot distinguish this case from the *McCollum* decision . . .

Thus, all three prongs of Lemon are violated and the Bible class fails constitutional muster.

B. The Endorsement Test

The government unconstitutionally endorses religion whenever it appears to "take a position on questions of religious belief," or makes adherence to a religion relevant in any way to a person's standing in the political community. This appearance is conveyed when the government implicates that religion is "favored," "preferred," or "promoted" over other beliefs. The District is clearly favoring religion over irreligion and preferring fundamentalist Christianity to the exclusion of all others.

C. The Coercion Test

The final test, and the Supreme Court's most recent attempt at analyzing Establishment Clause jurisprudence, was developed in *Lee* v. *Weisman*. In *Lee,* the Court expressly rejected invitations by many parties, including the United States, to abolish the *Lemon* test. Thus, *Lemon* remains in force. The Court, however, found the practice at issue violative of the Establishment Clause not through an analysis of *Lemon,* but through a finding of coercion. Although it appears clear that coercion is not a requirement to find a practice impermissible, if such a practice has coercive effects it would clearly violate the First Amendment. Thus, in *Lee* the Court did not need to consider *Lemon* because it found an even more egregious activity at work—the coercion of students.

The *Lee* Court noted that "there are heightened concerns with protecting freedom of conscience from subtle coercive pressure in the elementary and secondary public schools." In the elementary grades, the District has inserted into its rotational system a course which is manifestly religious in nature. The District has woven this course of study into a seamless transition from purely secular activities such as music or physical education, into a study of fundamentalist Christian doctrine. Thus, the plaintiff's young children are faced once a week with the difficult choice of conforming to the overwhelming majority's participation in the class or absenting themselves in protest. Furthermore, the lack of genuine alternative instruction elevates the coercive pressures placed on the plaintiff's children. As the Court in *Lee* stated, "we think the State may not, consistent with the Establishment Clause, place primary and secondary school children in this position."

The plaintiff urges the court to enjoin the District from allowing any teachers into the public schools who are recruited and paid by the Bible Committee of the several churches who have been funding the program. The court is disinclined to do so at this point. Although the court believes it will be very difficult for the course to be taught objectively and secularly by a teacher selected by a group which has traditionally selected teachers on the basis of their religious beliefs, both the plaintiff's expert and the defendants' expert testified that it was possible to teach an objective secular course of Middle East history if certain teaching outlines were followed. The defendants have, however, intentionally misled the MSDE by merely changing the name of its biblical history course but not the fundamentalist religious theme of the course in order to continue to receive state approval. It took the MSDE several years to react to that and disapprove the course, according to the school's witnesses at trial. The court declines to prohibit a church-paid teacher from teaching at this time on the assumption that the MSDE will be more aggressive in monitoring the course. Three years was obviously too long to allow a patently religious course to continue under the guise of a new name. The court also further assumes that the District will monitor the course closely and require any teacher to comply with the ruling herein, and that the District will satisfy itself that teachers it accepts have not been selected on the basis of a religious belief test and do not have an agenda to proselytize.

V. Religious Instruction in Classrooms

The final issue the court is called upon to review is the alleged proselytizing and airing of sectarian videotapes by eighth grade American History teacher Frank Cayson. As to any alleged proselytizing to his students, the District recognizes that such a practice, if occurring, would be unconstitutional and the District has instructed Cayson that he is not to preach or proselytize in his classroom. The District's policy against such practices is sufficient for the plaintiff. There being no cause of action against Cayson individually, the court will not comment further.

As to the District's authorization of certain videotapes to be shown to Cayson's students, the court finds that the videos are without question religious proclamation and cannot, in the context presently intended, be utilized constitutionally. At trial, Cayson testified that he shows the following videos: *The King Is Born, He Is Risen,* and *America's Godly Heritage.* According to Cayson, he shows the videotapes to explain the "real purpose" of the school holidays of Christmas and

Easter. He explains that many children believe they are dismissed from school in December because of exams or the pending arrival of Santa Claus and in April because of the Easter Bunny. Cayson states that by showing the films he is attempting to instruct his students on the "real" reason they are having the holiday—that is the "fact" that Jesus Christ was born and later died and was resurrected.

These practices obviously violate the neutrality that a public teacher is required to maintain toward religion, and constitute impermissible religious instruction and endorsement of religion by a public official which crosses the wall the Constitution erected between the scepter and the cross, and the defendants are directed to not allow any such activities by its teachers and to take swift and strong action if the District's policies are violated.

✤   ✤   ✤

. . . In accordance with the memorandum opinion this day issued, it is ORDERED:

That each of the defendants and anyone acting in concert with any of them are permanently ENJOINED AND RESTRAINED from (1) transmitting or authorizing the transmission of devotionals, including without limitation the recitation of Bible verses and/or prayers, over the school intercom system; (2) authorizing organized, vocal group prayers in classrooms during classroom hours at North Pontotoc; (3) authorizing the teaching of classes known as "Bible" or "A Biblical History of the Middle East," in their past or present form, in any grade; and (4) authorizing the showing of the videotapes *The King Is Born, He Is Risen,* and *America's Godly Heritage* during American History classes; and

That the defendants shall specifically direct all elementary teachers and other employees at North Pontotoc, and strictly enforce its directive, that they may not facilitate, participate in, endorse, encourage, invite, or sponsor classroom prayer by students, including but not limited to designating, facilitating or assisting in designating or enlisting individual students to lead vocal group prayer, delaying or slowing departure of students for the lunchroom to facilitate prayer, separating students who do and do not wish to engage in such prayer, or engaging in the conduct concerning the "Blessing for Lunch" contained in the instructions issued by defendant Flowers on or about January 3, 1995, . . . ; and

That if the Mississippi State Board of Education does give final approval to the new high school course "Biblical History of the Ancient Middle East," the defendants may offer that course in those grades (9–12), but the defendants and anyone acting in concert with them are permanently ENJOINED from teaching that or any other or successor course concerning the Bible or religion in any manner that is not consistent with this court's decision and the United States Constitution. This includes but is not limited to the following: (a) the course must be taught objectively as part of a secular program of education; (b) the course may not be taught using the Bible as the only source of historical fact or as if the Bible were actual literal history; (c) students must be assigned reading from non-biblical sources of ancient Middle East history; (d) the course may not teach religious doctrine or sectarian interpretation of the Bible; and (e) the District shall not accept an instructor for the Bible course who has been approved for employment based in whole or in part on a religious test, profession of faith, or criteria involving particular beliefs about the Bible in the selection process.

Appendix B

Decided: *ACLU* v. *Black Horse Pike Regional Board of Education*

The opposing decisions reached by the Fifth and Ninth Federal Circuit Courts have left uncertainly in the minds of Supreme Court observers respecting the ultimate resolution of the issues surrounding "student-initiated" prayers. In May 1996 the Third Circuit rendered an *en banc* opinion in *ACLU* v. *Black Horse Pike Regional Board of Education* that rejected the arguments and the decision in the Fifth Circuit *Clear Creek* case and endorsed the findings of the Ninth Circuit in the Harris case. If appealed, which is likely, it will provide the Supreme Court with an opportunity it evaded in the Harris and Clear Creek appeals. The request for the granting of certiorari may come as early as the fall of 1996. Pertinent sections of the *Black Horse* opinion are presented here.

THE AMERICAN CIVIL LIBERTIES UNION OF NEW JERSEY,
on behalf of its members; and Edward Ross v.
BLACK HORSE PIKE REGIONAL BOARD OF EDUCATION
United States Court of Appeals for the Third Circuit

May 24, 1996

We are asked to decide whether a policy adopted by the Black Horse Pike Regional Board of Education that allows a vote of the senior class to determine if prayer will be included in high school graduation ceremonies is constitutional. For the reasons that follow we hold that this policy is inconsistent with the First Amendment of the United States Constitution. Accordingly, we will affirm, but modify, the permanent injunction issued by the district court.

1. Factual Background

Two policies were presented to the Board at its May 23, 1993 meeting. One version (Version D) allowed graduating students to decide whether prayer would be included in the graduation ceremony as well as the nature of any such prayer. The other proposal would not have allowed "prayer" but would have allowed a "moment of reflection, during which pupils and parents [could] be asked to think silently about what has been and what is to come for each graduate." A group of students who had previously asked to address the Board on this issue attended the meeting and spoke in favor of Version D. At the conclusion of the meeting, the Board unanimously adopted Version D. That policy, as finally adopted, allowed the senior class officers to conduct a poll of the graduating class to determine whether seniors wanted "prayer, a moment of reflection, or nothing at all" to be included in their graduation ceremony. The policy was entitled, "Religion at Graduation Exercises," and the text began as follows:

> After reading recent decisions of the United States Supreme Court and interpretations of those decisions, the Board of Education concludes the long standing practice of conducting invocation and benediction prayer at graduation ceremonies and at other school functions is proper and legal under the following conditions:
> 1 The Board of Education, administration and staff of the schools shall not endorse, organize, or in any way promote prayer at school functions.
> 2. In the spirit of protected speech, the pupils in attendance must choose to have prayer conducted. Such prayer must be performed by a student volunteer and may not be conducted by a member of the clergy or staff.

The policy also allowed the students to decide how they would determine what form of prayer, if any, would be given at graduation, "so long as the process [was] conducted by duly elected class officers and the survey . . . provides pupils with an opportunity to choose prayer, a moment of reflection, or nothing at all." Version D further required that printed programs for the graduation include a disclaimer explaining that any presentation that may be given at commencement did not reflect the views of the School Board, the School District, administrators, staff, or other students.

11. Procedural History

On June 18, 1993, the ACLU and Edward Ross filed a Complaint in the District Court for the District of New Jersey, in which they asked the court to enjoin any student-led prayer at graduation. The Complaint alleged that the proposed prayer violated the First Amendment of the United States Constitution and Article I, Paragraph 4 of the New Jersey Constitution.

By Order entered June 24, 1993, the district court denied plaintiffs' request for a preliminary injunction. The court concluded that the proposed prayer was appropriate because it was given under circumstances that distinguished it from the prohibited prayer in *Lee* v. *Weisman*. The following day the plaintiffs filed an emergency appeal to this court where a two-judge panel reversed the district court and entered an order that stated in part:

> The graduation ceremony is a school-sponsored event; the fact that the school board has chosen to delegate the decision regarding one segment of the ceremony to the members of the graduating class does not alter that sponsorship, does not diminish the effect of a prayer on students who do not share the same or any religious perspective, and does not serve to distinguish, in any material way, the facts of this case from the facts of *Lee* v. *Weisman*: Now, therefore, . . . appellees, their agents and employees, and all those acting in concert with them are hereby enjoined from conducting a school sponsored graduation ceremony that includes a prayer whether it be an invocation, a benediction, or a prayer in any other form.

Thereafter, the School Board filed a motion in this court to vacate the preliminary injunction. That motion was denied. Additional motions were subsequently filed both in this court and in the United States Supreme Court. Finally, on March 29, 1994, the district court entered a final order, consistent with the aforementioned order of this court, reversing the court's previous denial of the preliminary injunction. The district court permanently enjoined the School Board from "conducting a school-sponsored graduation ceremony that included prayer, whether it be an invocation, a benediction or a prayer in any other form." On April 28, 1994, the School Board filed this appeal. The matter is now before this court *en banc.* . . .

IV. Discussion

A. The Free Speech Rights of Students

The Board relies upon the student referendum in an attempt to define the instant controversy as one impacting upon the students' right of free speech as opposed to a dispute over the constitutionality of prayer at a public high school graduation. Version D does state: "in the spirit of protected free speech, the pupils in attendance must choose to have prayer conducted." However, Version D allowed the 128 seniors who wanted verbal prayer at their graduation to impose their will upon 140 of their fellow classmates who did not. The Board's position would have us recognize a right in that plurality to do so, and ignore the right of others to worship in a different manner, or in no manner at all. This we cannot do because "the individual freedom of conscience protected by the First Amendment embraces the right to select any religious faith or none at all." . . . Therefore, the Board's emphasis on voting majorities is misplaced. "While in some societies the wishes of the majority might prevail, the Establishment Clause of the First Amendment is addressed to this contingency and rejects the balance urged upon us." . . .

An impermissible practice can not be transformed into a constitutionally acceptable one by putting a democratic process to an improper use. There should be no question "that the electorate as a whole, whether by referendum or otherwise, could not order [governmental] action violative of the [Constitution], and the [government] may not avoid the strictures of [the Constitution] by deferring to the wishes or objections of some fraction of the body politic." A policy that does this cannot be legitimized by arguing that it promotes the free speech of the majority. . . .

The very purpose of a Bill of Rights was to withdraw certain subjects from the vicissitudes of political controversy, to place them beyond the reach of majorities and officials and to establish them as legal principles to be applied by the courts. One's . . . fundamental rights may not be submitted to vote; they depend on the outcome of no elections.

High school graduation ceremonies have not been regarded, either by law or tradition, as public fora where a multiplicity of views on any given topic, secular or religious, can be expressed and exchanged. School officials at Highland did not allow a representative of the ACLU to speak about "safe sex" and condom distribution at graduation, as requested by one of the graduating seniors. The question was not submitted to referendum of the graduating seniors because the principal understandably determined that the proposed topic was not suitable for graduation. We do not suggest that the school's response to this request was inappropriate. However, we do note that the response illustrates the degree of control the administration retained over student speech at graduation. Version D was not intended to broaden the rights of students to speak at graduation, nor to convert the graduation ceremony into a public forum.

Accordingly, we fail to see how this particular policy, addressed only to providing an option for continuing prayer at graduation after *Lee,* can be legitimized as promoting the free speech rights of the students. . . .

The School Board argues that the student referendum here significantly distinguishes this case from *Lee.* We disagree. It is, of course, true that the state's entanglement with the graduation prayer in *Lee* was more obvious, pronounced, and intrusive than the School District's involvement here. In *Lee,* the principal decided prayer would be included in the ceremony, chose the clergy person who would give the prayer, and even determined part of the content of the prayer by giving the invited clergy guidelines for the substance of the prayer. It is no wonder then, that the resulting prayer "bore the imprint of the State."

Although the state's involvement here is certainly less evident, the student referendum does not erase the state's imprint from this graduation prayer. Graduation at Highland Regional High School, like graduation at nearly any other school, is a school-sponsored event. School officials decide the sequence of events and the order of speakers on the program, and ceremonies are typically held on school property at no cost to the students. The atmosphere at Highland's graduations is characterized by order and uniformity. School officials necessarily "retain a high degree of control over the precise contents of the program, the speeches, the timing, the movements, the dress, and the decorum of the students." Principal Palatucci testified before the district court that any student who attempted to give an unscheduled address at graduation in contravention of administrative direction would be arrested if police were available, even if a majority of the graduating students had previously approved. The district court carefully questioned the principal about what he would do if a majority of the student body, without administrative approval, voted to have a speaker who would not be included in the program but would be introduced by the valedictorian and allowed to give a one minute speech. The principal responded: "I couldn't allow that to happen. . . . If I have a police officer, I have her arrested." Thus, the school officials' involvement and control is not as limited, unintrusive, or neutral as the School Board suggests.

Delegation of one aspect of the ceremony to a plurality of students does not constitute the absence of school officials' control over the graduation. Students decided the question of prayer at graduation only because school officials agreed to let them decide that one question. Although the delegation here may appear to many to be no more than a neutral means of deciding whether prayer should be included in the graduation, it does not insulate the School Board from the reach of the First Amendment. "Courts must keep in mind both the fundamental place held by the Establishment Clause in our constitutional scheme and the myriad, subtle ways in which the Establishment Clause values can be eroded."

Furthermore, the text of Version D affirms that it was adopted in response to *Lee*. The Board's avowed purpose in reexamining its policy was to provide an option that might allow the "longstanding tradition" of graduation prayer to survive the prohibitions of that Supreme Court decision. We believe that the control exercised by state officials here, though different in degree than was present in *Lee,* is not sufficiently distinct to require a different result under the "first dominant fact" of *Lee.* . . .

The fact that attendance at the graduation ceremonies is voluntary in a legal sense does not save the religious exercise. The objector's presence at his or her graduation compels participation in the religious observance decreed by the results of the poll that is sanctioned under Version D. This the Constitution does not allow. What to most believers may seem nothing more than a reasonable request that the nonbeliever respect their religious practices, in a school context may appear to the nonbeliever or dissenter to be an attempt to employ the machinery of the State to enforce a religious orthodoxy. . . .

To say a teenage student has a real choice not to attend her high school graduation is formalistic in the extreme. . . . Everyone knows that in our society and in our culture high school graduation is one of life's most significant occasions. A school rule which excuses attendance is beside the point. . . .

The First Amendment is a shield that prohibits the state from interfering with a person's right to worship as he or she pleases. It is not a sword that can be used to compel others to join in a religious observance at a state sponsored event. "The First Amendment has lost much if the religious follower and the atheist are no longer to be judicially regarded as entitled to equal justice under law." . . .

The sole question presented is whether a religious exercise may be conducted at a graduation ceremony in circumstances where . . . young graduates who object are induced to conform. No holding by th[e Supreme Court] suggests a school can persuade or compel a student to participate in a religious exercise. That is being done here, and it is forbidden by the Establishment Clause of the First Amendment. . . .

The disclaimer required under Version D does help to recapture some of the separation between church and state that has been obscured by the state's control over the graduation. However, the Board cannot sanction coerced participation in a religious observance merely by disclaiming responsibility for the content of the ceremony. Given the protections inherent in the First Amendment, it is quite possible that parents of some graduating seniors chose public education precisely so that their children would not be compelled to follow the religious beliefs of others. Yet, that is exactly what Version D allows.

We recognize that the Court of Appeals for the Fifth Circuit has reached a result contrary to the one we reach today. (See *Jones* v. *Clear Creek Indep. Sch. Dist.* [1992].) Indeed, as stated earlier, the administration at Highland promulgated Version D pursuant to the Board's instruction to develop a policy that would parallel the holding of *Jones.* We are not, however, persuaded by that court's analysis. *Jones* also involved a challenge to a policy that allowed students to decide if they wanted prayer at a public school's graduation ceremony. The *Jones* court upheld the policy while acknowledging that "the practical result of [its] decision, viewed in light of *Lee,* is that a majority of students can do what the State acting on its own cannot do to incorporate prayer in public high school graduation ceremonies."

That court recently reaffirmed that ruling in affirming an order that enjoined enforcement of a Mississippi statute allowing prayer at compulsory and noncompulsory school events, "except as to nonsectarian, nonproselytizing student-initiated voluntary prayer at high school commencement as condoned by *Jones.*" . . . The court distinguished *Jones* by noting that graduation prayer occurred at a "once-in-a-lifetime event that could be appropriately marked with a prayer," that the students in *Jones* were mature seniors, and "that the challenged prayer was to be nonsectarian and nonproselytizing."[*]

We are not persuaded by these distinctions. *Lee* clearly established that the "once-in-a-lifetime event" does not justify allowing a public school to authorize collective prayer under the circumstances of that case. To the contrary, the significance of that "once-in-a-lifetime" event weighed heavily in favor of invalidating the prayer. It was precisely because graduation was a "once-in-a-lifetime" event that students were denied the option of foregoing the ceremony to avoid compromising their religious scruples. . . . Similarly, the Court in *Lee* was not convinced that the maturity level of high school students immunized them from the coercion endemic in coerced participation. ("For the dissenter of high school age, who has a reasonable perception that she is being forced by the State to pray in a manner her conscience will

---

*A similar case was decided in 1996 (*Ingebretsen* v. *Moore*) by the Fifth Circuit Court and a request for a rehearing *en banc* was denied. In an angry dissent to that denial, Judge Edith Jones wrote: "In overturning the Mississippi school prayer statute, leaving a sliver of liberty for student-initiated graduation ceremony prayers, the Fifth Circuit has transformed the Establishment Clause from a shield against government religious indoctrination to a sword attacking personal religious behavior." In light of the *Ingebretsen* decision, the Fifth Circuit has markedly curtailed the significance of its *Jones* v. *Clear Creek* opinion.

not allow, the injury is no less real.") Indeed, few would doubt the influence of peer pressure upon children in high school. Furthermore, we are not inclined to alter our analysis merely because Version D does not expressly allow proselytization. . . .

Instead, we find the reasoning of the Court of Appeals for the Ninth Circuit in *Harris* v. *Joint Sch. Dist.* (9th Cir. 1994) to be more persuasive. There, plaintiffs challenged a school district's policy of allowing graduating seniors to vote on whether prayer should be included in their graduation ceremony. The court concluded that the challenged practice violated the Establishment Clause even though any graduation prayer would have to be initiated, selected, and delivered by students.

We cannot allow the school district's delegate to make decisions that the school district cannot make. When the senior class is given plenary power over a state-sponsored, state-controlled event such as high school graduation, it is just as constrained by the Constitution as the state would be. . . .

(1) A Secular Purpose

The Board argues that Version D has the secular purpose of recognizing the students' rights to free speech and their desire to solemnize the occasion. As we noted earlier, the Board's proclamation of the purpose of promoting free speech must be viewed in context with the policy's emphasis on providing an option that would allow prayer to be delivered at graduation after *Lee*. . . .

In addition, Version D permits a student to give a sectarian, proselytizing address. If a student were to decide to give such an address after a student referendum "authorized" verbal prayer, the administration could not halt it without violating its own policy. If this were to occur, a proselytizing prayer (perhaps even degrading other religions) would be delivered in a forum controlled by the School Board. "A system which secures the right to proselytize religious . . . causes must also guarantee the concomitant right to decline to foster such concepts." Version D fails to achieve this balance.

The Board also argues that the inclusion of prayer solemnizes the graduation, but we are unable to understand why graduation would be any less solemn if students were not permitted to vote for prayer, a moment of silence, or no observance at graduation. Surely students who graduate in a year where students may chose to have no prayer at all would think their graduation to be a solemn event, and it is doubtful that the Board would disagree with that assessment.

Furthermore, assuming arguendo that Version D serves the secular purpose of solemnizing one's graduation, we believe it does so in a constitutionally impermissible manner. Students who are devoutly religious may feel that prayer is not something that should be put to a vote. Such students may even have a religious objection to such a vote and may, therefore, refuse to vote out of religious conviction. Version D puts such students on the horns of an impossible dilemma by forcing them to choose between doing violence to their own religious beliefs and voting, or abstaining and thereby risking that their forbearance may provide the margin of victory for those with a different religious preference. Regardless of how the referendum comes out, this state policy has forced such a student into an impossible, and impermissible, choice. . . . Still other students may face a similar predicament because they are atheists and refuse to vote out of conscience— as is their right. Such a Hobson's choice "sends a message to nonadherents that they are outsiders, not full members of the political community. . . ." The Constitution forbids that message, just as it forbids the procedure authorized by this policy. . . .

(2) The Endorsement of Religion

. . . "The question under endorsement analysis, in short, is whether a reasonable observer would view such longstanding practices as a disapproval of his or her particular religious choices." Thus, the viewpoint of the reasonable observer (adherent or nonadherent) helps us to determine if the "principal or primary effect [is] one that neither advances nor inhibits religion." In any such inquiry, "the 'history and ubiquity' of a practice is relevant because it provides part of the context in which a reasonable observer evaluates whether a challenged governmental practice conveys a message of endorsement of religion." . . .

The disclaimer that is required by Version D does weigh in favor of the Board's position under a *Lemon* analysis. However, it does not weigh so heavily as to neutralize the counterweight of the advantage the policy gives religious speech over secular speech. Despite the printed disclaimer, the reasonable observer here could not help but conclude that the Board favors the inclusion of prayer. . . .

Religious students cannot complain that omitting prayers from their graduation ceremony would, in any realistic sense, "burden" their spiritual callings. To be sure, many of them invest this rite of passage with spiritual significance, but they may express their religious feelings about it before and after the ceremony. They may even organize a privately sponsored baccalaureate if they desire the company of like-minded students. . . .

V. Conclusion

In closing, we emphasize the difficulty posed by the issue that we confront here and the intensity and sincerity of persons on both sides. Issues of religion touch litigants and interested observers of the law as few other issues can. For example, one of the students who opposed Version D testified before the district court that he received threatening letters in his school locker and threatening telephone calls at home after coming forward in this case.

References to, and images of, religion are to be found throughout this society. Yet, the prevalence of religious beliefs and imagery cannot erode the state's obligation to protect the entire spectrum of religious preferences from the most pious worshipper to the most committed atheist. Those preferences are the business of the individual, not the state nor the public schools it maintains. The First Amendment does not allow the state to erect a policy that only respects religious views that are popular because the largest majority can not be licensed to impose its religious preferences upon the smallest minority.

. . . The district court's order enjoined the School Board "from conducting a school-sponsored graduation ceremony that includes a prayer, whether it be an invocation, a benediction or a prayer in any other form." In context, we understand the district court's order to foreclose a school-sponsored graduation service involving an invocation, benediction or prayer pursuant to Policy IKFD Version D. As so read, we affirm the judgment of the district court.

Appendix C

Supreme Court Timeline

1791–The Bill of Rights is ratified by the states.

1803—*Marbury* v. *Madison* establishes the principle of judicial review of Congressional acts.

1868—Fourteenth Amendment adopted. Through the wording "No state shall make or enforce any law which shall abridge the privileges or immunities of citizens of the United States, nor shall any State deprive any person of life, liberty, or property, without due process of law," this amendment incorporates the Bill of Rights on a state and local level.

1940—*Cantwell* v. *Connecticut.* The religion clause of the First Amendment ("Congress shall make no law respecting the establishment of religion, or prohibiting free exercise thereof") is applied to the states for the first time.

1940—*Minersville School District* v. *Gobitis.* The Court decides 8–1 that the State of Pennsylvania has a right to provide for gestures of "respect for the symbol of national life," i.e., that it is legal to require people to salute the United States flag, even though they believe (as some Jehovah's Witnesses do) that it is a form of idolatry.

1943—*West Virginia State Board of Education* v. *Barnette* overturns the *Gobitis* decision.

1947—*Everson* v. *Board of Education.* The Court, in a 5–4 vote, found in favor of a New Jersey Board of Education by upholding that state's right to fund transportation to parochial schools. The separationist view was maintained in the written opinions of all nine of the justices, but it was narrowly ruled that the establishment clause had not been violated.

1948—*McCollum* v. *Board of Education.* In an 8–1 vote, the Court found that public schools in Champaign, Illinois, violated the establishment clause of the First Amendment by permitting religious groups to use classrooms during school hours to teach religion.

1952—*Zorach* v. *Clauson.* The Court supports "released time" in which students desiring religious education are transported, during school hours, from the campus to a nearby church building.

1954—*Brown* v. *Board of Education* calls for the desegregation of public schools.

1962—*Engel* v. *Vitale* bans the recitation of prayer in public school classrooms.

1963—*Abington Township* v. *Schempp* strikes down mandatory Bible reading and school-sanctioned prayer.

1963—*Murray* v. *Curlett,* which involved virtually identical issues to Schempp, was decided by the Supreme Court simultaneously with that case and the two were consolidated under the name *Abington Township* v. *Schempp.*

1971—*Lemon* v. *Kurtzman* provides a three-point test for deciding the constitutionality of a statute.

1973—*Committee for Public Education and Religious Liberty* v. *Nyquist* declares New York parochial school aid programs unconstitutional because they serve as government advancement of a religion.

1980—*Stone* v. *Graham.* The Court decided that a public school may not post the Ten Commandments on classroom walls because the purpose was "religious in nature."

1984—*Lynch* v. *Donnelly.* The Court decides that a creche displayed on public property is not unconstitutional as long as other symbols of the winter season (such as Santa Claus, snowmen, and menorahs) are also included.

1985—*Wallace* v. *Jaffree* declares that an Alabama law which calls for a moment of silence in order to return prayer to the classroom is unconstitutional. In his dissenting opinion, Judge William Rehnquist strongly recommends discarding the "Wall of separation" metaphor as a criterion for deciding such questions.

1990—*Board of Westside Schools* v. *Mergens* upholds the Equal Access act by finding that public schools must recognize the right of religious clubs to use school facilities if that right is granted to other noncurricular clubs.

1992—*Lee* v. *Weisman* declares school-sponsored prayer at graduation ceremonies unconstitutional.

Index